HUMOR FROM HARPER'S

HUMOR
FROM
HARPER'S

EDITED

BY JOHN FISCHER

AND LUCY DONALDSON

FOREWORD BY OGDEN NASH

HARPER & BROTHERS

NEW YORK

Grateful acknowledgment is made to the following for permission to reprint selections included in this book:

"The Extern" by Theodore Jacobs, by permission of the author.

"You, Too, Can Write the Casual Style" by William H. Whyte, Jr., by permission of the author.

"Nothing Difficult About a Cow" by A. B. Guthrie, Jr., by permission of Brandt & Brandt.

"Madame Rosette" by Roald Dahl, copyright 1945 by Roald Dahl, by permission of A. Watkins, Inc.

"The King and His Beasts" from *The Bafut Beagles* by Gerald M. Durrell, copyright 1954 by Gerald M. Durrell, by permission of The Viking Press, Inc. and Rupert Hart-Davis Limited.

"Aunt Jean's Marshmallow Fudge Diet" from *Please Don't Eat the Daisies* by Jean Kerr, by permission of Doubleday & Company, Inc. and William Heinemann Ltd.

Selections from *One Man's Meat* by E. B. White, copyright 1938, 1939, 1940 by E. B. White, by permission of Harper & Brothers.

"The Indians of the Colorado River" by Mario Prodan, by permission of Harold Matson Company.

"Easy Road to Culture, Sort of" by Eric Larrabee, by permission of the author.

"The Merciful Tenderizer" by Ralph McGill, by permission of the author.

Selection from *My Discovery of England* by Stephen Leacock, copyright 1922 by Dodd, Mead & Company, Inc., by permission of Dodd, Mead & Company, Inc., McClelland and Stewart Ltd. and The Bodley Head Ltd.

"Mr. K*A*P*L*A*N and the Glorious Pest" from *The Return of H*Y*M*A*N K*A*P*L*A*N* by Leo Rosten, copyright © 1959 by Leo Rosten, by permission of Harper & Brothers and Victor Gollancz Ltd.

"The Darlings at the Top of the Stairs" by James Thurber, by permission of the author.

"The Cracked Lens" by Sumner Locke Elliott, by permission of Annie Laurie Williams, Inc.

"A Wooden Darning Egg" from *The Carpentered Hen and Other Tame Creatures* by John Updike, copyright © 1956 by John Updike, by permission of Harper & Brothers and the author.

"My Father and His Pastors" from *God and My Father* by Clarence Day, copyright 1931, 1932 by Clarence Day, by permission of Alfred A. Knopf, Inc.

"A Lecturer at Large" by Ogden Nash, copyright 1952 by Ogden Nash, by permission of Curtis Brown, Ltd.

"My Career as a Lawbreaker" by Bernard DeVoto, by permission of Mrs. Bernard DeVoto.

"Dictionary of Charlestonese" by Ashley Cooper, by permission of *The News and Courier*, Charleston, S.C.

"Forget the Geraniums" by Max Steele, by permission of Elizabeth McKee.

"The Case for the Red Smith Irregulars" by Charles Einstein, by permission of Lurton Blassingame.

"How to Cure Bird-Watchers" by John Fischer, by permission of the author.

"Catkind" from *Food for Centaurs* by Robert Graves, copyright © 1959 by Robert Graves, by permission of Willis Kingsley Wing.

"The Girl from Sewickley, Pa." by Milton Mayer, by permission of the author.

"Philosophy of Punitive Action" by Parke Cummings, by permission of the author.

"The Third Baby's the Easiest" from *Life Among the Savages* by Shirley Jackson, copyright 1949, 1953 by Shirley Jackson, by permission of Farrar, Straus & Cudahy, Inc. and A. M. Heath & Company Ltd.

"The New Snobbism" from *Snobs* by Russell Lynes, by permission of Harper & Brothers.

"A Quartet of Elders" from *The Love Letters of Phyllis McGinley*, copyright 1952 by Phyllis McGinley, by permission of The Viking Press, Inc. and Secker & Warburg Ltd.

"The Death of Lady Mondegreen" from *Get Away from Me with Those Christmas Gifts* by Sylvia Wright, copyright © 1954, 1957 by Sylvia Wright, by permission of McGraw-Hill Book Company, Inc. and Elizabeth McKee.

"The Seal That Couldn't Swim" by Alexis Ladas, by permission of the author.

"The Young Man Who Came to Visit" from *The Dinner Party* by Gretchen Finletter, copyright 1954, 1955 by Gretchen Finletter, by permission of Harper & Brothers.

"Almost Strictly for the Birds" from *Report from Practically Nowhere* by John Sack, copyright © 1956 by John Sack, by permission of Harper & Brothers and Littauer & Wilkinson.

"These Intelligence Tests" by Frederick Lewis Allen, by permission of Agnes Rogers Allen.

"New Twilight on Old Gods" by David McCord, by permission of the author.

"Digging the Weans" from *The Weans* by Robert Nathan, copyright © 1956, 1960 by Robert Nathan, by permission of Alfred A. Knopf, Inc.

"Stranded in Kansas City, or a Fate Worse Than Vaudeville" from *Gypsy* by Gypsy Rose Lee, copyright © 1957 by Gypsy Rose Lee, by permission of Harper & Brothers.

"Conversation Piece" by Agnes Rogers, by permission of the author.

"The Man Who Walked Through Walls" from *Across Paris and Other Stories* by Marcel Aymé, by permission of Harper & Brothers and The Bodley Head Ltd.

"Who Needs No Introduction" by Kingsley Amis, by permission of the author.

"Protection for a Tough Racket" by Cordelia Baird Gross, by permission of the author.

"How to Tell When You Are Obsolete" from *Parkinson's Law* by C. Northcote Parkinson, by permission of Houghton Mifflin Co. and John Murray Ltd.

CONTENTS

FOREWORD
by Ogden Nash

"What is humor?" said the editor, not jesting; and clamored for an answer.

He may knock on my door until his knuckles ache, but he will knock in vain. I am not wise enough to define humor, or foolish enough to attempt to do so. I have, however, a few thoughts about the professors and panelists who are never at a loss when called on for a quotable analysis. Confronted by a frog, a high-hopping, light-leaping, erratic, unpredictable frog, a very frog of Calaveras, each says to himself, "I don't see no p'ints about that frog that's any better'n any other frog." Yet he has an uneasy sense that there must be some special p'ints about it, else why are all the other professors and panelists weighing, measuring, and analyzing? So they lay the frog on a slab in the laboratory, get out their dissecting tools, and start carving as the camera grinds. Off with the legs to reveal the secret of the lightning jumps; out with the eyes to discover the cause of that anomalistic point of view. The dissection complete, what are the results? A dead frog.

"What is humor?" said the editor, unheeding, this time provoking an answer, although an irrelevant one.

> Tell me where is Humor bred?
> What the happy marriage bed?
> Who in ardent bliss begets?
> Deodorants, or cigarettes?
> Mammon, with Vulgarity playing,
> As he met her once a-Maying,
> Filled her with Humor, idiot child,
> Who mops and mows in frenzy wild
> In interludes non-controversial
> Between commercial and commercial.
> Let us then ring Humor's knell,
> But first, a message from Jiffi-Jel.

If television seems to have popped up like a gopher in this paper, it is because television does offer us daily one exquisite example of humor which is no less hilarious because it is as unconscious as it is unconscionable. This is the "brief pause for station identification"; a brief pause elastic enough to include the lady shaving her legs, the lady losing her beloved because of food particles between her teeth, the lady stupefying her prey with a perfume of ineffable aphrodisiac powers, and a pitch for two Westerns and a Private Eye to be seen later on the network.

The writers whose work has been gathered here flourished before oral and visual gibberish had replaced the written word or have been able to keep their heads when all about them are losing theirs and blaming it on McCarthy, the Kremlin, Barry Goldwater, nuclear fallout, planned obsolescence, nonbooks, and the split-level ranch house. They view not with alarm, but with wonder; their mood ranges from rebelliousness to resignation (a journey some thirty or forty years long); and their wry smiles are never contorted into *risus sardonicus.*

"What is humor?" said the editor a third time.

Let me rather start again and try to define the humorist. I once saw a child dear to me perched precariously on the peaked roof of a barn, and asked her what she was doing there. Her answer covered the situation like a horse blanket: "Trying not to fall off."

I think the humorist writes as he does in an effort to resist the centrifugal force of daily life on this whirling planet; I think he is simply trying not to fall off.

INTRODUCTION

Some of the worst humor that ever reached print appeared in *Harper's Magazine*.

Or so, at least, it sounds today. At the time—roughly the half century after 1850—it apparently attracted an army of enthusiastic readers. They were devoted in those days to the arch little anecdote, stretched out to interminable length by such celebrated prose-stretchers as Anthony Trollope and The Hon. S. S. Cox. Even more popular was The Dialect Story, produced by the cord by Joel Chandler Harris, Owen Wister, and their scores of imitators. It was founded on the theory that nothing in the world was quite so funny as the mispronunciations and hamstrung syntax of the ignorant classes—including cowboys, waitresses, "darkies," Irishmen, farmers, and new-rich businessmen. Sometimes it achieved an apogee of corniness which remained unsurpassed until the invention of the radio. ("If George had not blowed into the muzzle of his gun," sighed a rural widow at the funeral of her late husband, "he might have got plenty of squirrels, it was such a day for them." 1875.)

This sort of comedy may still have a certain melancholy interest for two groups: (1) the wretches who have to work up Ph.D.s in literature in order to hold teaching jobs; (2) historians seeking to trace the vast changes in American taste and character during the past century. On the evidence of their jokes, our great-grandparents took a savage enjoyment in the embarrassments of the poor and handicapped. Not only did they bristle with racial and religious prejudice; they were proud of it. Their brash, by-jingo nationalism—and the national inferiority complex—were expressed in their derision of all foreigners, from Ah Sin to the Prince of Wales. Their loud-mouthed bragging about anything American sounded curiously like the noises now rising out of Castro's Cuba, and other new, unconfident societies. Witness Artemus Ward's announcement that the world would be permitted to "revolve around on her axle-tree onst in twenty-four hours, subjick to the Constitution of the United States."

With one exception, none of these primitive humorists are included in this anthology. It does not pretend to be an historical survey. It is intended primarily for the pleasure of contemporary readers. Consequently, all but one of the forty-four items in this book were chosen from issues of *Harper's* published within the last forty years. The exception is Mark Twain, the only writer of the previous century whose humor remains as fresh, wry, and relevant as ever. But then he was, in the essay reprinted here, dealing with an ageless subject: the War Between Men and Women, beginning with the first skirmish in the Garden of Eden.

The other selections range in subject matter from Clarence Day's *Life With Father* to Gypsy Rose Lee's redoubtable mother . . . from C. Northcote Parkinson's classic work on the decline and fall of corporations to A. B. Guthrie, Jr.'s unclassic encounters with a cow. Geographically they reach from the little Kingdom of Lundy, off the British coast, to the somewhat bigger Kingdom of Bafut in Africa (where the Fon reigns happily over his beasts, his hundred wives, and his all-girl band), with a Cairo bawdy house in between. The cast of characters includes H*Y*M*A*N K*A*P*L*A*N, a baby seal that couldn't swim, Hedda Hopper, a tribe of Colorado Indians, amateur bootleggers, Jack Kerouac, and a schoolteacher who also worked in a night club.

The authors represented here have only two things in common: (1) an eagerness to entice their readers with all the wit, grace, and narrative skill they can command; (2) a conviction that the purpose of humor is not merely to amuse, but to comment on the human condition. For the editors of *Harper's* have always tried, even in the genteel years of the nineteenth century, to publish humor that says something worth saying—about the shape of our culture, the zany habits of people presumed to be sane, the stuffed shirts which yearn for puncturing. So in each of these selections we hope the reader will find not only enjoyment but perhaps something else besides.

JOHN FISCHER

HUMOR FROM HARPER'S

THEODORE JACOBS

 The Extern

It's a funny thing about studying medicine. Sometimes you get to know a patient, and sometimes you don't. I mean really know him. Of course, if you do a decent job on your history and your physical, you can usually get a pretty good idea of where the trouble lies. But you can go over a patient all day, in fact you can go over him every day for weeks, and never get to know him, even when you've asked him every question in the whole history-taking manual. Even if he can tell you a story about every sore throat he's ever had, you might not get to know him. That's the way it was with Bluhm and me.

Bluhm was my first patient in medical school—and nearly my last. I was just starting, you understand. I had just finished two years of medical school and I was beginning in the clinics. To tell the truth, I almost didn't get that far. I was in academic trouble my second year, and they were all set to boot me out right then and there. But I told them how much I wanted to be a doctor, and finally they decided to see what I could do with patients. I was on the spot, though, let me tell you. One mistake and bingo—into my father's business.

So what happened? They threw me in with this wise apple Bluhm. My first morning in the hospital they assigned him to me. It was quite a shock. I hadn't even gotten to my locker yet when I heard my name over the telepage. That's the way they do it in our hospital. As soon as you get assigned to a patient, they start paging you. It really threw me when I heard that thing. If you've never heard your name over tele-page before, and all of a sudden at eight in the morning, on an empty stomach, someone starts paging you, it can throw you.

1

As soon as I found out what room Bluhm was in I got myself ready and started up there. There was a mirror on the wall just outside Bluhm's room and before I went in I checked my appearance. The one thing I remembered from the sophomore lectures was that no matter what, you had to look like a doctor. What it really came down to was you had to do a good job of fooling the patients. Of course no one said that, but you got the idea all right. If you looked enough like a doctor people might not catch on that you were a junior medical student.

Seeing myself in the mirror I hoped I might pass for a real doctor. I had on my white coat with a stethoscope slipped into one side pocket and fixed so that just enough of the tubing stuck out. That's a point of style I can't go into now, but take it from me, it makes a difference among doctors how much tubing sticks out. In the other pocket I had a notebook, a reflex hammer, and a tuning fork. I had noticed that all the successful clinicians in the hospital had a lot of things sticking out of their breast pockets, so I'd put a couple of pens in there along with a mechanical pencil, a ruler, and a few tongue depressors. It looked impressive all right. The only trouble was I had to walk slowly so that everything wouldn't jangle.

When I walked into Bluhm's room and saw him, at first I thought he was dead. I mean dead about a thousand years. He looked like one of these guys in an explorer picture that gets lost in a desert without any canteen, and his friends show up in Bermuda shorts later and find him just bones, with vultures flying around and all. Even his pajamas looked sort of pecked at. He was lying there giving me the eye, sort of squinty-like. Not too friendly, I'll tell you. I didn't know what to do. I had come to give this man medical attention, and he was looking at me as though I was intruding on his damn privacy. I felt like getting out of there and going to law school or some place. Finally, though, I asked him how he was feeling. I'd been standing there a couple of minutes without saying anything, and I was getting worried he might think I was a psychiatrist, so I put on this kind of professional cheery voice—you know, the nauseating kind, and I said:

"How are you feeling today, Mr. Bluhm?" Real cheery.

"To tell you the truth, I'm sick in bed today," said Bluhm. That's the way he was. You couldn't give him an inch.

Naturally I introduced myself as doctor, but I don't think it went over too well. In fact I *know* it didn't because right away Bluhm asked me what year I was in.

"What year you in?" he said, as though trying to show me he knew something. That burned me. Suppose I was really a doctor. He would have looked pretty stupid saying that. Bluhm could be a real smart alec when he wanted to. I didn't want to give myself away, though, so I said:

"I'm an extern, sir."

"Oh," said Bluhm, "that's different. Why didn't you say so? You should have said so when you first came in. For a minute I was thinking you was a regular doctor."

A real wise guy. The trouble was, Bluhm had been around university hospitals a lot. He knew all the medical school gimmicks.

"What's wrong with you, Mr. Bluhm?" I said. I said this sort of firmly. Not too firmly, understand, but enough to let him know that I wasn't holding any auditions for "Can You Top This?" or anything.

"What am I, an M.D.? Overnight they gave me a license? How do I know what's wrong with me? I'll tell you a secret. I ain't paying twenty-two dollars a day to tell you what's wrong with me."

"Well, what symptoms have you got?"

"What symptoms?"

"Yeah. You got headaches, pains in the stomach? Are you nervous, or what?"

"That's it."

"What's it?"

"I'm nervous. All the time I'm getting nervous."

"Nervous, eh? What are you nervous about?"

"Twenty-two dollars a day and he's asking me what I'm nervous about."

"Have you noticed any unusual sensations in your arms or legs, Mr. Bluhm?"

"Yeah, now you're mentioning it, since I'm here, my arms is feeling like pin cushions."

This guy's sense of humor could really devastate you.

"You've had quite a bit of blood drawn today, I imagine," I said. I was trying to be *cordial*, for God's sake.

"Why not? They see I'm an old man. I'm good to practice on." He always had a crack like that up his sleeve, Bluhm. Always with the kind word.

"It's not a matter of practice, Mr. Bluhm. That blood is taken for important tests. You'll be glad you had them."

Bluhm looked at me with that squinty eye of his.

"What are you, the chief *macher* around here or something? Maybe you're Dr. Salk from the vaccine, you know so much?"

I felt like giving him a wise answer when he said that. You know, something real sarcastic to shut him up. Still, I didn't want to antagonize him. After all, he was my first patient and you know how you always imagine that you are going to have a wonderful relationship with your first patient. You don't like to give up that idea. Besides, to tell the truth, I was plenty worried about what was liable to happen in this situation. If the attending doctors found out that I was not getting along with a patient, they'd go hard on me. I knew that. The way things were, it would probably mean the old heave-ho. So I tried to be nice to Bluhm. I laughed at his idiotic jokes, but I still couldn't get a history out of him. All he would tell was this fantastic stuff. With most of the patients on the gastro-intestinal service you get too much history. A lot of people with digestion trouble and constipation and things like to tell you all about it, especially the details. It can get you pretty sore. But not Bluhm. All he would tell me were these wild stories.

"Have you had any major illnesses?" I asked him.

"You don't know the half of it," said Bluhm. "I was born with a defective heart. Had an operation for it in the 'eighties." That was about sixty years before anyone ever heard of that kind of surgery. Whatever disease I asked about, he'd had it. High blood pressure, diabetes, tuberculosis, smallpox, malaria—anything. He'd had them all. If you started breathing in diseases like a chain smoker you couldn't have that many. It would be odds-on you'd never get past kindergarten, no less live to a mean old age, having half these things. But that didn't bother Bluhm. He'd just start telling stories of this or that disease and how it nearly wiped out the whole old country and how he survived by a miracle, and a lot of other lunatic stuff until I was really up to my neck.

"Have you ever had tularemia?" I finally asked him. That's some crazy disease no one ever gets. You have to live with a bunch of rabbits or something to get it.

"No," said Bluhm, "all my friends had it, but I never came down with it."

Well, finally I gave up trying to get the history. I just wasn't doing any business on that score at all. I figured maybe I'd have better luck with the physical.

"I'd like that very much," Bluhm said when I told him I would like to examine him. "It would be a pleasure. Only I can't do it."

"What do you mean, you can't do it?"

"My doctor wouldn't like it. He's the jealous type."

"Look, Mr. Bluhm," I said, "I've been sent here by the medicine department to go over you."

"I tell ya what. Go back to the medicine department and tell them I can't afford it. Blue Cross don't cover no treatment by undergraduates."

"Mr. Bluhm," I said, "in a hospital like this everyone is a student." I heard someone say that once about a British university.

"Would I deny it? Certainly everyone's a student. Only thing, I got a funny quirk. I like better the students around sixty years old. I feel sorry for them they been studying so many years."

I finally got to examine him, though. He did me a big favor and let me poke around, but to tell the truth I didn't get too much information. He had quite a few lumps, but I didn't know whether they were supposed to be there or not. It's hard to tell on old patients, especially if you got a "C" in anatomy to begin with. Besides, all the time he kept saying things to throw me off the track.

"Feel the goiter on my neck?" he asked. "Notice the liver is a little swollen?" Things like that just to mix me up. At first I believed him and I started poking around like mad—it's hell to pay if you miss a thyroid or a liver—but pretty soon I saw this stupid, apple-eating grin come on his face. So I cut it out. I could have kicked myself halfway around the ward and back for being such an idiot.

After I finished the physical I beat it out of Bluhm's room. I figured the best thing I could do for our relationship at that point was to get out of there and stay out. I felt depressed as hell. I had no history and I knew I'd done a pretty stinko physical, even by my flexible standards. It didn't help, either, to think of the bright remarks old Bluhm was liable to make to the doctors about me. They take very seriously any comment a patient makes about a student, even if the patient *is* a lunatic.

After that I tried to avoid Bluhm, but it seemed as though every time I passed his room to go to the lab or something he'd catch me. I'd be walking past there, and he'd spot me from his bed and call out. Naturally all he wanted was to aggravate me a little.

"I've got cutting pains across the middle," he'd call to me as I passed by, or, "Feels like that disc of mine has slipped again." Any plausible symptom he could think of to get me in there and give me the business for a little while.

He collected newspaper clippings, and whenever I came, he'd show me ones that he'd saved especially for me. Things like help-

wanted ads for veterinarians or stories about people that got jailed
for impersonating officers. He said he thought I'd appreciate them.

Actually I had almost gotten used to Bluhm's sterling personality.
In fact I had to admit that sometimes he could be pretty clever—in an
asinine way, of course. But I was getting a little tired of it all, too.
At one o'clock one morning, I was paged and told that I was wanted
in Bluhm's room. I was just about to go home for a little sack time
after doing lab work all night and I felt like saying the hell with it
and leaving, but like a dope, I didn't. I went up to his room.

Do you know what he wanted? You'll never believe this in a million
years. He wanted to know if I was Jewish or not. At one o'clock in
the morning. I told him I was a Buddhist and I was late for a prayer
meeting.

"No kiddin'," he says, "you been Bar Mitzvah?"

I told him I wasn't Bar Mitzvah and good night.

"Why not?" he wanted to know. "What's the matter, you're not
Jewish?"

"I'm terribly sorry, Mr. Bluhm," I said, "but I'm a Christian."

"What are you so sorry? You can't help it. Don't worry. Some
Christians are very nice."

"Thanks," I said.

I wasn't in the mood for that kind of thing. It was late and I was
beat and I wanted to go home. But old Bluhm just kept talking to me.
I don't know why. I suppose he just felt like talking to someone that
night. You got the idea he was a kind of lonely character anyway,
Bluhm. He told me he had no family and he lived alone in a hotel
room and I doubt if he had any real friends. With his personality
I don't think anyone could have taken him for very long. Anyway, he
just went on like that, talking to me for a couple of hours, until I
could hardly keep my eyes open. He talked about all kinds of things.
The Jewish religion, politics, television, chess, the movies, history—
everything. He wasn't really educated, but it seemed he had ideas
on a thousand different things. I listened as best I could, but I
couldn't help dozing a little, I was so pooped.

When I finally got out of there, it was after three, and I was disgusted with myself for having stayed that long. It was idiotic. I should
have walked out and let him try to trap some other screwball. But I
don't know, I just couldn't do it. He looked so damn skinny and
pecked at and everything, and I knew that he'd just gotten me up
there to have someone to listen to him. So I stayed. I'm a prize ass
when it comes to situations like that.

I didn't see Bluhm for a while after that, but about a week later I came into his room with a group of doctors. It was during what they call grand rounds, when the chief of the service takes his residents and a few medical students to see a slew of patients. It's usually quite a time, with the chief showing off to beat the band and everyone else giving him the old "yes, sir" until it's enough to stir up a little reverse peristalsis.

There were eight of us that morning and we marched into the patients' rooms in regular order. The chief first, the third-year resident second, the second-year resident third, and so on until you got down to the medical students, bringing up the rear. When we got near Bluhm's room, this Dr. Ackman, who's head of the G-I service and a real brain on bowel problems, suddenly asked me to tell the group what I knew about the case. I was caught by surprise. Usually Ackman didn't do things like that. Most of the time he was too busy to bother with the students' reports. But all of a sudden he wanted me to give him a summary of the case.

Well, I told him what I knew, which took about three minutes, and then for twenty minutes Ackman got me against the wall and started pumping me with questions, and every time I couldn't answer one, he got a little nastier. I really think he got a kick out of making me squirm.

When that friend of humanity finally got through with me, he led the parade into Bluhm's room. I was feeling awful. You could just tell the residents thought I was a low-grade moron.

As soon as we got in there Ackman took hold of Bluhm's hand and started playing the old family doctor in a voice that sounded as though he was announcing "The Firestone Hour." I really felt like leaving the room, it got so bad. All Ackman really said in the end was that Bluhm would have to have an exploratory operation—in other words that he was in the same situation, diagnostically speaking, as I was—but he threw in ten minutes' worth of polysyllables to make it sound good. Everyone crowded around him as though he was from the Nobel Prize committee, but I stood way in the back. I wasn't very keen on Ackman at that point, and besides I didn't want Bluhm to see me. Under the circumstances I didn't think it would be to my advantage for Bluhm to make one of his bright remarks about me.

He saw me, though. While the chief was talking he kept looking around with this puzzled expression on his face, as if he couldn't figure out who was Jewish and who wasn't. When he spotted me, though, he smiled a little. But I didn't smile back. I didn't want to start anything.

Through most of Ackman's talk Bluhm was quiet, but near the end, when he got to the part about the operation, Bluhm spoke up.

"Pardon me," he said. "I don't think I got that so well. You said an operation I need?"

"I'm afraid it's the only way to establish the diagnosis, Mr. Bluhm," said Ackman.

"I see. You couldn't maybe—maybe do without a diagnosis?"

"Not very well, I'm afraid. After all, we cannot treat intelligently if we do not know what entity we are dealing with."

"Sure. Sure, I could see that. But, well, to tell the truth, I wasn't planning it."

"I know, Mr. Bluhm, but it is the best way, believe me."

"You couldn't maybe take a few more pictures?"

"It wouldn't do any good."

"Okay. Well, listen. I don't know. There's something I would like to do first. I'd like to ask my own doctor, get his opinion. That's okay with you?"

"You have a physician on the outside you would like to consult?" asked Ackman, sounding slightly hurt.

"What on the outside? On the inside. There's my doctor over there." And with that apple-eating grin on his face Bluhm pointed at me.

"Sure, that's my doctor right there. Took care of me all the time."

"Is that right?" asked Ackman, grinning.

"Sure. Sure," said Bluhm. "All the time I'm here. Very fine doctor. He has a real heart, that doctor."

"Well, I feel confident he will give us permission to proceed," said Ackman, turning to me. "Won't you, Doctor?"

All I could do was nod. I nodded four times. I wanted to say something; to protest, to explain about Bluhm, but it was as though I'd had a stroke and had lost the ability to speak. I couldn't make a sound. I looked around. The residents were fighting laughter behind coughs and cupped hands. Even Ackman seemed to be smiling. I did not know what to do, or even what to think. All I knew for certain was that Bluhm was an out-and-out lunatic.

But you know, when I glanced over there he looked pretty normal. I swear he did. It was amazing. He didn't even look pecked at.

MARK TWAIN

Extracts
 from
Adam's Diary

Translated from the Original MS.

[NOTE.—I translated a portion of this diary some years ago, and a friend of mine printed a few copies in an incomplete form, but the public never got them. Since then I have deciphered some more of Adam's hieroglyphics, and think he has now become sufficiently important as a public character to justify this publication.—M. T.]

Monday.—This new creature with the long hair is a good deal in the way. It is always hanging around and following me about. I don't like this; I am not used to company. I wish it would stay with the other animals. . . . Cloudy today, wind in the east; think we shall have rain. . . . *We?* Where did I get that word? . . . I remember now—the new creature uses it.

Tuesday.—Been examining the great waterfall. It is the finest thing on the estate, I think. The new creature calls it Niagara Falls—why, I am sure I do not know. Says it *looks* like Niagara Falls. That is not a reason; it is mere waywardness and imbecility. I get no chance to name anything myself. The new creature names everything that comes

9

along, before I can get in a protest. And always that same pretext is offered—it *looks* like the thing. There is the dodo, for instance. Says the moment one looks at it one sees at a glance that it "looks like a dodo." It will have to keep that name, no doubt. It wearies me to fret about it, and it does no good, anyway. Dodo! It looks no more like a dodo than I do.

Wednesday.—Built me a shelter against the rain, but could not have it to myself in peace. The new creature intruded. When I tried to put it out it shed water out of the holes it looks with, and wiped it away with the back of its paws, and made a noise such as some of the other animals make when they are in distress. I wish it would not talk; it is always talking. That sounds like a cheap fling at the poor creature, a slur; but I do not mean it so. I have never heard the human voice before, and any new and strange sound intruding itself here upon the solemn hush of these dreaming solitudes offends my ear and seems a false note. And this new sound is so close to me; it is right at my shoulder, right at my ear, first on one side and then on the other, and I am used only to sounds that are more or less distant from me.

Friday.—The naming goes recklessly on, in spite of anything I can do. I had a very good name for the estate, and it was musical and pretty—GARDEN-OF-EDEN. Privately, I continue to call it that, but not any longer publicly. The new creature says it is all woods and rocks and scenery, and therefore has no resemblance to a garden. Says it *looks* like a park, and does not look like anything *but* a park. Consequently, without consulting me, it has been new-named— NIAGARA FALLS PARK. This is sufficiently high-handed, it seems to me. And already there is a sign up:

KEEP OFF
THE GRASS

My life is not as happy as it was.

Saturday.—The new creature eats too much fruit. We are going to run short, most likely. "We" again—that is *its* word; mine too, now, from hearing it so much. Good deal of fog this morning. I do not go out in the fog myself. The new creature does. It goes out in all weathers, and stumps right in with its muddy feet. And talks. It used to be so pleasant and quiet here.

Sunday.—Pulled through. This day is getting to be more and more trying. It was selected and set apart last November as a day of rest. I already had six of them per week, before. This morning found the new creature trying to clod apples out of that forbidden tree.

Monday.—The new creature says its name is Eve. That is all right, I have no objections. Says it is to call it by when I want it to come. I said it was superfluous, then. The word evidently raised me in its respect; and indeed it is a large, good word, and will bear repetition. It says it is not an It, it is a She. This is probably doubtful; yet it is all one to me; what she is were nothing to me if she would but go by herself and not talk.

Tuesday.—She has littered the whole estate with execrable names and offensive signs:

☞ THIS WAY TO THE WHIRLPOOL.
☞ THIS WAY TO GOAT ISLAND.
☞ CAVE OF THE WINDS THIS WAY.

She says this park would make a tidy summer resort, if there was any custom for it. Summer resort—another invention of hers—just words, without any meaning. What is a summer resort? But it is best not to ask her, she has such a rage for explaining.

Friday.—She has taken to beseeching me to stop going over the Falls. What harm does it do? Says it makes her shudder. I wonder why. I have always done it—always liked the plunge, and the excitement, and the coolness. I supposed it was what the Falls were for. They have no other use that I can see, and they must have been made for something. She says they were only made for scenery—like the rhinoceros and the mastodon.

I went over the Falls in a barrel—not satisfactory to her. Went over in a tub—still not satisfactory. Swam the Whirlpool and the Rapids in a fig-leaf suit. It got much damaged. Hence, tedious complaints about my extravagance. I am too much hampered here. What I need is change of scene.

Saturday.—I escaped last Tuesday night, and traveled two days, and built me another shelter, in a secluded place, and obliterated my tracks as well as I could, but she hunted me out by means of a beast which she has tamed and calls a wolf, and came making that pitiful noise again, and shedding that water out of the places she looks with. I was obliged to return with her, but will presently emigrate again, when occasion offers. She engages herself in many foolish things: among others, trying to study out why the animals called lions and tigers live on grass and flowers, when, as she says, the sort of teeth they wear would indicate that they were intended to eat each other. This is foolish, because to do that would be to kill each other, and that would introduce what, as I understand it, is called "death"; and death, as I have been told, has not yet entered the Park. Which is a pity, on some accounts.

Sunday.—Pulled through.

Monday.—I believe I see what the week is for: it is to give time to rest up from the weariness of Sunday. It seems a good idea. . . . She has been climbing that tree again. Clodded her out of it. She said nobody was looking. Seems to consider that a sufficient justification for chancing any dangerous thing. Told her that. The word justification moved her admiration—and envy too, I thought. It is a good word.

Thursday.—She told me she was made out of a rib taken from my body. This is at least doubtful, if not more than that. I have not missed any rib. . . . She is in much trouble about the buzzard; says grass does not agree with it; is afraid she can't raise it; thinks it was intended to live on decayed flesh. The buzzard must get along the best it can with what is provided. We cannot overturn the whole scheme to accommodate the buzzard.

Saturday.—She fell in the pond yesterday, when she was looking at herself in it, which she is always doing. She nearly strangled, and said it was most uncomfortable. This made her sorry for the creatures which live in there, which she calls fish, for she continues to fasten names onto things that don't need them and don't come when they are called by them, which is a matter of no consequence to her, as she is such a numskull anyway; so she got a lot of them out and brought them in last night and put them in my bed to keep warm, but I have noticed them now and then all day, and I don't see that they are any happier there than they were before, only quieter. When night comes I shall throw them outdoors. I will not sleep with them again, for I find them clammy and unpleasant to lie among when a person hasn't anything on.

Sunday.—Pulled through.

Tuesday.—She has taken up with a snake now. The other animals are glad, for she was always experimenting with them and bothering them; and I am glad, because the snake talks, and this enables me to get a rest.

Friday.—She says the snake advises her to try the fruit of that tree, and says the result will be a great and fine and noble education. I told her there would be another result, too—it would introduce death into the world. That was a mistake—it had been better to keep the remark to myself; it only gave her an idea—she could save the sick buzzard, and furnish fresh meat to the despondent lions and tigers.

I advised her to keep away from the tree. She said she wouldn't. I foresee trouble. Will emigrate.

Wednesday.—I have had a variegated time. I escaped that night, and rode a horse all night as fast as he could go, hoping to get clear out of the Park and hide in some other country before the trouble should begin; but it was not to be. About an hour after sunup, as I was riding through a flowery plain where thousands of animals were grazing, slumbering, or playing with each other, according to their wont, all of a sudden they broke into a tempest of frightful noises, and in one moment the plain was in a frantic commotion and every beast was destroying its neighbor. I knew what it meant—Eve had eaten that fruit, and death was come into the world. . . . The tigers ate my horse, paying no attention when I ordered them to desist, and they would even have eaten me if I had staid—which I didn't, but went away in much haste. . . . I found this place, outside the Park, and was fairly comfortable for a few days, but she has found me out. Found me out, and has named the place Tonawanda—says it *looks* like that. In fact I was not sorry she came, for there are but meagre pickings here, and she brought some of those apples. I was obliged to eat them, I was so hungry. It was against my principles, but I find that principles have no real force except when one is well fed. . . . She came curtained in boughs and bunches of leaves, and when I asked her what she meant by such nonsense, and snatched them away and threw them down, she tittered and blushed. I had never seen a person titter and blush before, and to me it seemed unbecoming and idiotic. She said I would soon know how it was myself. This was correct. Hungry as I was, I laid down the apple half eaten—certainly the best one I ever saw, considering the lateness of the season—and arrayed myself in the discarded boughs and branches, and then spoke to her with some severity and ordered her to go and get some more and not make such a spectacle of herself. She did it, and after this we crept down to where the wild-beast battle had been, and collected some skins, and I made her patch together a couple of suits proper for public occasions. They are uncomfortable, it is true, but stylish, and that is the main point about clothes. . . . I find she is a good deal of a companion. I see I should be lonesome and depressed without her, now that I have lost my property. Another thing, she says it is ordered that we work for our living hereafter. She will be useful. I will superintend.

Ten Days Later.—She accuses *me* of being the cause of our disaster! She says, with apparent sincerity and truth, that the Serpent assured

her that the forbidden fruit was not apples, it was chestnuts. I said
I was innocent, then, for I had not eaten any chestnuts. She said the
Serpent informed her that "chestnut" was a figurative term meaning
an aged and mouldy joke. I turned pale at that, for I have made many
jokes to pass the weary time, and some of them could have been of
that sort, though I had honestly supposed that they were new when
I made them. She asked me if I had made one just at the time of the
catastrophe. I was obliged to admit that I had made one to myself,
though not aloud. It was this. I was thinking about the Falls, and I
said to myself, "How wonderful it is to see that vast body of water
tumble down there!" Then in an instant a bright thought flashed into
my head, and I let it fly, saying, "It would be a deal more wonderful
to see it tumble *up* there!"—and I was just about to kill myself with
laughing at it when all nature broke loose in war and death, and I had
to flee for my life. "There," she said, with triumph, "that is just it;
the Serpent mentioned that very jest, and called it the First Chestnut,
and said it was coeval with the creation." Alas, I am indeed to blame.
Would that I were not witty; oh, would that I had never had that
radiant thought!

  Next Year.—We have named it Cain. She caught it while I was
up country trapping on the North Shore of the Erie; caught it in
the timber a couple of miles from our dug-out—or it might have been
four, she isn't certain which. It resembles us in some ways, and may
be a relation. That is what she thinks, but this is an error, in my
judgment. The difference in size warrants the conclusion that it is
a different and new kind of animal—a fish, perhaps, though when I
put it in the water to see, it sank, and she plunged in and snatched it
out before there was opportunity for the experiment to determine the
matter. I still think it is a fish, but she is indifferent about what it is,
and will not let me have it to try. I do not understand this. The
coming of the creature seems to have changed her whole nature and
made her unreasonable about experiments. She thinks more of it
than she does of any of the other animals, but is not able to explain
why. Her mind is disordered—everything shows it. Sometimes she
carries the fish in her arms half the night when it complains and wants
to get to the water. At such times the water comes out of the places
in her face that she looks out of, and she pats the fish on the back
and makes soft sounds with her mouth to soothe it, and betrays
sorrow and solicitude in a hundred ways. I have never seen her do
like this with any other fish, and it troubles me greatly. She used to
carry the young tigers around so, and play with them, before we lost

our property; but it was only play; she never took on about them like this when their dinner disagreed with them.

Sunday.—She doesn't work, Sundays, but lies around all tired out, and likes to have the fish wallow over her; and she makes fool noises to amuse it, and pretends to chew its paws, and that makes it laugh. I have not seen a fish before that could laugh. This makes me doubt. . . . I have come to like Sunday myself. Superintending all the week tires a body so. There ought to be more Sundays. In the old days they were tough, but now they come handy.

Wednesday.—It isn't a fish. I cannot quite make out what it is. It makes curious devilish noises when not satisfied, and says "goo-goo" when it is. It is not one of us, for it doesn't walk; it is not a bird, for it doesn't fly; it is not a frog, for it doesn't hop; it is not a snake, for it doesn't crawl; I feel sure it is not a fish, though I cannot get a chance to find out whether it can swim or not. It merely lies around, and mostly on its back, with its feet up. I have not seen any other animal do that before. I said I believed it was an enigma, but she only admired the word without understanding it. In my judgment it is either an enigma or some kind of a bug. If it dies, I will take it apart and see what its arrangements are. I never had a thing perplex me so.

Three Months Later.—The perplexity augments instead of diminishing. I sleep but little. It has ceased from lying around, and goes about on its four legs, now. Yet it differs from the other four-legged animals in that its front legs are unusually short, consequently this causes the main part of its person to stick up uncomfortably high in the air, and this is not attractive. It is built much as we are, but its method of traveling shows that it is not of our breed. The short front legs and long hind ones indicate that it is of the kangaroo family, but it is a marked variation of the species, since the true kangaroo hops, whereas this one never does. Still it is a curious and interesting variety, and has not been catalogued before. As I discovered it, I have felt justified in securing the credit of the discovery by attaching my name to it, and hence have called it *Kangaroorum Adamiensis*. . . . It must have been a young one when it came, for it has grown exceedingly since. It must be five times as big, now, as it was then, and when discontented is able to make from twenty-two to thirty-eight times the noise it made at first. Coercion does not modify this, but has the contrary effect. For this reason I discontinued the system. She reconciles it by persuasion, and by giving it things which she had previously told it she wouldn't give it. As already observed, I was not at home when it first came, and she told me she found it in the woods. It seems odd that it should be the only one, yet it must be so, for I have worn myself out these many weeks trying to find another one to add to my collection, and for this one to play with; for surely then it would be quieter, and we could tame it more easily. But I find none, nor any vestige of any; and strangest of all, no tracks. It has to live on the ground, it cannot help itself; therefore, how does it get about without leaving a track? I have set a dozen traps, but they do no good. I catch all small animals except that one; animals that merely go into the trap out of curiosity, I think, to see what the milk is there for. They never drink it.

Three Months Later.—The kangaroo still continues to grow, which is very strange and perplexing. I never knew one to be so long getting its growth. It has fur on its head now; not like kangaroo fur, but exactly like our hair, except that it is much finer and softer, and instead of being black is red. I am like to lose my mind over the capricious and harassing developments of this unclassifiable zoological freak. If I could catch another one—but that is hopeless; it is a new variety, and the only sample; this is plain. But I caught a true kangaroo and brought it in, thinking that this one, being lonesome, would rather have that for company than have no kin at all, or any animal it could feel a nearness to or get sympathy from in its forlorn condition here among strangers who do not know its ways or habits, or what to do to make it feel that it is among friends; but it was a mistake—it went into such fits at the sight of the kangaroo that I was convinced it had never seen one before. I pity the poor noisy little animal, but there is nothing I can do to make it happy. If I could tame it—but that is out of the question; the more I try, the worse I seem to make it. It grieves me to the heart to see it in its little storms of sorrow and passion. I wanted to let it go, but she wouldn't hear of it. That seemed cruel and not like her; and yet she may be right. It might be lonelier than ever; for since I cannot find another one, how could *it*?

Five Months Later.—It is not a kangaroo. No, for it supports itself by holding to her finger, and thus goes a few steps on its hind legs, and then falls down. It is probably some kind of a bear; and yet it has no tail—as yet—and no fur, except on its head. It still keeps on growing—that is a curious circumstance, for bears get their growth earlier than this. Bears are dangerous—since our catastrophe—and I shall not be satisfied to have this one prowling about the place much longer without a muzzle on. I have offered to get her a kangaroo if she would let this one go, but it did no good—she is determined to run us into all sorts of foolish risks, I think. She was not like this before she lost her mind.

A Fortnight Later.—I examined its mouth. There is no danger yet; it has only one tooth. It has no tail yet. It makes more noise now than it ever did before—and mainly at night. I have moved out. But I shall go over, mornings, to breakfast, and to see if it has more teeth. If it gets a mouthful of teeth it will be time for it to go, tail or no tail, for a bear does not need a tail in order to be dangerous.

Four Months Later.—I have been off hunting, and fishing a month, up in the region that she calls Buffalo; I don't know why, unless it is because there are not any buffaloes there. Meantime the bear has learned to paddle around all by itself on its hind legs, and says "poppa" and "momma." It is certainly a new species. This resemblance to words may be purely accidental, of course, and may have no purpose or meaning; but even in that case it is still extraordinary, and is a thing which no other bear can do. This imitation of speech, taken together with general absence of fur and entire absence of tail, sufficiently indicates that this is a new kind of bear. The further study of it will be exceedingly interesting. Meantime I will go off on a far expedition among the forests of the North and make an exhaustive search. There must certainly be another one somewhere, and this one will be less dangerous when it has company of its own species. I will go straightway; but I will muzzle this one first.

Three Months Later.—It has been a weary, weary hunt, yet I have had no success. In the meantime, without stirring from the home estate, she has caught another one! I never saw such luck. I might have hunted these woods a hundred years, I never should have run across that thing.

Next Day.—I have been comparing the new one with the old one, and it is perfectly plain that they are the same breed. I was going to stuff one of them for my collection, but she is prejudiced against it for some reason or other; so I have relinquished the idea, though I think it is a mistake. It would be an irreparable loss to science if they should get away. The old one is tamer than it was, and can laugh and talk like the parrot, having learned this, no doubt, from being with the parrot so much, and having the imitative faculty in a highly developed degree. I shall be astonished if it turns out to be a new kind of parrot; and yet I ought not to be astonished, for it has already been everything else it could think of, since those first days when it was a fish. The new one is as ugly now as the old one was at first; has the same sulphur-and-raw-meat complexion and the same singular head without any fur on it. She calls it Abel.

Ten Years Later.—They are boys; we found it out long ago. It was their coming in that small, immature shape that puzzled us; we were not used to it. There are some girls now. Abel is a good boy, but if Cain had staid a bear it would have improved him. After all these years, I see that I was mistaken about Eve in the beginning; it is better to live outside the Garden with her than inside it without her. At first I thought she talked too much; but now I should be sorry to have that voice fall silent and pass out of my life. Blessed be the chestnut that brought us near together and taught me to know the goodness of her heart and the sweetness of her spirit!

WILLIAM H. WHYTE, Jr.

You, Too, Can Write the Casual Style

A revolution has taken place in American prose. No longer the short huffs and puffs, the unqualified word, the crude gusto of the declarative sentence. Today the fashion is to write casually.

The Casual Style is not exactly new. Originated in the early Twenties, it has been refined and improved and refined again by a relatively small band of writers, principally for *The New Yorker*, until now their mannerisms have become standards of sophistication. Everybody is trying to join the club. Newspaper columnists have forsaken the beloved metaphors of the sports page for the Casual Style, and one of the quickest ways for an ad man to snag an award from other ad men is to give his copy the low-key, casual pitch; the copy shouldn't sing these days—it should whisper. Even Dr. Rudolf Flesch, who has been doing so much to teach people how to write like other people, is counseling his followers to use the Casual Style. Everywhere the ideal seems the same: be casual.

But how? There is very little down-to-earth advice. We hear about the rapier-like handling of the bromide, the keen eye for sham and pretension, the exquisite sense of nuance, the unerring ear for the vulgate. But not much about actual technique. The layman, as a consequence, is apt to look on the Casual Style as a mandarin dialect which he fears he could never master.

Nonsense. The Casual Style is within everyone's grasp. It has now become so perfected by constant polishing that its devices may readily be identified, and they change so little that their use need be no more difficult for the novice than for the expert. (That's not quite all there is to it, of course. Some apparently casual writers, Thurber and E. B. White, among others, rarely use the devices.)

The subject matter, in the first place, is not to be ignored. Generally speaking, the more uneventful it is, or the more pallid the writer's reaction to it, the better do form and content marry. Take, for example, the cocktail party at which the writer can show how bored everyone is with everyone else, and how utterly fatuous they all are anyhow. Since a non-casual statement—e.g., "The party was a bore" —would destroy the reason for writing about it at all, the Casual Style here is not only desirable but mandatory.

Whatever the subject, however, twelve devices are the rock on which all else is built. I will present them one by one, illustrating them with examples from such leading casual stylists as Wolcott Gibbs, John Crosby, John McCarten, and (on occasion) this magazine's "Mr. Harper." If the reader will digest what follows, he should be able to dash off a paragraph indistinguishable from the best casual writing being done today.

(1) *Heightened Understatement.* Where the old-style writer would say, "I don't like it," "It is not good," or something equally banal, the casual writer says it is *"something less than* good." He avoids direct statement and strong words—except, as we will note, where he is setting them up to have something to knock down. In any event, he qualifies. "Somewhat" and "rather," the bread-and-butter words of the casual writer, should become habitual with you; similarly with such phrases as "I suppose," "it seems to me," "I guess," or "I'm afraid." "Elusive" or "elude" are good, too, and if you see the word "charm" in a casual sentence you can be pretty sure that "eludes me," or "I find elusive," will not be far behind.

(2) *The Multiple Hedge.* Set up an ostensibly strong statement, and then, with your qualifiers, shoot a series of alternately negative and positive charges into the sentence until finally you neutralize the whole thing. Let's take, for example, the clause, "certain names have a guaranteed nostalgic magic." Challenge enough here; the names not only have magic, they have guaranteed magic. A double hedge reverses

the charge. "Names which have, *I suppose* [hedge 1], a guaranteed nostalgic magic, *though there are times that I doubt it* [hedge 2]. . . ."

We didn't have to say they were guaranteed in the first place, of course, but without such straw phrases we wouldn't have anything to construct a hedge on and, frequently, nothing to write at all. The virtue of the hedge is that by its very negating effect it makes any sentence infinitely expansible. Even if you have so torn down your original statement with one or two hedges that you seem to have come to the end of the line, you have only to slip in an anti-hedge, a strengthening word (*e.g.*, "definitely," "unqualified," etc.), and begin the process all over again. Witness the following quadruple hedge: "I found Mr. Home entertaining *from time to time* [hedge 1] on the ground, *I guess* [hedge 2], that the singular idiom and unearthly detachment of the British upper classes have *always* [anti-hedge] seemed reasonably [hedge 3] droll to me, *at least in moderation* [hedge 4]." The art of plain talk, as has been pointed out, does not entail undue brevity.

If you've pulled hedge on hedge and the effect still remains too vigorous, simply wipe the slate clean with a cancellation clause at the end. "It was all exactly as foolish as it sounds," says Wolcott Gibbs, winding up some 570 casual words on a subject, "and I wouldn't give it another thought."

(3) *Narcissizing Your Prose.* The casual style is nothing if not personal; indeed, you will usually find in it as many references to the writer as to what he's supposed to be talking about. For you do not talk about the subject; you talk about its impact on you. With the reader peering over your shoulder, you look into the mirror and observe your own responses as you run the entire range of the casual writer's emotions. You may reveal yourself as, in turn, listless ("the audience seemed not to share my boredom"); insouciant ("I was really quite happy with it"); irritated ("The whole thing left me tired and cross"); comparatively gracious ("Being in a comparatively gracious mood, I won't go into the details I didn't like"); or hesitant ("I wish I could say that I could accept his hypothesis").

(4) *Preparation for the Witticism.* When the casual writer hits upon a clever turn of phrase or a nice conceit, he uses this device to insure that his conceit will not pass unnoticed. Suppose, for example, you have thought of something to say that is pretty damn good if you say so yourself. The device, in effect, is to say so yourself. If you want to devastate a certain work as "a study of vulgarity in high

places," don't say this flat out. Earlier in the sentence prepare the reader for the drollery ahead with something like "what I am tempted to call" or "what could best be described as" or "If it had to be defined in a sentence, it might well be called. . . ."

Every writer his own claque.

(5) *Deciphered Notes Device; or Cute-Things-I-Have-Said*. In this one you are your own stooge as well. You feed yourself lines. By means of the slender fiction that you have written something on the back of an envelope or the margin of a program, you catch yourself good-humoredly trying to decipher these shrewd, if cryptic, little jottings. *Viz.:* "Their diagnoses are not nearly as crisp as those I find in my notes"; ". . . sounds like an inadequate description, but it's all I have on my notes, and it may conceivably be a very high compliment."

(6) *The Kicker*. An echo effect. "My reactions [included] an irritable feeling that eleven o'clock was past Miss Keim's bedtime,"— and now the Kicker—"*not to mention my own.*" This type of thing practically writes itself. "She returns home. She should never have left home in the first place. —— —— —— —." [1]

(7) *Wit of Omission*. By calling attention to the fact that you are not going to say it, you suggest that there is something very funny you could say if only you wanted to. "A thought occurred to me at this point," you may say, when otherwise stymied, "but I think we had better not go into *that*."

(8) *The Planned Colloquialism*. The casual writer savors colloquialisms. This is not ordinary colloquial talk—nobody is more quickly provoked than the casual writer by ordinary usage. It is, rather, a playful descent into the vulgate. Phrases like "darn," "awfully," "as all getout," "mighty," and other folksy idioms are ideal. The less you would be likely to use the word normally yourself the more pointed the effect. Contrast is what you are after, for it is the facetious interplay of language levels—a blending, as it were, of the East Fifties and the Sticks—that gives the Casual Style its off-hand charm.

(9) *Feigned Forgetfulness*. Conversation gropes; it is full of "what I really meant was" and "maybe I should have added," backings and fillings and second thoughts of one kind or another. Writing is different; theoretically, ironing out second thoughts beforehand is one of the things writers are paid to do. In the Casual Style, however, it is exactly this exposure of the writer composing in public that makes it so casual. For the professional touch, then, ramble, rebuke yourself in print ("what I really meant, I guess"), and if you have something

[1] "And neither should I."

you feel you should have said earlier, don't say it earlier, but say later that you guess you should have said it earlier.

(10) *The Subject-Apologizer, or Pardon-Me-for-Living.* The Casual Stylist must always allow for the possibility that his subject is just as boring to the reader as it is to him. He may forestall this by seeming to have stumbled on it by accident, or by using phrases like: "If this is as much news to you as it is to me," or "This, in case you've been living in a cave lately, is. . . ."

(11) *The Omitted Word.* This all began modestly enough the day a *New Yorker* writer dropped the articles "the" and "a" from the initial sentence of an anecdote (*e.g.,* "Man we know told us"; "Fellow name of Brown"). Now even such resolutely lowbrow writers as Robert Ruark affect it, and they are applying it to any part of speech anywhere in the sentence. You can drop a pronoun ("Says they're shaped like pyramids"); verb ("You been away from soap opera the last couple of weeks?"); or preposition ("Far as glamour goes . . .").

(12) *The Right Word.* In the lexicon of the casual writer there are a dozen or so adjectives which in any context have, to borrow a phrase, a guaranteed charm. Attrition is high—"brittle," "febrile," "confected," for example, are at the end of the run. Ten, however, defy obsolescence: *antic, arch, blurred, chaste, chill, crisp, churlish, disheveled, dim, disembodied.*

They are good singly, but they are even better when used in tandem; cf., "In an arch, antic sort of way"; "In an arch, blurred sort of way"; "In an arch, crisp sort of way." And so on.

Finally, the most multi-purpose word of them all: "altogether." Frequently it is the companion of "charming" and "delightful," and in this coupling is indispensable to any kind of drama criticism. It can also modify the writer himself (*e.g.,* "Altogether, I think . . ."). Used best, however, it just floats, unbeholden to any other part of the sentence.

Once you have mastered these twelve devices, you too should be able to write as casually as all getout. At least it seems to me, though I may be wrong, that they convey an elusive archness which the crisp literary craftsman, in his own dim sort of way, should altogether cultivate these days. Come to think of it, the charm of the Casual Style is something less than clear to me, but we needn't go into *that.* Fellow I know from another magazine says this point of view best described as churlish. Not, of course, that it matters.

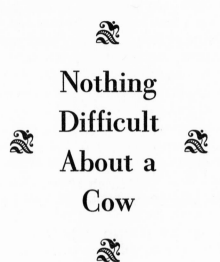

Nothing Difficult About a Cow

My wife contracted for the Montana ranch while I was away from our home in Kentucky. We had talked about it before, though. We both thought it would be good to have a summer hideaway in the West I write about. We even knew the place we wanted—a section of rock-and-jack-pine land with a house that sat on the edge of a small lake. So when my wife's sister called from Montana to say that Twin Lakes finally was for sale and that she still wanted a piece of it, my wife told her to proceed.

That much had been agreed upon. What hadn't been discussed with me was the cow and calf that the girls bought while they were about it.

On my return to Kentucky my wife broke the news. A registered Brown Swiss, newly freshened, and the calf by her side! Brown Swiss, a breed famed for placidity. Won't it be wonderful, she asked, her breath already a little milky, to have cream and home-made cottage cheese and butter fresh from the churn?

In my boyhood I had had some experience with milk cows. We had one roan animal, in appearance a cross between a buffalo and a Texas longhorn, that had suffered frostbite of the udder while hiding out with her newborn calf during a blizzard. She had to be milked in a tin cup, in takes, from behind a sheep panel. Though in time her udder healed, her disposition was frosty ever after. As safely approach a lion without a chair as approach her without a panel.

Her successor was a faun-like Jersey, a trim and fetching creature that we called Deerie at first. This one, Father said, wouldn't kick. Her butterfat content was terrific. He was right. The fault with Deerie, we were to discover, was her unalterable conviction that, once she had finished her bran, proceedings was over. So, often, was the milk pail. If not tied, she just ran off. Tied, she sashayed. To get her to stand, I had to give her second helpings and even thirds. At its final best, milking was an exact operation, a synchronization of consumption and production to the split second at which I'd whisk the milk pail away and she'd whisk away. Once, sensing that she would finish before I did, I got up, set the bucket aside and went for more bran. While I was gone, she drank the milk I'd milked. It bemused me that I couldn't squeeze it right out again.

But fine, I said to my wife, out of memories gentled by the years. I even caught a little of her enthusiasm. Maybe we would want to build a springhouse. We went to Montana.

The cow wasn't big, as Brown Swiss usually are. She had no horns. She seemed quite accustomed to people. And yet, looking at her while my wife chattered of oceans of milk and cream too thick to pour, I had the feeling that this was a fated encounter. At some level we seemed to communicate. I know now that that level was the level of instant and implacable antagonism.

There are drawbacks to the keeping of milk cows, regardless of animal or place. If a man has one, he ought to be up before the flies, which is early in any case and earlier than that in the northern latitudes. Also to escape the flies, he ought to milk in the cool of the evening, at about the time the flies knock off and the mosquitoes take over. A dawn and dusk chore, milking is a seven-day-a-week chore. Nothing short of jail is more confining than a cow. You can employ baby sitters, but who'll milk for you? The final complaint is this: to associate with a cow is to smell like one. Wash with soap and water, scour with abrasives, apply perfumes and deodorants, change clothes—a residual effluvium remains. I doubt even that chlorophyll would work. The cow is full of it, isn't she?

These trials I endured with my fellow milkmen the world over, if with less regularity and resignation. I do not like to go to bed early.

Neither did my guests, of whom the summer provided quite a few. They acted as if no man had to give thought to the morrow. I do not like to get up early. I do not like to be tied to a chore. I do not like to be chained to one spot, or to have to heed the bidding of a clock. I do not like to smell.

The consequence was a compromise except for the last item. I milked in the mornings at about eight-thirty or nine or ten o'clock, which is early enough for anyone of good conscience and honorable purpose. Often I would have ignored the evening's ordeal but for my wife, who worried lest the cow be suffering. This is a possibility that appears to distress women particularly. It did no good to answer that if Bossie was suffering it was a shabby appreciation she showed for relief. On rare occasions, which became less rare with time, I was permitted to put the cow and calf together and let nature take its course. This dereliction of duty, I confess, always made me feel pretty guilty though it fattened the calf. After all, as my wife often re-marked, there was right on the place more milk than we could use if we'd just take pains to get it.

A deceptive amity marked the first engagement between Bossie and me. She kicked a couple of times, but almost idly. I responded quietly, blaming my own lack of practice. No one likes to be pinched anywhere. I strode to the house with a full bucket of good Brown Swiss milk. Thereafter the situation deteriorated with great rapidity.

I want to be fair about this. There were, I know, extenuating cir-cumstances. The cow was chapped. She got worse as with increasing frequency I sneaked the calf to her. Of mornings the flies were big and numerous and resolute. Having no barn, I had to milk outside. I was, indeed, unpracticed. But beyond all allowances there was, I'm convinced, that spontaneous hostility.

Bossie's manifestations of it were confined to the rear, though her gaze was slow and brooding, as if she wished for horns. She allowed me to put a halter on her and tie her up. She ate cottonseed cake out of my hand. Only once did she butt my wind out, and then she was swinging for a fly. It was, indeed, hard to reconcile the forward tolerance and the backward passion. I fancied sometimes that the front end was the conscious and the rear the unconscious, which will kick the hell out of you if you don't watch out.

It kicked the hell out of me. That cow, improving with practice, scuffed my forearm, barked my knuckles, bruised my leg, batted me off the stool, belted pail after pail from between my knees. It got so I didn't have to be in operating position to have a pass made at me.

Just let me look at her flank and up came her leg. She also had a way with her tail, though it was by comparison unimportant.

There are patented substances, promoted as unguents and balms for the relief of chap, fly bites, and general inflammation. I tried these, though applying them was like working through an electric fan.

I bought cow hobbles. These are metal brackets, connected by a short piece of chain, that fit over the back legs. With them in place —if you can get them in place—a cow can't kick, they say. Mine could. Within two or three days she caught the trick of slipping the left clamp as she swung the right foot. And whereas I'd faced only the foot before, now I had to reckon with flying metal. The hobbles strengthened and extended her fire power.

Often now we bought milk when we happened to drive the twenty-three miles to town. More and more I left my duties to the calf, though the cow had sunk so low as to try to kick her own child's head off. But I was of bad conscience and in bad grace. My wife and my wife's sister and my children looked at me with something close to contempt, though none of them offered to sub for me. They aired my troubles in our little town, with the result that fun-loving friends were forever making innocent inquiry about that nice animal I'd bought. They asked if I really didn't enjoy juicing a cow again. My own flesh and blood listened with appreciation.

And so, one morning, I took a lariat with me when I went out to milk. I stepped the cow's back legs into the loop of it after I had haltered and tied her. I pulled the loop tight and strained the rope around an aspen. To cap my mastery, I tied Bossie's tail with a sash cord and anchored the cord to a tent peg. Now I had her. Spread-eagled, she couldn't do a thing. You think so, do you? Two resources, needing no elaboration, remain to a cow when all else is gone. These my cow used deliberately, I know, out of no physical and inward need, out of malice beyond cure or check.

My wife came out while I was squeezing away. Her sister was with her. They took sober note of the tied legs. They sized up the pegged tail.

My wife said to my sister-in-law, "I feel sorry for the poor thing."

My sister-in-law said to my wife, "I know she was all right when we bought her."

The girls sold Bossie a day or two afterward. Good deal, too, they agreed. Got as much for the cow as they had paid for the cow and calf. I suggested strongly that they throw in the calf as boot. It's a heifer, name of Brownie.

Madame Rosette

"Oh, this is wonderful," said the Stag. He was lying back in the bath with a scotch and soda in one hand and a cigarette in the other. The water was right up to the brim, and he was keeping it warm by turning the tap with his toes.

He raised his head and took a little sip of his whiskey, then he lay back and closed his eyes.

"For God's sake, get out," said a voice from the next room. "Come on, Stag, you've had over an hour." Stuffy was sitting on the edge of the bed with no clothes on, drinking slowly and waiting his turn.

The Stag said, "All right. I'm letting the water out now," and he stretched out a leg and flipped up the plug with his toes.

Stuffy stood up and wandered into the bathroom holding his drink in his hand. The Stag lay in the bath for a few moments more, then, balancing his glass carefully on the soap rack, he stood up and reached for a towel. His body was short and square, with strong thick legs and exaggerated calf muscles. He had coarse, curly ginger hair and a thin, rather pointed face covered with freckles.

"I've brought half the desert with me," he said, looking down into the bathtub.

Stuffy said, "Wash it out and let me get in. I haven't had a bath for five months."

This was back in the early days when we were fighting the Italians in Libya. One flew very hard in those days because there were not

28

many pilots. They certainly could not send any out from England because there they were fighting the Battle of Britain. So one remained for long periods out in the desert, living the strange unnatural life of the desert, living in the same dirty little tent, washing and shaving every day in a mug full of one's own spat-out tooth water, all the time picking flies out of one's tea and out of one's food, having sandstorms which were as much in the tents as outside them, so that placid men became bloody-minded and lost their tempers with their friends and with themselves; having dysentery and gippy tummy and mastoid and desert sores, having some bombs from the Italian S.79's, having no water and no women; having very little except sand sand sand. One flew old Gloster Gladiators against the Italian C.R.42's, and when one was not flying, it was difficult to know what to do.

Occasionally one would catch scorpions, put them in empty petrol cans and match them against each other in fierce mortal combat. Always there would be a champion scorpion in the squadron, a sort of Joe Louis who was invincible and won all his fights. He would have a name; he would become famous and his training diet would be a great secret known only to the owner. Training diet was considered very important with scorpions. Some were trained on corned beef, some on a thing called Machonachies, which is an unpleasant canned meat stew, some on live beetles, and there were others who were persuaded to take a little beer just before the fight on the premise that it made the scorpion happy and gave him confidence. These last ones always lost. But there were great battles and great champions, and in the afternoons when the flying was over, one could often see a group of pilots and airmen standing around in a circle on the sand, bending over with their hands on their knees, watching the fight, exhorting the scorpions and shouting at them as people shout at boxers or wrestlers in a ring. The greatest scorpion of all was owned by a sergeant called Wishful who fed him only on marmalade. The animal had an unmentionable name, but he won forty-two consecutive fights and then died quietly in training just when Wishful was considering the problem of retiring him to stud.

So you can see that because there were no great pleasures while living in the desert, the small pleasures became great pleasures and the pleasures of children became the pleasures of grown men. That was true for everyone; for the pilots, the fitters, the riggers, the corporals who cooked the food and the men who kept the stores. It was true for the Stag and for Stuffy, so true that when the two of them wangled a forty-eight-hour pass and a lift by air into Cairo, and when they got to the hotel, they were feeling about having a bath rather as you would feel on the first night of your honeymoon.

The Stag had dried himself and was lying on the bed with a towel round his waist, with his hands up behind his head, and Stuffy was in the bath, lying with his head against the back of the bath, groaning and sighing with ecstasy.

The Stag said, "Stuffy."

"Yes."

"What are we going to do now?"

"Women," said Stuffy. "We must find some women to take out to supper."

The Stag said, "Later. That can wait till later." It was then early afternoon.

"I don't think it can wait," said Stuffy.

"Yes," said the Stag, "it can wait."

The Stag was very old and wise; he never rushed any fences. He was twenty-seven, much older than anyone else in the squadron, including the C.O., and his judgment was respected by the others in much the same way as the judgment of a university professor is respected by the students.

"Let's do a little shopping first," he said.

"Then what?" said the voice from the bathroom.

"Then we can consider the other situation."

There was a pause.

"Stag?"

"Yes."

"Do you know any women here?"

"I used to. I used to know a Turkish girl with very white skin called Wenka, and a Yugoslav girl who was six inches taller than I, called Kiki, and another who I think was Syrian. I can't remember her name."

"Ring them up," said Stuffy.

"I've done it. I did it while you were getting the whiskey. They've all gone. It isn't any good."

Stuffy said, "It's never any good."

The Stag said, "We'll go shopping first. There is plenty of time."

In an hour Stuffy got out of the bath. They both dressed themselves in clean khaki shorts and shirts and wandered downstairs, through the lobby of the hotel and out into the bright hot street. The Stag put on his sunglasses.

Stuffy said, "I know. I want a pair of sunglasses."

"All right. We'll go and buy some."

They stopped a gharri, got in, and told the driver to go to Cicurel's. Stuffy bought his sunglasses and the Stag bought some poker-dice, then they wandered out again onto the hot crowded street.

"Did you see that girl?" said Stuffy.

"The one that sold us the sunglasses?"

"Yes. That dark one."

"Probably Turkish," said Stag.

Stuffy said, "I don't care what she was. She was terrific. Didn't you think she was terrific?"

They were walking along the Sharia Kasr-el-Nil with their hands in their pockets, and Stuffy was wearing the sunglasses which he had just bought. It was a hot dusty afternoon, and the sidewalk was crowded with Egyptians and Arabs and small boys with bare feet, and the small boys pattered along beside the Stag and Stuffy shouting "baksheesh," "baksheesh" in shrill insistent voices, and the flies followed the small boys. There was the smell of Cairo, which is not like the smell of any other city. It comes not from any one thing or from any one place; it comes from everything everywhere; from the gutters and the sidewalks, from the houses and the shops and the things in the shops and the food cooking in the shops, from the horses and the dung of the horses in the streets and from the drains. It is a rare, pungent smell like the smell of something which is sweet and rotting and hot and salty and bitter all at the same time, and it is never absent, even in the cool of the early morning.

The two pilots walked along slowly through the crowd.

"Didn't you think she was terrific?" said Stuffy. He wanted to know what the Stag thought.

"She was all right."

"Certainly she was all right. You know what, Stag?"

"What?"

"I would like to take that girl out tonight."

They crossed over a street and walked on a little further.

The Stag said, "Well, why don't you? Why don't you ring up Rosette?"

"Who in the hell's Rosette?"

"Madame Rosette," said the Stag. "She is a great woman."

They were passing a place called Tim's Bar. It was run by an Englishman called Tim Gilfillan, who had been a quartermaster sergeant in the last war and who had somehow managed to get left behind in Cairo when the army went home.

"Tim's," said the Stag. "Let's go in."

There was no one inside except Tim, who was arranging his bottles on shelves behind the bar.

"Well, well, well," he said, turning around. "Where you boys been all this time?"

"Hello, Tim."

He did not remember them, but he knew by their looks that they were in from the desert.

"How's my old friend Graziani?" he asked, turning around and leaning his elbows on the counter.

"He's bloody close," said the Stag. "He's outside Mersa."

They got their whiskey and carried the glasses over to a table in the corner.

Stuffy said, "Who's this Rosette?"

The Stag took a long drink and put down the glass.

"She's a great woman," he said.

"Who is she?"

"She's a filthy old Syrian bitch."

"All right," said Stuffy, "but what about her?"

"Well," said Stag, "I'll tell you. Madame Rosette runs the biggest brothel in the world. It is said that she can get you any girl that you want in the whole of Cairo. You just ring her up and tell her where you saw the woman, where she was working, what shop and at which counter, together with an accurate description, and she will do the rest."

"Don't be such a bloody fool," said Stuffy.

"It's true. It's absolutely true. Thirty-three Squadron told me about her."

"They were pulling your leg."

"All right. You go and look her up in the phone book."

"She wouldn't be in the phone book under that name."

"I'm telling you she is," said Stag. "Go and look her up under Rosette. You'll see I'm right."

Stuffy did not believe him, but he went over to Tim and asked him for a telephone directory and brought it back to the table. He opened it and turned the pages until he came to R-o-s. He ran his finger down the column. Roseppi . . . Rosery . . . Rosette. There it was, Rosette, Madame, and the address and number, clearly printed in the book. The Stag was watching him.

"Got it?" he said.

"Yes, here it is. Madame Rosette."

"Well, why don't you go and ring her up?" The Stag picked up his drink.

"What shall I say?"

The Stag looked down into his glass and poked the ice with his finger.

"Tell her you are a colonel," he said. "Colonel Higgins. She mistrusts pilot officers; and tell her that you have seen a beautiful dark girl selling sunglasses at Cicurel's and that you would like, as you put it, to take her out to dinner."

"There isn't a telephone here."

"Oh, yes, there is. There's one over there."

Stuffy looked around and saw the telephone on the wall at the end of the bar.

"Tim will hear everything I say."

"What the hell does that matter? He probably rings her up himself."

Stuffy was just a child. He was nineteen, eight whole years younger than the Stag. He was fairly tall and he was thin with a lot of black hair and a handsome wide-mouthed face which was coffee brown from the sun of the desert. He was unquestionably the finest pilot in the squadron, and already in these early days his score was fourteen Italians confirmed destroyed. On the ground he moved slowly and lazily like a tired person, and he thought slowly and lazily like a sleepy child, but when he was up in the air his mind was quick and his movements were quick, so quick that they were like reflex actions which happened automatically and instantaneously as a result of something else having happened before. It seemed when he was on the ground almost as though he was resting, dozing a little in order to make sure that when he got into the cockpit he would wake up ready for that two hours of high concentration. But now he had something on his mind which had waked him up almost like flying. For the moment, anyway, he was concentrating.

Stuffy looked again in the book for the number, got up and walked slowly over to the telephone. He put in a piastre, dialed the number and heard it ringing at the other end. The Stag was sitting at the table looking at him and Tim was still behind the bar arranging his bottles. Tim was only about five yards away and he was obviously going to listen to everything that was said. Stuffy felt rather foolish. He leaned against the bar and waited, hoping that no one would answer.

Then there was a click and he heard a woman's voice saying "Allo."

He said, "Hello, is Madame Rosette there?" He was watching Tim. Tim went on arranging his bottles, pretending to take no notice, but Stuffy knew that he was listening.

"This ees Madame Rosette. Oo ees it?" Her voice was petulant and gritty, and she sounded as if she did not want to be bothered with anyone just then.

Stuffy tried to sound casual. "This is Colonel Higgins."

"Colonel oo?"

"Colonel Higgins." He spelled it.

"Yes, Colonel. What do you want?" She sounded impatient. He still tried to sound casual.

"Well, Madame Rosette, I was wondering if you could help me over a little matter."

Stuffy was watching Tim. He was listening all right, moving the bottles quickly from one shelf to another, watching the bottles, making no noise, never looking around into the room. Over in the far corner the Stag was leaning forward with his elbows on the table, smoking a cigarette, enjoying the whole business and knowing that Stuffy was embarrassed because of Tim. Stuffy had to go on.

"I was wondering if you could help me," he said. "I was in Cicurel's today buying a pair of sunglasses and I saw a girl there whom I would very much like to take out to dinner."

"What's 'er name?" The hard, rasping voice was more business-like than ever.

"I don't know," he said sheepishly.

"What's she look like?"

"Well, she's got dark hair, and tall and, well, she's very beautiful."

"What sort of a dress was she wearing?"

"Er, let me see. I think it was a kind of white dress with red flowers printed all over it." Then, as a brilliant afterthought, he added, "She had a red belt."

There was a pause. Then the loud gritty voice again, "It may cost you a lot."

"That's all right." Suddenly he didn't like the conversation any more. He wanted to finish it and get away quickly.

"Might cost you six pounds, might cost you eight or ten. I don't know till I've seen her. That all right?"

"Yes, yes, that's all right."

"Where you living, Colonel?"

"Metropolitan Hotel," he said without thinking.

"All right, I give you a ring later." And she put down the receiver bang.

Stuffy hung up, went slowly back to the table and sat down.

"Well," said Stag, "what did she say?"

"She said she would call me back at the hotel."

"You mean she'll call Colonel Higgins at the hotel."

Stuffy swore.

Stag said, "It's all right. We'll tell the desk that the Colonel is in our room, and to put his calls through to us. What else did she say?"

"She said it may cost me a lot, six or ten pounds."

"Rosette will take ninety per cent of it," said Stag. "She's a filthy old Syrian bitch."

"How will she work it?" Stuffy asked.

He was really a gentle person, and now he was feeling worried about having started something which might become complicated.

"Well," said Stag, "she'll dispatch one of her pimps to locate the girl and find out who she is. If she's already on the books, then it's easy. If she isn't, the pimp will proposition her there and then over the counter at Cicurel's. If the girl tells him to go to hell, he'll up the price, and if she still tells him to go to hell, he'll up the price still more, and in the end she'll be tempted by the cash and probably agree. Then Rosette quotes you a price three times as high and takes the balance herself. You have to pay her, not the girl. Of course, after that the girl goes on Rosette's books, and once she's in her clutches she's finished. Next time Rosette will dictate the price, and the girl will not be in a position to argue."

"Why?"

"Because if she refuses, Rosette will say, 'All right, my girl, I shall see that Cicurel's are told about what you did last time, and how you've been working for me and using their shop as a marketplace. Then they'll fire you.' That's what Rosette will say, and the wretched girl will be frightened and do what she's told."

Stuffy said, "Sounds like a nice person."

"Charming," said Stag. "She's a charming person."

It was hot. Stuffy wiped his face with his handkerchief.

"More whiskey," said Stag. "Hi, Tim, two more of those."

Tim brought the glasses over and put them on the table without saying anything. He picked up the empty glasses and went away at once. To Stuffy it seemed as though he was different from what he had been when they first came in. There wasn't any more hi, you fellows, where you been all this time, about him now, and when he got back behind the counter, he turned around and went on arranging the bottles.

The Stag said, "How much money you got?"

"Nine pounds, I think."

"May not be enough. You gave her a free hand, you know. You ought to have set a limit. She'll sting you now."

"I know," Stuffy said.

They went on drinking for a little while without talking. Then Stag said, "What you worrying about, Stuffy?"

"Nothing," he answered. "Nothing at all. Let's go back to the hotel. She may ring up."

They paid for their drinks and said good-by to Tim who nodded but didn't say anything. They went back to the Metropolitan and as they went past the desk the Stag said to the clerk, "If a call comes in for Colonel Higgins, put it through to our room. He'll be there." The Egyptian said, "Yes, sir," and made a note of it.

Stuffy had been quiet all the way back to the hotel. He hadn't said a word. Now, in the bedroom, he sat down on the edge of the bed with his hands still in his pockets and said, "Look, Stag, I'm not very keen on this Rosette deal any more. It may cost too much. Can't we put it off?"

The Stag sat up. "Hell no," he said. "You're committed. You can't back out."

"Well, wait and see."

Stuffy got up, went over to the parachute bag and took out the bottle of whiskey. He poured out two, filled the glasses with water from the tap in the bathroom, came back and gave one to the Stag.

"Stag," he said. "Ring up Rosette and tell her that Colonel Higgins has had to leave town urgently to rejoin his regiment in the desert. Ring her up and tell her that. Say the Colonel asked you to deliver the message because he didn't have time."

"Ring her up yourself."

"She'd recognize my voice. Come on, Stag, you ring her."

"No," he said, "I won't."

"Listen," said Stuffy suddenly. It was the child Stuffy speaking. "I don't want to go out with that woman and I don't want to have any dealings with Madame Rosette tonight. We can think of something else."

The Stag looked up quickly. Then he said, "All right. I'll ring her."

He reached for the telephone book, looked up her number, and spoke it into the telephone. Stuffy heard him get her on the line and he heard him giving her the message from the Colonel. There was a pause, then the Stag said, "I'm sorry, Madame Rosette, but it's nothing to do with me. I'm merely delivering a message." Another pause; then the Stag said the same thing over again and that went on for quite a long time, until he must have got tired of it because in the end he put down the receiver and lay back on his bed. He was roaring with laughter.

"The lousy old woman," he said, and he laughed some more. Stuffy said, "Was she angry?"

"Angry," said Stag. "Was she angry? You should have heard her. Wanted to know the Colonel's regiment and God knows what else and said he'd have to pay. She said you boys think you can fool around with me but you can't."

"Hooray," said Stuffy. "The filthy old Syrian bitch."

"Now what are we going to do?" said the Stag. "It's six o'clock already."

"Let's go out and do a little drinking in some of those Gyppi places."

"Fine. We'll do a Gyppi pub-crawl."

They had one more drink, then they went out. They went to a place called the Excelsior, then they went to a place called the Sphinx, then to a small place called by an Egyptian name, and by ten o'clock they were sitting happily in a place which hadn't got a name at all, drinking beer and watching a kind of stage show. At the Sphinx they had picked up a pilot from Thirty-three Squadron who said that his name was William. He was about the same age as Stuffy but his face was younger, for he had not been flying so long. It was especially around his mouth that he was younger. He had a round schoolboy face and a small turned-up nose, and his skin was brown from the desert.

The three of them sat happily in the place without a name drinking beer. It was a long wooden room with an unpolished wooden sawdust floor and wooden tables and chairs. At the far end there was a raised wooden stage where there was a show going on, and the room was full of Egyptians, sitting drinking black coffee with the red tarbooshes on their heads. There were two fat girls on the stage dressed in shiny silver pants and silver brassieres. The one was waggling her bottom in time to the music, and the other was waggling her bosom in time to the music. The bosom-waggler was most skillful, and the Egyptians were spellbound and kept giving her a big hand. The more they clapped, the more she waggled, waggling with the music, never losing the tempo, never losing the fixed brassy smile that was upon her face, and the Egyptians clapped more and more and louder and louder as the speed increased. Everyone was very happy.

When it was over William said, "Why do they always have those dreary fat women? Why don't they have beautiful women?"

The Stag said, "The Gyppies like them fat. They like them like that."

"Impossible," said Stuffy.

"It's true," Stag said. "It's an old business. It comes from the days when there used to be lots of famines here, and all the poor people were thin, and all the rich people and the aristocracy were well fed and fat. If you got someone fat you couldn't go wrong; she was bound to be high-class."

"Ridiculous," said Stuffy.

William said, "I don't believe it either, but we'll soon find out. I'm going to ask those Gyppies." He jerked his thumb toward two middle-aged Egyptians who were sitting at the next table, only about four feet away.

"No," said Stag. "No, William. We don't want them over here."

"Yes," said Stuffy.

"Yes," said William. "We've got to find out why the Gyppies like fat women."

He was not drunk. None of them was drunk, but they were happy with a fair amount of beer and whiskey and William was the happiest. His brown schoolboy face was radiant with happiness, his turned-up nose seemed to have turned up a little more and he was probably relaxing for the first time in many weeks. He got up, took three paces over to the table of the Egyptians and stood in front of them, smiling.

"Gentlemen," he said, "my friends and I would be honored if you would join us at our table."

The Egyptians had dark skin and podgy faces. They were wearing the red hats, and one of them had a gold tooth. At first, when William addressed them, they looked a little alarmed. Then they caught on, looked at each other, grinned and nodded.

"Pleess," said one.

"Pleess," said the other, and they got up, shook hands with William, and followed him over to where the Stag and Stuffy were sitting.

William said, "Meet my friends. This is the Stag. This is Stuffy. I am William."

The Stag and Stuffy stood up, they all shook hands, the Egyptians said "Pleess" once more and then everyone sat down.

The Stag knew that their religion forbade them to drink. "Have a coffee," he said.

The one with the gold tooth grinned broadly, raised his hands, palms upward, and hunched his shoulders a little. "For me," he said,

"I am accustomed. But for my frient," and he spread out his hands toward the other, "for my frient—I cannot speak."

The Stag looked at the friend. "Coffee?" he asked.

"Pleess," he answered. "I am accustomt."

"Good," said Stag. "Two coffees."

He called a waiter. "Two coffees," he said. "And, wait a minute. Stuffy, William, more beer?"

"For me," Stuffy said, "I am accustomed. But for my friend," and he turned toward William, "for my friend—I cannot speak."

William said, "Please. I am accustomed." None of them smiled.

The Stag said, "Good. Waiter, two coffees and three beers." The waiter fetched the order and the Stag paid. The Stag lifted his glass toward the Egyptians and said, "Bung ho."

The Egyptians seemed to understand, and they lifted their coffee cups. "Pleess," said the one. "Thank you," said the other. They drank.

The Stag put down his glass and said, "It is an honor to be in your country."

"You like?"

"Yes," said the Stag. "Very fine."

The music had started again, and the two fat women in silver tights were doing an encore. The encore was a knock-out. It was surely the most remarkable exhibition of muscle control that has ever been witnessed. The Egyptians all stamped their feet and screamed with delight. Then it was over. The applause gradually died down.

"Remarkable," said the Stag.

"You like?"

"Please, it was remarkable."

"Those girls," said the one with the gold tooth, "very special."

William couldn't wait any longer. He leaned across the table and said, "Might I ask you a question?"

"Pleess," said the Egyptian with the gold tooth. "Pleess."

"Well," said William, "how do you like your women? Like this— slim?" and he demonstrated with his hands. "Or like this—fat?" He demonstrated again.

The gold tooth shone brightly behind a big grin. "For me, I like like this—fat," and a pair of podgy hands drew a big circle in the air.

"And your friend?" said William.

"For my frient," he answered, "I cannot speak."

"Pleess," said the friend. "Like this." He grinned and drew a fat girl in the air with his hands.

Stuffy said, "Why do you like them fat?"

Golden Tooth thought for a moment, then he said, "You like them slim, eh?"

"Please," said Stuffy. "I like them slim."

"Why you like them slim? You tell *me*."

Stuffy rubbed the back of his neck with the palm of his hand. "William," he said, "why do we like them slim?"

"For me," said William, "I am accustomed."

"Yes, yes, I know," Stuffy said. "So am I. But why?"

William considered. "I don't know," he said. "I don't know why we like them slim."

"Ha," said Golden Tooth, "you don't know." He leaned over the table toward William and said triumphantly, "And me, I do not know either."

But that wasn't good enough for William. "The Stag," he said, "says that all rich people in Egypt used to be fat and all poor people were thin."

"No," said Golden Tooth. "No, no, no. Look those girls up there. Very fat; very poor. Look queen of Egypt, Queen Farida. Very thin; very rich. Quite wrong."

"Yes, but what about years ago?" said William.

"What is this, years ago?"

William said, "Oh, all right. Let's leave it."

The Egyptians drank their coffee and the noise was like water running out of the bathtub. When they had finished, they got up to go.

"Going?" said the Stag.

"Pleess," said Golden Tooth.

William said, "Thank you." Stuffy said, "Please." The other Egyptian said, "Pleess," and the Stag said, "Thank you." They all shook hands, and the Egyptians departed.

"Ropy types," said William.

"Very," said Stuffy. "Very ropy types."

The three of them sat on drinking happily until midnight when the waiter came up and told them that the place was closing and that there were no more drinks. They were still not really drunk, because they had been taking it slowly, but they were feeling healthy.

"He says we've got to go."

"All right. Where shall we go? Where shall we go, Stag?"

"I don't know. Where do you want to go?"

"Let's go to another place like this," said William. "This is a fine place."

There was a pause. Stuffy was stroking the back of his neck with his hand. "Stag," he said slowly, "I know where I want to go. I want to go to Madame Rosette's and I want to rescue all the girls there."

"Who's Madame Rosette?" William said.

"She's a great woman," said the Stag.

"She's a filthy old Syrian," said Stuffy.

"She's a lousy old bitch," said the Stag.

"All right," said William. "Let's go. But who is she?"

They told him who she was. They told him about their telephone calls and about Colonel Higgins, and William said, "Come on, let's go. Let's go and rescue all the girls."

They got up and left. When they went outside, they remembered that they were in a rather remote part of the town.

"We'll have to walk a bit," said Stag. "No gharris here."

It was a dark starry night with no moon. The street was narrow and blacked-out, and it smelled strongly with the smell of Cairo. They walked on, the three of them abreast; square, short, ginger-haired Stag, tall dark Stuffy, and tall young William who went bareheaded because he had lost his cap. They headed roughly toward the center of the town where they knew that they would find a gharri to take them on to Rosette.

Stuffy said, "Oh, won't the girls be pleased when we rescue them."

The Stag said, "It ought to be a party."

"Does she actually keep them locked up?" William said.

"Well, no," said Stag. "Not exactly. But if we rescue them now, they won't have to work any more tonight anyway. You see, the girls she has at her place are nothing but ordinary shop girls who still work during the day in the shops. They have all of them made some mistake or other which Rosette either engineered or found out about, and now she has put the screws on them; she makes them come along in the evening. But they hate her and they do not depend on her for a living. They would kick her in the teeth if they got the chance."

Stuffy said, "We'll give them the chance."

They crossed over a street. William said, "How many girls will be there, Stag?"

"I don't know. I suppose there might be thirty."

"Good God," said William. "This *will* be a party. Does she really treat them very badly?"

The Stag said, "Thirty-three Squadron told me that she pays them nothing, about twenty akkers a night. She charges the customers about a hundred or two hundred akkers each."

"Good God," said William. "She must be a millionaire."

"She is. Someone calculated that she makes the equivalent of about fifteen hundred pounds a week. That's, let me see, that's between five and six thousand pounds a month. Sixty thousand pounds a year."

Stuffy came out of his dream. "Good God," he said, "the filthy old Syrian bitch."

Then they saw a gharri and hailed it.

Stuffy said, "We don't know the address."

"He'll know it," said Stag. "Madame Rosette," he said to the driver.

The driver grinned and nodded. Then William said, "I'm going to drive. Give me the reins, driver, and sit up here beside me and tell me where to go."

The driver protested vigorously, but when William gave him ten piastres, he gave him the reins. William sat high up on the driver's seat with the driver beside him. The Stag and Stuffy got in the back of the carriage. They went off at a gallop, with the terrified driver shrieking directions to William and the gharri careening around corners, until at last they pulled up in another of those narrow, dark streets.

"How much?" said William to the driver.

"Pleess, twenty piastres."

William gave him forty and said, "Thank you very much. Fine horses." The little man took the money, jumped up onto the gharri, and drove off. He was in a hurry to get away.

Though the street was narrow, the houses, what they could see of them, looked huge and prosperous. The one which the driver had said was Rosette's was wide and thick and three stories high, built of gray concrete, and it had a large thick front door, which stood wide open. As they went in the Stag said, "Now leave this to me. I've got a plan."

Inside there was a cold gray dusty stone hall, lit by a bare electric light bulb in the ceiling, and there was a man standing in the hall. He was a mountain of a man, a huge Egyptian with a flat face and two cauliflower ears. In his wrestling days he had probably been billed as Abdul the Killer or The Poisonous Pasha, but now he wore a dirty white cotton suit.

The Stag said, "Good evening. Is Madame Rosette here?"

Abdul looked hard at the three pilots, hesitated, then said, "Madame Rosette top floor."

"Thank you," said Stag. "Thank you very much." Stuffy noticed that the Stag was being polite. There was always trouble for somebody when he was like that.

They went up the bare stone steps which had iron railings. They went past the first landing and the second landing, and the place was as bare as a cave. At the top of the third flight of steps, there was no landing; it was walled off, and the stairs ran up to a door. The Stag pressed the bell. They waited a while, then a little panel in the door was slid back and a pair of small black eyes peeked through. A woman's voice said, "What you boys want?" Both the Stag and Stuffy recognized the voice from the telephone. The Stag said, "We would like to see Madame Rosette." He pronounced the Madame in the French way, because he was being polite.

"You officers? Only officers here," said the voice. She had a voice like a broken board.

"Yes," said Stag. "We are officers."

"You don't look like officers. What kind of officers?"

"R.A.F."

There was a pause. The Stag knew that she was considering. She had probably had trouble with pilots before, and he hoped only that she would not see William and the light that was dancing in his eyes, for William was still feeling the way he had felt when he drove the gharri. Suddenly the panel closed and the door opened.

"All right, come in," she said. She was too greedy, this woman, even to pick her customers carefully.

They went in and there she was. Short, fat, greasy, with wisps of untidy black hair straggling over her forehead; a large, mud-colored face, a large wide nose and a small fish mouth, with just the trace of a black mustache above the mouth. She had on a loose black satin dress.

"Come into the office, boys," she said, and started to waddle down the passage to the left. It was a long, wide passage, and all the way down there were doors, about eight or ten of them on each side. If you turned right as you came in from the stairs, you ran into the end of the passage, but there was one door there too, and as the three of them walked in, they heard a babble of female voices from behind that door. The Stag noted that it was the girls' dressing room.

"This way, boys," said Rosette, and she turned left and slopped down the passage, away from the door with the voices. The three followed her. They got about halfway down the passage when there was a yell from the dressing room behind them. Rosette stopped and looked around.

"You go on, boys," she said, "into the office, last door on the left. I won't be a minute," and she turned and went back toward the dressing room door. They didn't go on. They stood and watched her, and just as she got to the door it opened and a girl rushed out. From where they stood, they could see that her fair hair was all over her face and that she had on an untidy-looking green evening dress. They heard Rosette say something angry and quick spoken and they heard the girl shout something back at her. Rosette raised her right arm and they saw her hit the girl smack on the side of the face with the palm of her hand. She hit her twice. The girl put her hands up to her face and began to cry. Rosette opened the door of the dressing room and pushed her back inside.

"My God," said the Stag, "she's tough." William said, "So am I." Stuffy didn't say anything.

Rosette came back to them and said, "Come along, boys. Just a bit of trouble, that's all." She led them to the end of the passage and into her office. It was a medium-sized room with two red plush sofas, two or three red plush armchairs, and a thick red carpet on the floor. In one corner was a small desk, and Rosette sat herself behind it, facing the room.

"Sit down, boys," she said.

The Stag took an armchair, Stuffy and William sat on a sofa.

"Well," she said, and her voice became sharp and urgent. "Let's do business."

The Stag leaned forward in his chair. His short ginger hair looked somehow wrong against the bright red plush. "Madame Rosette," he said, "it is a great pleasure to meet you. We have heard so much about you." Stuffy looked at the Stag. He was being polite again. Rosette looked at him too, and her little black eyes were suspicious. "Believe me," the Stag went on, "we've really been looking forward to this for quite a time now."

His voice was so pleasant and he was so polite that Rosette took it. "That's nice of you boys," she said. "You'll always have a good time here. I see to that. Now—business."

William couldn't wait any longer. He said slowly, "The Stag says that you're a great woman."

"Thanks, boys."

Stuffy said, "The Stag says that you're a filthy old Syrian."

William said quickly, "The Stag says that you're a lousy old bitch."

"And I know what I'm talking about," said the Stag.

Rosette jumped to her feet. "What's this?" she shrieked, and her face was no longer the color of mud; it was the color of red clay. The men sat quite still, leaning forward a little in their seats, watching her.

Rosette had had trouble before, plenty of it, and she knew how to deal with it. But this was different. They didn't seem drunk, it wasn't about money, and it wasn't about one of her girls. It was about herself and she didn't like it.

"Get out," she yelled. "Get out unless you want trouble." But they did not move.

For a moment she paused, then she stepped quickly from behind her desk and made for the door. But the Stag was there first, and when she went for him, Stuffy and William each caught one of her arms from behind.

"We'll lock her in," said the Stag. "Let's get out."

Then she really started yelling, and the words which she used cannot be written down on paper, for they were terrible words. They poured out of her small fish mouth in one long unbroken high-pitched stream. Stuffy and William pulled her back by the arms toward one of the big chairs, and gave her a quick push so that she fell backwards into it. Stuffy nipped across to her desk, bent down quickly and jerked the telephone cord from its connection. The Stag had the door open and all three of them were out of the room before Rosette had time to get up. The Stag had taken the key from the inside of the door, and now he locked it. The three of them stood outside in the passage.

"My God," said the Stag. "What a woman!"

"Mad as hell," William said. "Listen to her."

They stood outside in the passage and they listened. They heard her yelling, then she began banging on the door, but she went on yelling and her voice was not the voice of a woman, it was the voice of an enraged but articulate bull.

The Stag said, "Now quick. The girls. Follow me. And from now on you've got to act serious."

He ran down the passage toward the dressing-room, followed by Stuffy and William. Outside the door he stopped. They could still hear Rosette yelling from her office. The Stag said, "Now don't say anything. Just act serious as hell," and he opened the door and went in.

There were about a dozen girls in the room. They all looked up. They stopped talking and looked up at the Stag who was standing in the doorway. The Stag clicked his heels and said, "This is the Military Police. Les Gendarmes Militaires." He said it in a stern voice and with a straight face and he was standing there in the doorway at attention with his cap on his head. Stuffy and William stood behind him.

"This is the Military Police," he said again, and he produced his identification card and held it up between two fingers.

The girls didn't move or say anything. They stayed still in the middle of what they were doing and they were like a tableau because they stayed so still. One had been pulling on a stocking and she stayed like that, sitting on a chair with her leg out straight and the stocking up to her knee with her hands on the stocking. One had been doing her hair in front of a mirror and when she looked round she kept her hands up to her hair. One was standing up and had been applying lipstick and she raised her eyes to the Stag but still held the lipstick to her mouth. Several were just sitting around on plain wooden chairs, doing nothing, and they raised their heads and turned them to the door, but they went on sitting. One or two of them were half clothed, but most of them were in shiny green or shiny blue or shiny red or shiny gold evening dress, and when they turned to look at the Stag they were so still that they were like a tableau.

The Stag paused. Then he said, "I am to state on behalf of the authorities that they are sorry to disturb you. My apologies, mesd'moiselles. But it is necessary that you come with us for purposes of registration, etcetera. Afterwards you will be allowed to go. It is a mere formality. But now you must come, please. I have conversed with Madame." The girls stared.

The Stag stopped speaking, but still the girls did not move.

"Please," said the Stag, "get your coats. We are the military." He stepped aside and held open the door. Suddenly the tableau dissolved, the girls got up, puzzled and murmuring, and two or three of them moved toward the door. The others followed, and the ones that were half-clothed quickly slipped on a dress, patted their hair with their hands, and came too. None of them had a coat.

"Count them," said the Stag to Stuffy as they filed out of the door. Stuffy counted them aloud and there were fourteen.

"Fourteen, sir," said Stuffy, who was trying to talk like a sergeant-major.

The Stag said, "Correct," and he turned to the girls who were crowded in the passage. "Now, mesd'moiselles, I have the list of your names from Madame, so please do not try to run away. And do not worry. This is merely a formality of the military."

William was out in the passage opening the door which led to the stairs, and he went out first. The girls followed and the Stag and Stuffy brought up the rear. The girls were quiet and puzzled and worried and a little frightened and they didn't talk; none of them talked except for a tall one with black hair who said, "Mon Dieu, a formality of the military. Mon Dieu, mon Dieu, what next?" But that was all, and they went on down. In the hall they met the Egyptian who had a flat face and two cauliflower ears, and for a moment it looked as though there would be trouble. But the Stag waved his identification card in his face and said, "The Military Police," and the man was so surprised that he did nothing and let them pass.

And so they came out onto the street, and the Stag said, "It is necessary to walk a little way, but only a very little way," and they turned right and walked along the sidewalk with the Stag leading, Stuffy at the rear, and William walking out on the road guarding the flank. There was some moon now. One could see quite well, and William tried to keep in step with the Stag and Stuffy tried to keep in step with William, and they swung their arms and held their heads up high and looked very military, and the whole thing was a sight to behold. Fourteen girls in shiny evening dresses, fourteen girls in the moonlight in shiny green, shiny blue, shiny red, and shiny gold, marching along the street with the Stag in front, William alongside, and Stuffy at the rear. It was a sight to behold.

The girls had started chattering. The Stag could hear them, although he didn't look round. He marched on at the head of the column and when they came to the crossroads he turned right. The others followed and they had walked fifty yards down the block when they came to an Egyptian café. The Stag saw it and he saw the lights burning behind the blackout curtains and he turned around and shouted "Halt!"

"Mesd'moiselles," said the Stag, "listen to me." But there was mutiny in the ranks and the girls were talking and the tall one with dark hair was saying, "Mon Dieu, what is this? What in hell's name sort of a thing is this?"

"Quiet," said the Stag. "Quiet!" and the second time he shouted it as a command. The talking stopped.

"Mesd'moiselles," he said, and now he became polite. "With the military there always has to be formality. It is something unavoidable. It is something that I regret exceedingly. But there can be chivalry also. And you must know that with the R.A.F. there is great chivalry. So now it will be a pleasure if you will all come in here and take with us a glass of beer. It is the chivalry of the military." He stepped forward, opened the door of the café and said, "Oh, for God's sake, let's have a drink. Who wants a drink?"

Suddenly the girls saw it all. They saw the whole thing as it was, all of them at once. It took them by surprise. For a second they considered. Then they looked at one another, then they looked at the Stag, then they looked around at Stuffy and at William, and when they looked at those two they caught their eyes and the laughter that was in them. All at once the girls began to laugh, and they moved forward and poured into the café.

The tall one with dark hair took the Stag by the arm and said, "Mon Dieu, Military Police, mon Dieu, oh, mon Dieu," and she threw her head back and laughed and the Stag laughed with her. William said, "It is the chivalry of the military," and they moved into the café.

The place was rather like the one that they had been in before, wooden and sawdusty, and there were a few coffee-drinking Egyptians sitting around with the red tarbooshes on their heads. William and Stuffy pushed three round tables together and fetched chairs. The girls sat down. The Egyptians at the other tables put down their coffee cups, turned around in their chairs and gaped.

A waiter came up and the Stag said, "Seventeen beers. Bring us seventeen beers." The waiter said "Pleess," went away and returned with the beer.

William raised his glass and said, "To the chivalry of the military." The dark girl said, "Oh, mon Dieu." Stuffy didn't say anything. He was busy looking around at the girls, sizing them up, trying to decide now which one he liked best so that he could go to work at once. The Stag was smiling and the girls were sitting there in their shiny evening dresses, and once again it was almost a tableau, certainly it was a picture, and the girls were sitting there sipping their beer, seeming quite happy not seeming suspicious any more because to them the whole thing now appeared exactly as it was and they understood.

The Stag put down his glass and looked around him. "My God, there's enough here for the whole squadron. How I wish the whole squadron was here!" He took another drink, stopped in the middle of it, and put down his glass quickly. "I know what," he said. "Waiter, oh, waiter."

"Pleess."

"Get me a big piece of paper and a pencil."

"Pleess." The waiter went away and came back with a sheet of paper, and he took a pencil from behind his ear and handed it to the Stag. The Stag banged the table for silence.

"Mesd'moiselles," he said, "for the last time there is a formality. It is the last of all the formalities."

"Oh, mon Dieu," said the dark girl.

"It is nothing," the Stag said. "You are required to write your name and your telephone number on this piece of paper. It is for my friends in the squadron." One could see that the girls liked the Stag's voice. "You would be very kind if you would do that," he went on, "for they too would like to meet you. It would be a pleasure."

"Wonderful," said William.

"Crazy," said the dark girl, but she wrote her name and number on the paper and passed it on. The Stag ordered another round of beer. The girls were writing their names down on the paper. They looked happy and William particularly looked happy, but Stuffy looked serious because the problem of choosing was a weighty one and it was heavy on his mind. They were good-looking girls, young and good-looking, all different, completely different from each other because they were Greek and Syrian and French and Italian and light Egyptian and Yugoslav and many other things, but they were all good-looking.

The piece of paper had come back to the Stag now and they had all written on it, fourteen strangely written names and fourteen telephone numbers. The Stag looked at it slowly. "This will go on the squadron notice-board," he said, "and I will be regarded as a great benefactor."

William said, "It should go to headquarters. It should be mimeographed and circulated to all squadrons. It would be good for morale."

"Oh, mon Dieu," said the dark girl. "You are crazy."

Slowly Stuffy got up to his feet, picked up his chair, carried it round to the other side of the table and pushed it between two of the girls. All he said was, "Excuse me. Do you mind if I sit here?" At last he had made up his mind, and now he turned toward the one on his right and quietly he went to work. He began to talk to her, completely oblivious to the rest of the company, turning toward her and leaning his head on his hand. Watching him, it was not so difficult to understand why he was the greatest pilot in the squadron. He was a young concentrator, this Stuffy.

Meanwhile the Stag was thinking. He was thinking about the next move, and when everyone was getting toward the end of their third beer, he banged the table again for silence.

"Mesd'moiselles," he said, "it will be a pleasure for us to escort you home. I will take five of you"—he had worked it all out—"Stuffy will take five, and Jamface will take four. We will take three gharris and

I will take five of you in mine and I will drop you home one at a time."

William said, "It is the chivalry of the military."

"Stuffy," said the Stag. "Stuffy, is that all right? You take five. It's up to you whom you drop off last."

Stuffy looked around. "Yes," he said. "Oh, yes. That suits me."

"William, you take four. Drop them home one by one; you understand."

"Perfectly," said William. "Oh, perfectly."

They all got up and moved toward the door. The tall one with dark hair took the Stag's arm and said, "You take me?"

"Yes," he answered. "I take you."

"You drop me off last?"

"Yes. I drop you off last."

"Oh, mon Dieu," she said. "That will be fine."

Outside they got three gharris, and they split up into parties. Stuffy was moving quickly. He got his girls into the carriage quickly, climbed in after them and the Stag saw the gharri drive off down the street. Then he saw William's gharri move off, but it seemed to start away with a sudden jerk, with the horses breaking into a gallop at once, and the Stag looked again and he saw that William once again was perched high up on the driver's seat with the reins in his hands.

The Stag said, "Let's go," and his five girls got into their gharri. It was a squash, but everyone got in. The Stag sat back in his seat and then he felt an arm pushing under and linking with his. It was the tall one with dark hair. He turned and looked at her.

"Hello," he said. "Hello, you."

"Ah," she whispered. "You are such goddam crazy people." And the Stag felt a warmness inside him and he began to hum a little tune as the gharri rattled on through the dark streets.

JOHN E. McMILLIN

 For Penelope

. . . And there was Polyphemus,
A very rugged character.
Bellowed like a bull when we stuck the spit in his eye.
Scared the bloody blazes out of the crew.
Me? No, why should I be?
He was just a man, wasn't he?

And the Lotos Eaters.
And that damned fruit.
All we wanted to do was eat and eat
And sit on our tails under the trees
Forever.

And Circe. Circe and her swine,
Rooting and wallowing and squealing and—
Yes, I guess you'd call her beautiful.
Sort of hippy, bosomy, oriental.
No, I didn't say that.
I didn't mean that either.
You're beautiful, too, but in a different way.
You're beautiful, well, like Ithaca.
You're—no, no, I don't mean that.
I don't mean "bony, rocky, small."
I mean—well, dammit, listen to me then!
I mean you're beautiful like home,
And I came home, didn't I?

GERALD M. DURRELL

The King

 and

His Beasts

The Cross River picks its way down from the great mountains of the Cameroons, until it runs sprawling and glittering into the great bowl of forest land around Mamfe. After being all froth, waterfalls, and eager chattering in the mountains, it settles down when it reaches this forest, and moves along majestically, its brown waters full of hippo and crocodile. The forest on the bank gives way to the small grassfield that surrounds the village of Mamfe; and it was here, on the edge of the forest, above the smooth brown river, that we chose to have our base camp. . . .

I was not certain which part of the grasslands would be the best for me to operate in, and so I went to the District Officer for advice. I explained my dilemma, and he produced a map of the mountains, and together we pored over it. Suddenly he dabbed his forefinger down, and glanced at me.

"What about Bafut?" he asked.

"Is that a good place? What are the people like?"

"There is only one person you have to worry about in Bafut, and that's the Fon," he said. "Get him on your side and the people will help you all they can."

"Is he the chief?"

"He's the sort of Nero of this region," said the DO, marking a great circle on the map with his finger, "and what he says goes. He's the most delightful old rogue, and the quickest and surest way to his heart is to prove to him that you can carry your liquor. He's got a wonderful great villa there, which he built in case he had any European visitors, and I'm sure if you wrote to him he would let you stay there. It's worth a visit, is Bafut, even if you don't stay."

"Well, I'll drop him a note and see what he says."

"See that your communication is . . . er . . . well lubricated," said the DO.

So, that afternoon, a messenger went off to the mountains, carrying with him my note and a bottle of gin. Four days later he returned, bearing a letter from the Fon, a masterly document that encouraged me tremendously.

Fon's Office Bafut,
Bafut Bemenda Division,
5th March, 1949.

MY GOOD FRIEND,

Yours of 3rd March, 1949, came in hand with all contents well marked out.

Yes, I accept your arrival to Bafut in course of two month stay about your animals and too, I shall be overjoyed to let you be in possession of a house in my compound if you will do well in arrangement of rentages.

Yours cordially,
FON of BAFUT

I arranged to leave for Bafut at once.

We drove for some hours, and by the time we were nearing our destination the valleys were washed with deep purple shadow and the sun was sinking leisurely into a thousand scarlet and green feathers of cloud behind the highest range of western hills. We knew when we reached Bafut, for there the road ended. On our left lay an enormous dusty courtyard surrounded by a high red-brick wall. Inside was a great assembly of circular huts with high thatched roofs clustered round a small, neat villa. But all these structures were dominated and dwarfed by an edifice that looked like an old-fashioned beehive magnified a million times. It was a huge circular hut, with a massive dome roof of thatch, black and mysterious with age. On the opposite side of the road the ground rose steeply, and a wide flight of some seventy steps curved upward to a large villa—shoebox shaped, its upper and lower stories completely surrounded by wide verandas, the pillars of which were profusely hung with bougainvillaea and other creepers. This I realized was to be my home for the next few months.

As I stiffly got out of the lorry, an arched doorway in the far wall of the great courtyard opened, and a small procession made its way across to where I stood. It was a group of men, most of them elderly, clad in flowing multicolored robes that swished as they moved; on their heads they wore little skullcaps thickly embroidered in a riot of colored wools. In the midst of this group walked a tall, slim individual with a lively, humorous face. He was dressed in a plain white robe, and his skullcap was innocent of decoration; yet you at once singled him out as the only one of any importance in the little cavalcade, so regal was his manner. He was the Fon of Bafut, ruler of the great grassland kingdom we had been traveling through and of its immense population of black subjects. He was incredibly wealthy, and he ruled his kingdom, I knew, with an intelligent, if slightly despotic, cunning. He stopped in front of me, smiling gently, and extended an incredibly large, slender hand.

"Welcome," he said.

It was not until later that I learned he could speak pidgin English as well as any of his subjects, so we talked through an interpreter. The Fon listened politely to my speech of welcome and then waved one huge hand at the villa on top of the slope above me.

"Foine!" he said, grinning.

I got out a bottle and drank his health in whiskey and water, while he drank mine in neat whiskey. As the level of the whiskey fell the Fon started to speak pidgin English.

For two hours I was fully occupied in explaining my mission in his country. I brought out books and photographs of the animals I wanted. I drew them on bits of paper and made noises like them when all else failed.

He said he thought I should be able to get most of the animals I had shown him, and he promised that, the next day, he would send some good hunters to work for me. But, he went on, the best thing for him to do was to spread the word among his people so that they would all try to catch beef—the pidgin term for any sort of animal. . . .

I agreed heartily, thanked him profusely, and refilled his empty glass. The level in the bottle fell lower and lower, until it was obviously innocent of even the most reluctant drops of liquid. The Fon rose majestically to his feet, stifled a hiccup, and held out a hand. . . .

A few days after my arrival at the Fon's village, this good-natured old monarch assembled most of the people of his Kingdom of Bafut and made them a speech about my animal-collecting enterprise. It produced astonishing results.

The next afternoon I lay down for a couple of hours to catch up on some sleep. When I awoke, I decided that some tea would help to restore me to a more amiable frame of mind, and so I staggered off the bed and made my way to the door, intending to shout my instructions down to the kitchen from the veranda. I opened the door and then stopped dead, wondering if I was dreaming, for the whole veranda was literally covered with a weird assortment of sacks, palm-leaf baskets, and calabashes—all of which shook and quivered gently. Leaning up against the wall were four or five long bamboos to the ends of which were tied writhing and infuriated snakes. At the top of the steps squatted my native assistant, Jacob, scowling at me.

"Masa wake up?" he said mournfully, "why Masa wake up?"

"What's all this?" I asked, waving my hand at the collection of bags and baskets.

"Beef," said Jacob succinctly.

I examined the snakes' bonds to make sure they were secure.

"Which man done bring dis beef?" I asked, feeling rather stunned by the profusion of the arrivals.

"Dis men done bring um," said Jacob. I stepped over and saw that the seventy-five steps up to the villa, and a good deal of the road beyond, were jammed with a great variety of Bafutians of all ages and sexes. There must have been about a hundred and fifty of them, and they gazed up at me, unmoving and strangely quiet. As a rule, a small group of four or five Africans can make more noise than any other race on earth, yet this great crowd might have been composed of deaf mutes for all the sound it was making.

"What's the matter with them?" I asked Jacob.

"Sah?"

"Why dey no make noise, eh?"

"Ah!" said Jacob, light dawning, "I done tell um Masa 'e sleep."

This was the first of many examples I was to have of the courtesy and good manners of the Bafut people. For nearly two hours, I discovered, they had sat there in the hot sun, curbing their natural exuberance so that my slumbers might not be disturbed.

"Why you no wake me before?" I said to Jacob. "You no savvay na bad ting for dis beef to wait, eh?"

"Yes, sah. Sorry, sah."

"All right, let's get on with it and see what they've brought."

I picked up the first basket and peered into it: it contained five mice with pale ginger fur, white tummies and long tails. I handed the basket to Jacob, who carried it to the top of the steps and held it aloft.

"Who done bring dis beef?" he shouted.

"I done bring um," called an old woman shrilly. She fought her way up onto the veranda, bargained with me breathlessly for five minutes, and then fought her way down the steps again, clutching her money.

The next item was a squirrel who created a considerable diversion. He was confined in a palm-leaf bag, and as soon as I opened it he shot out like a jack-in-the-box, bit my hand, and then galloped off across the veranda. Jacob gave chase, and as he drew near to it, the squirrel suddenly darted to one side and then ran down the steps, weaving his way skillfully through the dozens of black legs that stood there.

The panic he created was tremendous: those on the first step leaped into the air as he rushed at their feet, lost their balance, and fell backward against those on the next step. They, in turn, fell against the ones below them, who went down like grass before a scythe. In a matter of seconds, the steps were covered with a tangled mass of struggling bodies, with arms and legs sticking out at the oddest angles. I thought that the unfortunate squirrel would be crushed to death under this human avalanche—but to my surprise he appeared at the bottom of the steps apparently unhurt, flipped his tail a couple of times and set off down the road.

At the top of the steps, I was fuming impotently and struggling to push my way down through the tangle of Africans, for the squirrel was a rarity, and I was determined that he should not escape. Halfway down someone clutched my ankle and I sat down abruptly on top of a large body which, judging from the bits I could see, was female. I glanced desperately down at the road as I endeavored to regain my feet, and to my joy I saw a band of some twenty young men approaching. They saw the squirrel and stopped short, and the squirrel sat up and sniffed suspiciously.

"You!" I roared, "you dere for de road . . . catch dat beef."

The young men put down their bundles and advanced determinedly upon the squirrel, who took one look at them and then turned and fled. They set off in hot pursuit, each determined that he should be the one to recapture the rodent. The squirrel ran well, but he was no match for the long legs of his pursuers. They drew level with him in a tight bunch, their faces grim and set. Then, to my horror, they launched themselves at my precious specimen in a body, and for the second time the squirrel disappeared under a huge pile of struggling Africans. This time, I thought, the poor beast really *would* be crushed, but that squirrel seemed indestructible. When the heap in the road had sorted itself out a bit, one of the young men stood up, holding the chattering and panting squirrel by the scruff of its neck.

"Masa!" he called, beaming up at me, "I done catch um!"

I threw down a bag for him to put the animal in, and then it was passed up the steps to me. Hastily, I got the beast into a cage, so that I could examine him. He seemed all right, except that he was in an extremely bad temper. He was a Black-eared Squirrel, one of the most beautiful of the Cameroon squirrels.

Placed in a cage he flipped his dazzling tail at me once or twice, and then squatted down to the stern task of devouring a mango which I had put in there for him. I watched him fondly, thinking what a lucky escape he had had, and how pleased I was to have got him.

I turned my attention back to the various containers that littered the veranda, and picked up a large calabash at random. As usual, its neck was stuffed with a tightly packed plug of green leaves; I removed these and peered into the depths, but the calabash was so capacious and so dark that I could not see what was inside. I carried it to the head of the steps and held it up.

"Which side de man who done bring dis calabash?" I asked.

"Na me, sah, na me!" shouted a man halfway down the steps.

It was always a source of astonishment to me how the Africans could distinguish their own calabashes out of hundreds of others. Except for a difference in size, I could never tell one from the other, but the Africans knew at a glance which was theirs.

"What beef 'e dere for inside?" I asked, negligently swinging the calabash by its cord.

"Snake, sah," said the man, and I hastily replaced the plug of green leaves.

"What kind of snake, my friend?"

"Na Gera, sah."

I consulted my list of local names and found this meant a Green Leaf Viper. These were common and beautiful snakes, about eighteen inches long, a startlingly bright grass green in color, with canary yellow bellies and broad diagonal white stripes along their sides. I carried the calabash over to empty the new arrival into the shallow, gauze-topped box in which I kept vipers.

Now, emptying a snake from a calabash into a cage is one of the simplest of operations, providing you observe one or two rudimentary rules. First, make sure that any inmates of the cage are far away from the door. This, I did. Secondly, make sure how many snakes you have in the calabash before starting to shake them out. This I omitted to do.

I opened the door of the cage, unplugged the mouth of the calabash, and began to shake gently. Jacob stood behind me, breathing heavily down my neck, and behind him stood a solid wall of Africans, watching open-mouthed. I shook a bit harder with no results. I had never known a viper to cling with such tenacity to the interior of a receptacle. Becoming irritated, I gave the calabash a really vigorous shaking, and it promptly broke apart in two pieces.

An intricately tangled knot of Green Leaf Vipers—composed of about half a dozen large, vigorous, and angry snakes—fell out onto the cage with what can only be described as a sickening thud.

They were plaited together in such a large and solid ball that instead of falling through the door and into the cage, they got jammed halfway, so that I could not slam the door on them. Then, with a fluid grace which I had no time to admire, they disentangled themselves and wriggled determinedly onto the floor. Here they spread out fanwise, with an almost military precision, and came toward us.

Jacob, and the Africans who had been jammed behind him, disappeared with the startling suddenness of a conjuring trick. I could hardly blame them, for none of them were wearing shoes. But I was not clad to gallivant with a tribe of vipers either, for I was wearing shorts and a pair of sandals. Leaving the snakes in sole charge of the veranda, I shot into my bedroom. Here I found a stick, and then went cautiously out again. The snakes had scattered widely, and so they were quite easy to corner, pin down with the stick, and then pick up. One by one I dropped them into the cage, and then shut and locked the door with a sigh of relief. The Africans reappeared, all chattering and laughing and clicking their fingers as they described to each other the great danger they had been in. I fixed the snake bringer sternly with a very cold eye indeed.

"You!" I said, "why you no tell me dere be plenty snake for inside dat calabash, eh?"

"Wah!" he said, looking surprised, "I done tell Masa dere be snake for inside."

"Snake, yes. *One* snake. You no tell me dere be six for inside."

"I done tell Masa dere be snake for inside," he said indignantly.

"I done ask you what beef you done bring," I explained patiently, "and you say, 'snake.' You no say dere be six snake. How you tink I go savvay how many snake you bring, eh?"

"Stupid man," said Jacob, joining in the fray, "sometime dis snake bite Masa, and Masa go die. Den how you go do, eh?" I turned on Jacob.

"I noticed that you were conspicuous by your absence, my noble and heroic creature."

"Yes, sah!" said Jacob, beaming.

It was quite late that evening when the last hunter had been paid, and I was left with such a weird assortment of live creatures on my hands that it took me until three o'clock the following morning to cage them. Even so, there were five large rats left over, and no box from which to make a cage. I was forced to release them in my bedroom, where they spent the entire night trying to gnaw through the leg of the table for some obscure reason of their own.

The next morning, when I arose and cleaned out and fed my now considerable collection, I thought that probably nothing more would turn up that day. I was wrong. The Bafutians had thrown themselves wholeheartedly into the task of providing me with specimens, and by ten o'clock the roadway and the seventy-five steps were black with people. By lunchtime it was obvious that the supply of animals had far exceeded my store of wood and boxes to make cages for them, so I was forced to employ a team of small boys to tour Bafut, buying up any and every box or plank of wood they could find. . . .

When I had finished the work, before buying any fresh specimens, I made a speech to the assembled Bafutians from the top of the steps. I pointed out that they had brought me a vast quantity of beef of all shapes, sizes, and descriptions. This proved that the Bafutians were by far the best hunters I had come across, and I was very grateful to them. However, I went on, as they would realize, there was a limit to the amount of beef I could purchase and house in any one day. So, I would be glad if they would stop hunting for three days. There was no sense, I pointed out, in my buying beef from them if it was going to die for lack of adequate housing; that was just simply a waste of money. The African is nothing if not a businessman, and at this remark the nodding heads sent a ripple over the crowd, and a chorus of "Arrrrr!" arose. Having thus driven the point home, I purchased the animals they had brought, and once more set about the task of cage building.

At four o'clock the caging was under control, and I was having a break for a cup of tea. As I leaned on the veranda rail I saw the arched doorway in the red brick wall fly open, and the Fon appeared. He strode across the great courtyard with enormous strides, his robes fluttering and hissing as he moved. He was scowling and muttering to himself.

"Iseeya, my friend," I said politely as he reached me.

"My friend!" he said, enveloping my hand in his and peering earnestly into my face, "some man done tell me you no go buy beef again. Na so!"

"No be so," I said.

"Ah! Good, good!" he said in a relieved voice; "sometime I fear you done get enough beef an' you go lef' dis place."

I explained the reason for my three-day suspension of business.

"Ah! I savvay," said the Fon, smiling at me affectionately. Then he peered anxiously round in a conspiratorial fashion.

"Ma friend," he said in a hoarse whisper, "I done find beef for you. Na fine beef, na beef you never get."

"What kind beef?" I asked curiously.

"Beef," said the Fon explicitly, "you go like *too much*. We go catch um now, eh?"

"You never catch up yet?"

"No, my friend, but I savvay which side dey de hide."

Eagerly he led me across the great courtyard, through a maze of narrow passages, until we reached a small hut.

"Wait here small time, my friend, I go come," he said, and then disappeared hurriedly into the hut's gloomy interior. I waited outside, wondering where he had gone to, and what kind of beef it was that he had discovered. He had an air of mystery about him which made the whole thing rather intriguing.

When he eventually reappeared, for a moment I did not recognize him. He had removed his robes, his skullcap, and his sandals, and was now naked except for a small and spotlessly white loin cloth. In one hand he held a long and slender spear. His thin, muscular body gleamed with oil, and his feet were bare. He approached me, twirling his spear professionally, beaming with delight at my obvious surprise.

"You done get new hunter man," he said, chuckling.

"I tink dis hunter man be best for all," I said, grinning at him.

"I savvay hunting fine," he said, nodding. "Sometime my people tink I get ole too much for go bush. My friend, if some man get hunting for 'e eye, for 'e nose, an' for 'e blood, 'e *never* get ole too much for go bush, no be so?"

"You speak true, my friend," I said.

He led me out of the environs of his compound, along the road for perhaps half a mile, and then branched off through some maize fields. He walked at a great pace, twirling his spear and humming to himself, occasionally turning to grin at me with a mischievous delight illuminating his features. Presently, we left the fields, passed through a small thicket of mimbo palms—dark and mysterious and full of the rustling of the fronds—and then started to climb up the golden hillside.

When we reached the top, the Fon paused, stuck his spear into the ground, folded his arms, and surveyed the view. Presently, he sighed deeply, and, turning toward me, he smiled and swept his arms wide.

"Na my country dis," he said, "na foine, dis country."

I nodded and we stood there in silence for a few minutes and looked at the view. Below us lay a mosaic of small fields, green and silver and fawn, broken up by small palm thickets and an occasional patch of rust red where the earth of a field had been newly hoed. This small area of cultivation was like a colored handkerchief laid on the earth and forgotten, surrounded on all sides by the great ocean of mountains. The Fon gazed slowly round, an expression on his face that was a mixture of affection and childlike pleasure. He sighed again, a sigh of satisfaction.

"Foine!" he murmured. Then he plucked his spear from the earth and led the way down into the next valley, humming tunefully to himself.

The valley was shallow and flat, thickly overgrown with a wood of small stunted trees, some only about ten feet high. A sleepy throbbing drone came from a thousand bees that hovered round the flowers. The Fon surveyed the trees for a moment, and then moved quietly to a better vantage point.

"Na for here we go see beef," he whispered, pointing at the trees, "we sit down an' wait small time."

He squatted down on his haunches and waited with a relaxed immobility; I squatted down beside him and found my attention equally divided between watching him and watching the trees. As the trees remained devoid of life, I concentrated on my companion. He sat there, clutching his spear upright in his large hands, and on his face was a look of eager expectancy, like that of a child at a pantomime before the curtain goes up. When he had appeared out of that dark little hut in Bafut, it seemed as though he had not only left behind his robes and trappings of state, but also had shed that regal air which had seemed so much part of his character. Here, crouching in this quiet warm valley with his spear, he appeared to be just another hunter, his bright dark eyes fixed on the trees, waiting for the quarry he knew would come.

But, as I looked at him, I realized that he was not just another hunter; there was something different about him which I could not place. It came to me what it was: any ordinary hunter would have crouched there, patient, a trifle bored, for he would have done the same thing so many times before. But the Fon waited, his eyes gleaming, a half smile on his wide mouth, and I realized that he was thoroughly enjoying himself. I wondered how many times in the past he had become tired of his deferential councilors and his worshiping subjects, and felt his magnificent robes to be hot and cumbersome, and his pointed shoes cramping and hard. Then perhaps the urge had come to him to feel the soft red earth under his bare feet, and the wind on his naked body—and so he would steal off to his hut, put on the clothes of a hunter and stride away over the hills, pausing on the hill tops to admire the beautiful country over which he ruled.

My meditations on the Fon's character were interrupted: he leaned forward and gripped my arm, pointing a long finger at the trees.

"Dey done come," he whispered, his face wreathed in smiles. I followed the pointing of his finger, and for a moment I could see nothing but a confused net of branches. Then something moved, and I saw the animal that we had been awaiting.

It came drifting through the tangled branches with all the gentle, airy grace of a piece of thistledown. When it got nearer, I discovered that it looked exactly like my idea of a leprechaun: it was clad in a little fur coat of greenish-gray, and it had a long slender furry tail. Its hands, which were pink, were large for its size, and its fingers tremendously long and attenuated. Its ears were large and the skin so fine that it was semi-transparent; these ears seemed to have a life of their own, for they twisted and turned independently, sometimes crumpling and folding flat to the head as if they were fans.

The face of the little creature was dominated by a pair of tremendous dark eyes that would have put any self-respecting owl to shame. Moreover, the creature could twist its head round and look over its back in much the same way that an owl does. It ran to the tip of a slender branch that scarcely dipped beneath its weight, and there it sat, clutching the bark with its long slender fingers, peering about with its great eyes, and chirruping dimly to itself. It was, I knew, a galago, but it looked much more like something out of a fairy tale.

It sat on the branch, twittering vaguely to itself, for a minute; then an astonishing thing happened. Quite suddenly, the trees were full of galagos—of every age and size, ranging from babies little bigger than a walnut, to fully adult ones that could have fitted themselves quite comfortably into an ordinary drinking glass. They jumped from branch to branch, grasping the leaves and twigs with their large, thin hands, twittering softly to each other and gazing round them with the wide-eyed innocence of a troupe of cherubim.

The babies, who seemed to be composed almost entirely of eyes, kept fairly close to their parents; occasionally, they would sit up on their hind legs and hold their tiny pink hands up, fingers spread wide, as though in horror at the depravity they were seeing in the world of leaves around them. One of these babies discovered, while I watched, that he was sitting on the same branch as a large and succulent locust. It was evening time, and the insect was drowsy and slow to realize its danger. Before it could do anything, the baby galago had flitted down the branch and grabbed it firmly round the middle.

The locust woke up abruptly and decided that something must be done. He was a large insect, almost as big as the baby galago; also he possessed a pair of long and muscular hind legs, and he started to kick out vigorously with them. It was a fascinating fight to watch: the galago clasped the locust desperately in his long fingers, and tried to bite it. Each time it tried to bite, the locust would give a terrific kick with its hind legs and knock its adversary off balance, so it would fall off the branch and hang beneath, suspended by its feet.

When this had happened several times, I decided that the galago must have adhesive soles. Even when hanging upside down and being kicked in the stomach by a large locust, the galago maintained its expression of wide-eyed innocence.

The end of the fight was unexpected: when they were hanging upside down, the locust gave an extra hefty kick, and the galago's feet lost their grip, so they fell through the leaves, clasped together. As they tumbled earthward, the galago loosened one hand from its grip round the locust's waist and grabbed a passing branch with the effortless ease of a trained acrobat. He hauled himself onto the branch and bit the locust's head off before the insect could recover sufficiently to continue the fight.

Holding the decapitated, but still kicking, body in one hand, the galago stuffed the insect's head into his mouth and chewed it with evident enjoyment. Then he sat, clasping the twitching body in one hand and contemplated it with his head on one side, giving vent to shrill and excited screams of delight. When the corpse had ceased to move and the big hind legs had stiffened in death, the galago tore them off, one by one, and ate them. He looked ridiculously like a diminutive elderly gourmet, clasping in one hand the drumstick of some gigantic chicken.

Soon the valley was filled with shadow, and it became difficult to see the galagos among the leaves, though we could hear their soft chittering. We rose from our cramped positions, and made our way back up the hillside. At the top, the Fon paused and gazed down at the woods below, smiling delightedly.

"Dat beef!" he chuckled, "I like um too much. All time 'e make funny for me, an' I go laugh."

"Na fine beef," I said, "how you call um?"

"For Bafut," said the Fon, "we call um Shilling."

"You think sometimes my hunter men fit catch some?"

"Tomorrow you go have some," promised the Fon, but he would not tell me how they were to be captured, nor who was to do the capturing. We reached Bafut in the dusk, and when the Fon was respectably clothed once more he came and had a drink. As I said good night to him, I reminded him of his promise to get me some of the galagos.

"Yes, my friend, I no go forget," he said, "I go get you some Shilling."

Four days passed, and I began to think that either the Fon had forgotten, or else the creatures were proving more difficult to capture than he had imagined.

Then, on the fifth morning, my tea was brought in, and reposing on the tray was a small, highly colored raffia basket. I pulled off the lid and looked sleepily inside, and four pairs of enormous, liquid, innocent eyes peered up at me with expressions of gentle inquiry.

It was a basketful of Shillings from the Fon.

My stay in Bafut eventually drew to a close. I had collected a vast quantity of animal life, and it was time to take it all back to the base camp, where it could be recaged and got ready for the voyage. Reluctantly I informed the hunters that I would be leaving in a week, so that they would not bring in any specimens after I had left. The Fon, when he heard the news, came flying over, clasping a bottle of gin, and did his best to persuade me to stay on. But, as I explained to him, I could not stay any longer, much as I would like to; our return passages were booked, and that meant the whole collection had to be ready to move down country on the prescribed date. If there was any hitch we would miss the ship, and we might not be able to get another one for a couple of months, a delay which the trip's budget was not designed to cope with.

"Ah! My friend, I sorry too much you go," said the Fon, pouring gin into my glass with the gay abandon of a fountain.

"I sorry too much as well," I said with truth, "but I no get chance for stay Bafut any more."

"You go remember Bafut," said the Fon, pointing a long finger at me. "You go remember Bafut fine. Na for Bafut you done get plenty fine beef, no be so?"

"Na so," I said, pointing at my vast piles of cages. "I done get beef too much for Bafut."

The Fon nodded benignly, leaned forward, and clasped my hand. "When you go for your country, sometime you go tell your people de Fon of Bafut na your friend, and 'e done get you all dis fine beef, eh?"

"I go tell um all," I promised, "and I go tell um dat de Fon be fine hunter man, better pass all hunter for Cameroons."

"Foine, foine!" said the Fon delightedly. . . .

The Fon and I sat drinking in the misty moonlight until it was late. Then he turned to me, pointing toward his village. "I tink sometime you like to dance," he said, "so I done tell um to make musica. You like we go dance before you leave, eh?"

"Yes, I like to dance," I said.

The Fon lurched to his feet and, leaning perilously over the veranda rail, shouted an order to someone waiting below. In a short time a cluster of lights moved across the great courtyard, and the Fon's all-female band assembled in the road below and started to play. Soon they were joined by numerous others, including most of the council members.

The Fon listened to the music for a bit, waving his hands and smiling, and then got up and held out his hand to me.

"Come!" he said, "we go dance, eh?"

"Foine, foine!" I mimicked him, and he crowed with glee.

We crossed the moon-misty veranda to the head of the steps, the Fon draped a long arm over my shoulders, partly out of affection and partly for support, and we started to descend. Halfway down my companion stopped to execute a short dance to the music. His foot got tangled up in his impressive robes, and, but for his firm grip round my neck, he would have rolled down the steps into the road. As it was, we struggled there for a moment, swaying violently, trying to regain our balance. The crowd of wives, offspring, and councilors gasped in horror and consternation, and the band stopped playing.

"Musica, musica!" roared the Fon, as we reeled together on the steps. "Why you done stop, eh?"

The band started up again. We regained our equilibrium and walked down the rest of the way without mishap. The Fon was in fine fettle, and he insisted on holding my hand and dancing across the courtyard, splashing through the puddles, while the band trotted behind, playing a trifle short-windedly. When we reached the dancing hut, he sat down on his throne for a rest while his court took the floor. Presently, when there was a slight lull in the dancing, I asked the Fon if he would call the band over, so that I could examine the instruments more closely. They trooped over and stood in front of the dais.

I tried each instrument in turn and was shown the correct way of playing it. To everyone's surprise, including my own, I succeeded in playing the first few bars of "The Campbells Are Coming" on a bamboo flute. The Fon was so delighted he made me repeat it several times, while he accompanied me on a big drum, and one of the council members on the strange foghorn-like instrument. The effect was not altogether musical, but we rendered it with great verve and feeling. Then we had to repeat it all over again, with a full band accompaniment. Actually, it sounded rather good, as most of my flat notes were drowned by the drums.

When we had exhausted the musical possibilities of the tune, the Fon sent for another bottle, and we settled down to watch the dancers. The inactivity soon told on my companion, and after an hour or so he started to shift on his throne and to scowl at the band.

"Dis dance no be good," he confided at last.

"Na fine," I said. "Why you no like?"

" 'E slow too much," he pointed out and smiled at me disarmingly. "You like we go dance your special dance?"

"Special dance?" I queried, slightly fuddled. "What dance?"

"One, two, three, keek—one, two, three, keek," yodeled the Fon.

"Ah, dat dance you de talk. Yes, we go dance um if you like."

"I like too much," said the Fon firmly.

He led the way to the dance floor and clutched my waist in a firm grip, while everyone else, chattering and grinning with delight, joined on behind. To add a little variety to the affair I borrowed a flute and piped noisily and inaccurately on it as I led them a wild dance round the dance hall and out among the huts of the Fon's wives. The night was warm, and half an hour of this exercise made me stream with sweat and gasp for breath.

We stopped for a rest and some liquid refreshment. It was obvious, however, that my conga had got into the Fon's blood. He sat on his throne, his eyes gleaming, feet tapping, humming reminiscently to himself—and waiting with ill-concealed impatience until I had recovered my breath before suggesting that we repeat the whole performance. I decided that I would have to head him off in some way, for I found the conga too enervating for such a close night, and I had barked my shin most painfully on a doorpost during our last round. I cast around in my mind for another dance I could teach him which would be less strenuous to perform, and yet whose tune could be easily mastered by the band. I made my choice, called once more for a flute, and practiced on it for a few minutes.

Then I turned to the Fon, who had been watching me with great interest. "If you go tell de band 'e go learn dis special music I go teach you other European dance," I said.

"Ah! Foine, foine!" He roared the band to silence, then marshaled them round the dais.

I played the tune to them, and in a surprisingly short space of time they picked it up and were even adding little variations.

The Fon stamped his feet delightedly. "Na fine music dis," he said, "now you go show me dis dance, eh?"

I looked round and singled out a young damsel who, I had noticed, seemed exceptionally bright, and, clasping her as closely as propriety would permit (for her clothing was nonexistent), I set off across the dance floor in a dashing polka. My partner after only a momentary hesitation picked up the step perfectly, and we bobbed and hopped around in great style. To show his appreciation the Fon started to clap, and immediately the rest of the court followed suit; it started off as normal, ragged applause, but, being Africans, they kept clapping and worked it into the rhythm of the dance. The girl and I circled round the large floor five times, and then we were forced to stop for a rest.

When I reached the dais, the Fon held out a brimming glass of whiskey and clapped me on the back as I sat down. "Na foine dance!"

I nodded and gulped down my drink. As soon as I had put my glass down the Fon seized me by the hand and pulled me onto the floor again. "Come," he said persuasively, "you go show me dis dance."

Clasped in each other's arms, we polkaed round, but it was not a great success, owing chiefly to the fact that my partner's robes became entangled with my feet and jerked us both to a standstill. We would then have to stand patiently while a crowd of council members unwound us, after which away we would go again: one, two, three, hop, only to end up in the opposite corner entwined together like a couple of maypoles.

Eventually I glanced at my watch and discovered to my dismay that it was three o'clock. Reluctantly I had to take my leave of the Fon and retire to bed. He and the court followed me out into the great courtyard. As I climbed up the steps to the villa I looked back at them. In among the twinkling hurricane lanterns they were all dancing the polka. In the center the Fon was jigging and hopping by himself, waving one long arm and shouting, "Good night, my friend! Good night!" I waved back, and then went and crawled thankfully into my bed.

By eight-thirty the next morning the lorry had arrived and the collection had been stacked on it. An incredible number of Bafutians had come to say good-by and to see me off; they had been arriving since early that morning, and now lined the roadside, chattering together, waiting for me to depart. The last load was hoisted onto the lorry, and the sound of drums, flutes, and rattles heralded the arrival of the Fon to take his leave of me. He was dressed as I had seen him on the day of my arrival, in a plain white robe and a wine-red skullcap. He was accompanied by his retinue of councilors. He strode up and embraced me and then, holding me by the hand, addressed the assembled Bafutians in a few rapid sentences. When he stopped the crowd broke into loud "arrr's" and started to clap rhythmically.

The Fon turned to me and raised his voice. "My people 'e sorry too much you go leave Bafut. All dis people dey go remember you, and you no go forget Bafut, eh?"

"I never go forget Bafut," I said truthfully, making myself heard with difficulty above the steady clapping of hundreds of black hands.

"Good," he said with satisfaction. He clasped my hand firmly in his and wrung it. "My friend, always I go get you for my eye. I no go forget dis happy time we done get. By God Power you go reach your own country safe. Walker good, my friend, walker good."

As the lorry started off down the road the clapping got faster and faster, until it sounded like rain on a tin roof. We jolted our way slowly along until we reached the corner. Looking back, I saw the road lined with naked black humanity, their hands fluttering as they clapped, and at the end of this avenue of moving hands and flashing teeth stood a tall figure in dazzling white. The Fon raised a long arm, and a huge hand waved a last farewell as we rounded the corner and started up the red earth road that wound over the golden hills.

JEAN KERR

Aunt Jean's
 Marshmallow
Fudge Diet

Fred Allen used to talk about a man who was so thin he could be dropped through a piccolo without striking a single note. Well, I'm glad I never met *him;* I'd hate to have to hear about *his* diet.

I can remember when I was a girl—way back in Truman's Administration—and No-Cal was only a gleam in the eye of the Hirsch Bottling Company. In those days it was fun to go to parties. The conversation used to crackle with wit and intelligence because we talked about *ideas*—the aesthetic continuum in Western culture, Gary Cooper in Western movies, the superiority of beer over lotion as a wave-set, and the best way to use left-over veal.

Go to a party now and the couple next to you won't say a word about the rich, chocolate texture of their compost heap or how practical it's been to buy bunk-beds for the twins. They won't talk about anything except their diets—the one they've just come off, the one they're on now, or the one they're going to have to start on Monday if they keep lapping it up like this.

I really blame science for the whole business. Years ago when a man began to notice that if he stood up on the subway he was immediately replaced by *two* people, he figured he was getting too fat.

So he went to his doctor and the doctor said, "Quit stuffing yourself, Joe." And Joe either stopped or he didn't stop, but at least he kept his big mouth shut. What was there to talk about?

Today, with the science of nutrition advancing so rapidly, there is plenty of food for conversation, if for nothing else. We have the Rockefeller diet, the Mayo diet, high-protein diets, low-protein diets, "blitz" diets which feature cottage cheese and something that tastes like thin sandpaper, and—finally—a liquid diet that duplicates all the rich, nourishing goodness of mother's milk. I have no way of knowing which of these takes off the most weight, but there's no question that as a conversation-stopper the Mother's Milk Diet is way out ahead.

Where do people get all these diets, anyway? Obviously from the magazines; it's impossible to get a diet from a newspaper. For one thing, in a newspaper you can never catch the diet when it *starts*. It's always the fourth day of Ada May's Wonder Diet and, after a brief description of a simple slimming exercise that could be performed by anybody who has had five years' training with the ballet, Ada May gives you the menu for the day. One glass of skim milk, eight prunes, and three lamb's kidneys. This settles the matter for most people, who figure—quite reasonably—that if this is the *fourth* day, heaven deliver them from the first.

However, any stoics in the group who want to know just how far Ada May's sense of whimsy will take her can have the complete diet by sending twenty-five cents in stamps to the newspaper. But who has twenty-five cents in stamps? And if you're going to go out and get the stamps you might as well buy a twenty-five-cent magazine which will give you not only the same diet (now referred to as *Our Wonder Diet*) but will, in addition, show you a quick and easy way to turn your husband's old socks into gay pot holders.

In a truly democratic magazine that looks at all sides of the picture you will also find a recipe for George Washington's Favorite Spice Cake which will replace any weight you may have haphazardly lost on that wonder diet.

If you have formed the habit of checking on every *new* diet that comes along, you will find that, mercifully, they all blur together, leaving you with only one definite piece of information: French fried potatoes are out. But once in a great while a diet will stick in your mind. I'll never forget one I read about last summer. It urged the dieter to follow up his low-calorie meals by performing a series of calisthenics in the bathtub. No, not in the bath*room*. I read it twice, and it said in the bath*tub*. What a clever plan! Clearly, after you've broken both your arms you won't be able to eat as much (if at all) and the pounds will just melt away. In fact, if you don't have a co-operative husband who is willing to feed you like a two-year-old you may be limited to what you can consume through a straw, in which case let me suggest that Mother's Milk Formula.

The best diet I've heard about lately is the simplest. It was perfected by the actor Walter Slezak after years of careful experimentation. Under the Slezak plan, you eat as much as you want of everything you don't like. And if you should be in a hurry for any reason (let's say you're still wearing maternity clothes and the baby is eight months old) then you should confine yourself to food that you just plain hate.

Speaking about hateful food, the experts used to be content with merely making food pallid—by eliminating butter, oil, and salt. Not any more. Nowadays we are taught that, with a little imagination and a judicious use of herbs, anyone can turn out a no-calorie dish that's downright ghastly. Just yesterday I came across a dandy recipe for sprucing up good old boiled celery. You just simmer the chopped celery (with the tops) in a little skim milk. When it's tender, you add chopped onion, anise, chervil, marjoram, a dash of cinnamon, and you have a dish fit for the Dispose-All. And you'd better have a Dispose-All, because it's awfully messy if you have to dump it into a newspaper and carry it out to the garbage can.

And where is all this dieting getting us? No place at all. It's taken all the fun out of conversation and all the joy out of cooking. Furthermore, it leads to acts of irrational violence. A friend of mine keeps all candy and other luscious tidbits in the freezer, on the theory that by the time they thaw out enough to be eaten she will have recovered her will power. But the other night, having been driven berserk by a four-color advertisement for Instant Brownies, she rushed out to the freezer, started to gnaw on a frozen Milky Way, and broke a front tooth.

But let's get to the heart of the matter. All these diets that appear so monotonously in the flossy magazines—who are they for? Are they aimed at men? Certainly not; most men don't read these magazines. Are they intended for fat teen-agers? Probably not; teen-agers can't afford them. Do not ask for whom the bell tolls. It tolls for you—Married Woman, Mother of Three, lumpy, dumpy, and the source of concern to practically every publication in the United States. And why, why is the married woman being hounded into starvation in order to duplicate an ideal figure which is neither practical nor possible for a person her age? I'll tell you why.

First, it is presumed that when you're thinner you live longer. (In any case, when you live on a diet of yogurt and boiled grapefruit, it *seems* longer. Second, it is felt that when you are skin and bones you have so much extra energy that you can climb up and shingle the roof. Third—and this is what they're really getting at—when you're thin you are so tasty and desirable that strange men will pinch you at the A & P and your husband will not only follow you around the kitchen breathing heavily but will stop and smother you with kisses as you try to put the butter back in the icebox. This—and I hope those in the back of the room are listening—is hogwash.

Think of the happy marriages you know about. How many of the ladies are still wearing size twelve? I've been giving this a lot of thought in the last twenty minutes, and I have been examining the marriages in my own troubled circle. What I have discovered is that the women who are being ditched are one and all willowy, wand-like, and slim as a blade. In fact, six of them require extensive padding even to look flat-chested.

That the fourteen divorcees, or about-to-be divorcees, whom I happen to know personally are all thin may be nothing more than a coincidence. Or it may just prove that men don't divorce fat wives because they feel sorry for them. Then again—and this is rather sinister—men may not divorce fat wives because they imagine that the poor, plump dears will never locate *another* husband and they'll be paying alimony to the end of their days. (I mention this possibility, but my heart's not in it.)

The real reason, I believe, that men hang onto their well-endowed spouses is because they're comfy, and nice to have around the house. In a marriage there is nothing that stales so fast as physical beauty— as we readers of *Modern Screen* have observed. What actually holds a husband through thick and thick is a girl who is fun to be with. And any girl who has had nothing to eat since nine o'clock this morning but three hard-boiled eggs will be about as jolly and companionable as an income-tax inspector.

So I say, ladies, find out why women everywhere are switching from old-fashioned diets to the *modern* way: no exercise, no dangerous drugs, no weight loss. (And what do they mean "ugly fat"? It's *you*, isn't it?) For that tired, run-down feeling, try eating three full meals a day with a candy bar after dinner and pizza at eleven o'clock. Don't be intimidated by pictures of Audrey Hepburn. That girl is nothing but skin and bones. Just sit there smiling on that size twenty backside and say, "Guess what we're having for dinner, dear? Your favorite—stuffed breast of veal and corn fritters."

All your friends will say, "Oh, Blanche is a mess, the size of a house, but he's crazy about her, just *crazy* about her!"

E. B. WHITE

One
Man's
Meat

December, 1938

It is not likely that a person who changes his pursuits will ever succeed in taking on the character or the appearance of the new man, however much he would like to. I am farming, to a small degree and for my own amusement, but it is a cheap imitation of the original. I have fitted myself out with standard equipment, dungarees and a cap; but I would think twice before I dared stand still in a field of new corn. In the minds of my friends and neighbors who really know what they are about and whose clothes really fit them, much of my activity has the quality of a little girl playing house. My routine is that of a husbandman, but my demeanor is that of a high-school boy in a soft-drink parlor. This morning, carrying grain to my birds, I noticed that I was unconsciously imitating the young roosters— making a noise in my throat like a cock learning to crow. No farmer has the time or the temperament for vaudeville of this sort. He feeds his flock silently, sometimes attentively, sometimes absent-mindedly, but never banteringly. He doesn't go round his place making noises in his throat.

Another time I caught myself carrying a paper napkin in my hand, as I wandered here and there. I have never seen a farmer carrying a paper napkin around his barnyard.

For all its implausibility, however, my farming has the excitement, the calamities, and sometimes the nobility of the real thing. For sheer surprise there is nothing to beat this life. For example, I had read widely on the subject of lice and mites, had treated my flock diligently. The specter of infestation was with me constantly. Yet when trouble finally came to my farm, it was not my hens that developed lice, but my Victrola. The old machine, I discovered the other day, is fairly alive with parasites—in the seams where the old needles lodge, and running in and out the little cup where old and new needles mingle in democratic equality. I use Black Leaf 40 (nicotine sulphate) for my hens, smearing it on the roosts according to directions on the bottle. But I'm damned if I know how to apply nicotine sulphate to a Victrola, and there is nothing in my agricultural bulletins which covers the subject. I suppose I could rub the stuff on a Benny Goodman record and let him swing it, but it sounds like a mess. It is this sort of thing that makes the land so richly exciting: you never know where the enemy is going to strike.

July, 1939

I would like to hand down a dissenting opinion in the case of the Camel ad which shows a Boston terrier relaxing. I can string along with cigarette manufacturers to a certain degree, but when it comes to the temperament and habits of terriers, I shall stand my ground.

The ad says: "A dog's nervous system resembles our own." I don't think a dog's nervous system resembles my own in the least. A dog's nervous system is in a class by itself. If it resembles anything at all, it resembles the New York Edison Company's power plant. This is particularly true of Boston terriers, and if the Camel people don't know that, they have never been around dogs.

The ad says: "But when a dog's nerves tire, he obeys his instincts —he relaxes." This, I admit, is true. But I should like to call attention to the fact that it sometimes takes days, even weeks, before a dog's nerves tire. In the case of terriers it can run into months.

I knew a Boston terrier once (he is now dead and, so far as I know, relaxed) whose nerves stayed keyed up from the twenty-fifth of one June to the sixth of the following July, without one minute's peace for anybody in the family. He was an old dog and he was blind in one eye, but his infirmities caused no diminution in his nervous power. During the period of which I speak, the famous period of his greatest excitement, he not only raised a type of general hell which startled even his closest friends and observers, but he gave a mighty clever excuse. He said it was love.

"I'm in love," he would scream. (He could scream just like a hurt child.) "I'm in love and I'm going *crazy*."

Day and night it was all the same. I tried everything to soothe him. I tried darkness, cold water dashed in the face, the lash, long quiet talks, warm milk administered internally, threats, promises, and close confinement in remote locations. At last, after about a week of it, I went down the road and had a chat with the lady who owned the object of our terrier's affection. It was she who finally cleared up the situation.

"Oh," she said, wearily, "if it's that bad, let him out."

I hadn't thought of anything as simple as that myself, but I am a creature of infinite reserve. As a matter of record, it turned out to be not so simple—the terrier got run over by a motor car one night while returning from his amorous adventures, suffering a complete paralysis of the hip but no assuagement of the nervous system; and the little Scotty bitch returned to Washington, D. C., and a Caesarian.

I am not through with the Camel people yet. Love is not the only thing that can keep a dog's nerves in a state of perpetual jangle. A dog, more than any other creature, it seems to me, gets interested in one subject, theme, or object, in life, and pursues it with a fixity of purpose which would be inspiring to Man if it weren't so troublesome. One dog gets absorbed in one thing, another dog in another. When I was a boy there was a smooth-haired fox terrier (in those days nobody ever heard of a fox terrier that *wasn't* smooth-haired) who became interested, rather late in life, in a certain stone. The stone was about the size of an egg. As far as I could see, it was like a million other stones—but to him it was the Stone Supreme.

He kept it with him day and night, slept with it, ate with it, played with it, analyzed it, took it on little trips (you would often see him three blocks from home, trotting along on some shady errand, his stone safe in his jaws). He used to lie by the hour on the porch of his house, chewing the stone with an expression half tender, half petulant. When he slept he merely enjoyed a muscular suspension: his nerves were still up and around, adjusting the bed clothes, tossing and turning.

He permitted people to throw the stone for him and people would. But if the stone lodged somewhere he couldn't get to he raised such an uproar that it was absolutely necessary that the stone be returned, for the public peace. His absorption was so great it brought wrinkles to his face, and he grew old before his time. I think he used to worry that somebody was going to pitch the stone into a lake or a bog, where it would be irretrievable. He wore off every tooth in his jaw, wore them right down to the gums, and they became mere brown vestigal bumps. His breath was awful (he panted night and day) and his eyes were alight with an unearthly zeal. He died in a fight with another dog. I have always suspected it was because he tried to hold the stone in his mouth all through the battle. The Camel people will just have to take my word for it: that dog was a living denial of the whole theory of relaxation. He was a paragon of nervous tension, from the moment he first laid eyes on his slimy little stone till the hour of his death.

The advertisement speaks of the way humans "prod" themselves to endeavor—so that they keep on and on working long after they should quit. The inference is that a dog never does that. But I have a dog right now that can prod himself harder and drive himself longer than any human I ever saw. This animal is a dachshund, and I shall spare you the long dull inanities of his innumerable obsessions. His particular study (or mania) at the moment is a black-and-white kitten that my wife gave me for Christmas, thinking that what my life needed was something else that could move quickly from one place in the room to another. The dachshund began his research on Christmas eve when the kitten arrived "secretly" in the cellar, and now, five months later, is taking his Ph.D., still working late at night on it, every night. If he could write a book about that cat, it would make *Middletown* look like the work of a backward child.

I'll be glad to have the Camel people study this animal in one of his relaxed moods, but they will have to bring their own seismograph. Even curled up cozily in a chair, dreaming of his cat, he quivers like an aspen.

June, 1940

When I invested in a band of sheep last fall (they cost seven dollars apiece) I had no notion of what I was letting myself in for in the way of emotional involvements. I knew there would be lambs in spring, but they seemed remote. Lambing, I felt, would take place automatically and would be the sheep's business, not mine. I forgot that sheep come up in late fall and join the family circle. At first they visit the barn rather cautiously, eat some hay, and depart. But after one or two driving storms they abandon the pasture altogether, draw up chairs around the fire, and settle down for the winter. They become as much a part of your group as your dog, or your Aunt Maudie. Our house and barn are connected by a woodshed, like the Grand Central Station and the Yale Club; and without stepping out of doors you can reach any animal on the place, including the pig. This makes for greater intimacy than obtains in a layout where each farm building is a separate structure. We don't encourage animals to come into the house, but they get in once in a while, particularly the cosset lamb, who trotted through this living room not five minutes ago looking for an eight-ounce bottle. Anyway, in circumstances such as ours you find yourself growing close to sheep. You give them names not for whimsy but for convenience. And when one of them approaches her confinement you get almost as restless as she does.

The birth of a mammal was once a closed book to me. Except for the famous "Birth of a Baby" picture and a couple of old receipted bills from an obstetrician, I was unacquainted with the more vivid aspects of birth. All that is changed. For the past six weeks I have been delivering babies with great frequency, moderate abandon, and no little success. Eighteen lambs from thirteen sheep isn't bad. I lost one pair of twins—they were dropped the first week of February, before I expected them, and they chilled. I also lost a single lamb, born dead.

A newcomer to the realm of parturition is inclined to err on the side of being too helpful. I have no doubt my early ministrations were as distasteful to the ewe as those of the average night nurse are to an expectant mother. Sheep differ greatly in their ability to have a lamb and to care for it. They also differ in their attitude toward the Shepherd. Some sheep enjoy having you mincing around, arranging flowers and adjusting the window. Others are annoyed beyond words. The latter, except in critical cases, should be left to work out their problem by themselves. They usually get along. If you've trimmed the wool around their udders the day before with a pair of desk shears, the chances are ten to one they will feed their lambs all right when they arrive.

At first, birth strikes one as the supreme example of bad planning —a thoroughly mismanaged and ill-advised functional process, something thought up by a dirty-minded fiend. It appears cluttery, haphazard. But after you have been mixed up with it for a while, have spent nights squatting beneath a smoky lantern in a cold horse stall helping a weak lamb whose mother fails to own it; after you have grown accustomed to the odd trappings and by-products of mam-

malian reproduction and seen how marvelously they contribute to the
finished product; after you've broken down an animal's reserve and
have identified yourself with her and no longer pull your punches,
then this strange phenomenon of birth becomes an absorbingly
lustrous occasion, full of subdued emotion, like a great play, an
occasion for which you unthinkingly give up any other occupation that
might be demanding your attention. I've never before in my life put
in such a month as this past month has been—a period of pure creation, vicarious in its nature, but extraordinarily moving.

I presume that everything a female does in connection with birth-
ing her young is largely instinctive, not rational. A sheep makes a
hundred vital movements and performs a dozen indispensable and
difficult tasks, blissfully oblivious of her role. Everything is important, but nothing is intelligent. Before the lamb is born she paws
petulantly at the bedding. Even this is functional, for she manages
to construct a sort of nest into which the lamb drops, somewhat to
the lamb's advantage. Then comes the next miraculous reflex. In
the first instant after a lamb is dropped, the ewe takes one step ahead,
turns, and lowers her head to sniff eagerly at her little tomato surprise.
This step ahead that she takes is a seemingly trivial thing, but I have
been thinking about it and I guess it is not trivial at all. If she were
to take one step backward it would be a different story—she would
step on her lamb, and perhaps damage it. I have often seen a ewe step
backward while laboring, but I never remember seeing one take
a backward step after her lamb has arrived on the ground. This is
the second instinctive incident.

The third is more important than either of the others. A lamb,
newly born, is in a state of considerable disrepair; it arrives weak and
breathless, with its nose plugged with phlegm or covered with a sac.
It sprawls, suffocated, on the ground, and after giving one convulsive
shake, is to all appearances dead. Only quick action, well directed, will
save it and start it ticking. The ewe takes this action, does the next
important thing, which is to open the lamb's nostrils. She goes for
its nose with unerring aim and starts tearing off the cellophane. I can't
believe that she is intelligently unstoppering these air passages for
her child; she just naturally feels like licking a lamb on the nose. You
wonder (or I do, anyway) what strange directional force impels her
to begin at the nose, rather than at the other end. A lamb has two
ends, all right, and before the ewe gets through she has attended to
both of them; but she always begins with the nose, and with almost
frenzied haste. I suppose Darwin is right, and that a long process of

hereditary elimination finally produced sheep which began cleaning the forward end of a lamb, not the after end. It is an impressive sight, no matter what is responsible for it. It is literally life-giving, and you can see life take hold with the first in-draught of air in the freed nostril. The lamb twitches and utters a cry, as though from a long way off. The ewe answers with a stifled grunt, her sides still contracting with the spasms of birth; and in this answering cry the silver cord is complete and takes the place of the umbilicus, which has parted, its work done.

These are only the beginnings of the instinctive events in the maternal program. The ewe goes on to dry her lamb and boost it to its feet. She keeps it moving so that it doesn't lodge and chill. She finally works it into position so that it locates, in an almost impenetrable jungle of wool, the indispensable fountain and the early laxative. One gulp of this fluid (which seems to have a liberal share of brandy in it) and the lamb is launched. Its little tail wiggles and satisfaction is written all over it, and your heart leaps up.

Even your own technic begins to grow more instinctive. When I was a novice I used to work hard to make a lamb suck by forcing its mouth to the teat. Now I just tickle it on the base of its tail.

MARIO PRODAN

The Indians
of the

Colorado
River

It is astonishing how really personal a matter truth is. I remember
when we were children there was a stereoscope in Father's study and
a heavy box neatly filled with double photographs. One set of these
was our favorite. It was progressive. A beautiful lady dressed in the
style of a Gibson Girl is sitting in a drawing room brimful of furniture, potted plants, hangings, pictures, porcelain, and lamps. There
is a little girl there too, dressed in white with long black stockings,
reading a large book. A gentleman comes in, with mustaches. He
shakes hands all around and is seated. The little girl is asked to leave.
She leaves. The grown-up people talk and laugh. Then they stand
up and, while the gentleman looks on, the lady begins to undress.
One by one, photograph by photograph, she takes off her clothes
until she is left in a voluminous chemise and no less voluminous
bloomers. At this point the gentleman walks over to her and lifts
the back of her chemise. There, on the small of the lady's back, is
a perforated plaster about the size of a handkerchief. While the lady
registers hilarious agony on her beautiful face the gentleman pro-
ceeds to pull away the plaster. The stereoscope adventure ends there.

But this is what it did to me: it brought me the conviction that all ladies, for some obscure grown-up reason, wore perforated plasters on the small of their backs. It remained my personal truth right into my fourteenth year.

I possess personal truths at this very moment, certain truths that are almost exclusively my own. But who has not? And, are we who have them to be condemned? There is a very strong extenuating circumstance, if not indeed grounds for complete exoneration, that we can turn to. It is that the other truths, the so-called absolute truths, have received tremendous jolts of late.

I have a personal truth about the Indians of the Colorado River, and I wish to relate how I came upon it.

People who travel from the Far East to Europe via America invariably say: "Oh, you must see the Grand Canyon," so, when I went to Europe via the United States, I went to see it.

We made the trip to the Canyon by special tourist train. On the way from Los Angeles, I became acquainted with three young men who, by an odd coincidence, were also from the Far East. One was an American mining engineer, the other an English student at Oxford, and the third a Dutch lieutenant of the Netherlands East Indies artillery. Our Oriental background made acquaintance easy, and the moment we began to talk politics and to take sides we found ourselves on excellent terms.

As the train pulled in and we descended, the pastel country that surrounded the station was bathed in a mist that hung in the air like silver powder. The open-air platform was deserted—except for three figures who were walking toward us from the head of the train. They were walking slowly and now, as they came nearer, we discovered what they were. They were Indians. Red Indians. The black glossiness of their hair, the severe but colorful decorations on the blankets, the honey-colored leather moccasins assured it. We gazed at them, enthralled. Red Indians as we had imagined them—somber, dignified, silent. They were carrying their arms crossed and high, so that their eyes and broad foreheads alone looked over that scaffolding of arms from which, austere, the heavy cloth hung down. They approached us and we made way for them to pass. The Indian in front acknowledged this attention with a dignified nod. As he drew level we noticed that he was the only man of the party, for the Indian behind him was a woman, and the Indian behind her a boy.

They went by silently, the whole length of the platform. At the point where it dipped to the level of the rails they swung off, and then were gone from our sight.

They had made us feel very warm inside. They filled us with anticipation of drama, recalled to us a forgotten flavor from the books of our childhood.

We were taken by bus to the hotel, where an excellent breakfast awaited us. At 8:45, however, we were commanded to attend a sun worship ceremony by the Indians of the Colorado River.

Even though only three Indians performed it, it turned out to be very impressive. Two of them, encased in their woolen blankets, sat on the rock a little behind the third who, standing erect like a statue, attired in nothing but a loin cloth, his sinewy brown arms raised to the sky, emitted from time to time a succession of sounds. They were a low gutteral murmur, followed, after a short interval, by a high-pitched yell. The trio was at a distance from us, up on a shelf of rock in that amazing terrain. All three faced the sun, now still hidden from them by a sharp boulder which, the guide pointed out, had the shape of an eagle crouching. But, as the sun rose up, up, and the rays began to cast their light on the face of the man, he began to tremble. It was fairly chilly as a matter of fact, and I remember wondering that he had not started shivering sooner. The succession of moans and yells became more immediate and went up into a crescendo until the sun was full on him, and on the two behind him. They stood up then and handed the standing Indian his blanket. After him, with surprising dignity under the circumstances, they climbed the sheer wall of rock to mount the flat terrain that over-hung it. There, they formed an Indian file. I borrowed the Dutch-man's binoculars. The three Indians were a man, a woman, and a boy. The boy was in the middle.

At 9:15 we were ordered to go through a little Indian hut where hand-wrought jewelry was on sale. It was attractive, turquoise and coral chips held together by a black paste, made up into brooches, rings, and bracelets. A woman and a boy, Indians, wearing those handsome leather jackets with fringed edges, were selling them. The boy was an attractive youth, long-haired, with a diadem on his brow held there by a metal ring round his head. They did not speak a word; they only pointed to the jewelry and to the price-tags that were on it. But they knew how to add up sums quickly, on odd pieces of paper, and they wrote out the totals for you in an easy hand. At the end of the shop a door was ajar and from it came the sound of a small hammer beating metal. Some of the tourists went in. A man, an Indian, his back to the shop, was hammering strips of silver. You would have had to lie down in front of him in order to see his face, for he was sitting on the ground, bent double over his work.

At 10:10 we were summoned to the bus for the tour of the Grand Canyon's rim. Deep down in the yawning abyss, the Colorado River . . . Heavens, I wish I could go on like this for a page at least. I know that the Colorado River, the Grand Canyon absolutely deserve it. They are stupendous. But to me the whole thing was a bore. We had the Grand Canyon and the Colorado River when we were children, in the stereoscope in my father's study, forty double-photographs of them. It was a bore then and it was a bore now. The Grand Canyon in the stereoscope is not much different from the Grand Canyon in reality. You can't jump into either one, safely—they're both at such a tremendous distance. I prefer the lady with the perforated plaster. The power of the human element is really very great. I wanted to see people, Indians, not monstrous geological formations. That is why I kept looking forward: we had been told that we were to visit another Indian hut and see the Indians weaving their blankets on their primitive looms.

The hut was low, completely made of stone. Outside the door were three earthenware vessels amazingly similar to the neolithic pottery of China. We went in, stooping. It was quite dark after the glare outside.

Three Indians were weaving, seated on the earth in front of their looms which were lined against the wall. Unless you had sandwiched yourself between the looms and the wall and then thrust your face through the warp at them, you could not have seen their faces. But from behind you could tell their approximate size and their sex. They were a man, a woman, and a boy. We stayed and watched them for a time. Not once did those impassive Indians turn to look at us. One could not help feeling that it was noble of them to be so impervious to our inquisitive presence. But I would have liked to glean a spark from them. A look, a smile, a frown even: to let me know that they were molded as I was molded of sensitive human stuff. . . . But no. Instead we were led back to the bus and to the jokes of the guide. His humor was like Mark Twain's and as worn as the bed of the Colorado River.

12:45: We had lunch in a sort of stone observatory-*cum*-museum. 1:50: A young geologist dressed in uniform gave us a lecture. The guide told us that the young man's grandfather had come to the Canyon in a covered wagon. That cheered us somehow.

At 3:50, after a roll call, we were ordered once more to the bus and the peripatetic geological pilgrimage continued till 6:10, when we were suddenly back at the hotel again. We were allowed to rest for an hour. At 7:10 we were summoned to an Indian dance in front of the hotel.

It was inspiring. A wood fire was burning in the center of the cleared space as we came out of the house. The fire was low, almost embers. The orange-ruby glow gave the settling blueness of the night a deeper velvet, a greater intensity. Quietly at first, out of the night, rose the rhythmic beat of a drum like the blood thrumming through your body. It grew louder, and then louder. Out of the darkness a man appeared. He was almost naked. Shuffling almost imperceptibly, he penetrated deeper into the splash of light around the dying fire. Over and behind him flashing out of the shadow of his own body, was a crest of snow-white feathers. They rose up and away from his temples, flowed down his sinewy loins to trail on the ground. As he shuffled along, the feathers made that noise that turkey feathers make when the bird is aroused. The man stood still. But his long and bony fingers, as though they had a life of their own, beat on and on in steady rhythm. The suspense was at a high pitch. Now it was fulfilled. From the darkness a woman came into the zone of light. She was dressed. With measured steps she walked to the fire and, turning her back to it, stood still—but only for an instant. As if the rhythm of the drum were irresistible, she, too, began to shuffle her rather large feet back and forth, back and forth, until another dancer appeared out of the shadow. A boy, naked but for a breech clout and an eagle's feather in his hair. The woman stopped her shuffling, but the boy went on from where she left off. While he shuf-fled he moved, in a circle, around the fire. Soon he began to lift his head and to lower it, to lift his arms and to lower them, and then to ululate. At this the woman shuffled again. I thought there was a little too much shuffling; after all there is not much to it. But the spectacle was splendid. They shuffled, all three of them, for another fifteen minutes, and then the fire went out, and the dance was over.

We went in to dinner and had another excellent meal.

At 10:15 we were put on the bus and by 11:05 we were on the train. As it pulled slowly out of the station, we saw three Indians under a station light—a man, a woman, and a boy.

We arrived in New York and each went his own way. I stayed on in the city, and one day I went into a Trans-Lux. This was in 1940 and news theatres were interesting in those days. Whenever anything German came on, everybody hooted. A race developed to see who would hoot first. They showed a dog show. It was won by a German police dog, and everybody hooted.

Then, heralded by martial music and a stentorian voice, airplanes— large, powerful, beautiful—flew diagonally across the screen. The voice was saying: "Uncle Sam's air force is making test flights of new types of bombers over the Grand Canyon!" and I saw the Grand Canyon again, yards and yards of it. And then I saw the three Indians gazing up at the planes under distended hands. They wore, two of them, feathers, many feathers. But the third did not, for she was a woman.

Sometimes I read a book, a pamphlet, an article, which tells me of the vast reservations, of the innumerable, romantic names of Indian tribes, and I am absorbed and interested. But as I turn the last page I smile and gently shake my head. *I know the truth about the Colorado Indians. . . .*

ERIC LARRABEE

Easy Road
 to Culture,
Sort of

No modern scholar, whatever his special competence, can ignore the impact on educational practice of those two British authorities, W. C. Sellar and R. J. Yeatman, the authors of *1066 and All That*. It fell to these courageous innovators to redefine the word "memorable" to mean not what *should* be remembered but what *can* be remembered.

This realistic principle has since been increasingly applied in the colleges and universities. Notable achievements have been made in reducing the number of Great Ideas and Men to a manageable figure, and in compressing the body of organized knowledge into at most two or three more-or-less manageable departments. Strange as it may seem, however, until my own study of the matter no effort had been made to reduce all of higher education to *one course*.

The following syllabus is purely tentative. Exact research under rigidly controlled conditions will undoubtedly reveal that some elements in it are *not* memorable. The author will in that event welcome deletions or emendations of a negative character, but it must be understood that no proposal to *add* to the outline can be entertained. The survey course described below therefore replaces all others.

First Semester: Western Thought

Western thought was invented by the Greeks, who were the first people to realize they were thinking. The most memorable Greek thinker was Aristotle, author of the *Metataphysica* ("After Physics, What?"). One day while he was walking in the shade with King Midas (*cf.* Golden Mean, peripatetics), he fell into a bathtub and tried to pass it off by shouting "Eureka!" This is known as the Hypocritical Oath. Attention should also be paid to Greek Art, which is very classical and represented by the Wingless de Mille (Nike the Greek).

The Greek period was followed by the Roman period, which may roughly be divided into Decline and Fall. This period is somewhat decadent and noteworthy for such authors as Suetonius, Apuleius, Petronius, and Henry Miller (his *Nexus, Plexus,* and *Sexus* are especially memorable). The cruelty of the Roman period is typified by Floradora, mother of Cato the Elder, Cato the Younger, Marcus Cato, and Neiman Marcus (*"Timeo dallas, et panem circenses"*). Having set fire to Rome, she asked Julius Caesar to put his hand in the flame to see if it was hot enough.

"You brute," he replied.

This brings us to the Medieval period and to St. Thomas Aquinas, the author of *Theologica, Indian Summa.* According to Henry Adams, Aquinas may have been the architect of the Cathedral of Beauvais, which collapsed. Aquinas was consequently banished to St. Heloise, where he wrote entertaining letters under the name of Abelard. Adams, who was also an architect (Mont St. Michel and Chartres), was thus the original Doubting Thomist.

The Medieval period was followed in quick succession by the Renaissance, the Reformation, the counter-Renaissance, and the counter-Reformation. The Renaissance was started by Erasmus of Rotterdam, author of *Moriae Encomium,* a rather poor biography of his friend Sir Thomas More. Erasmus is the subject of an eggtempera portrait by Holstein ("that Jersey cow," as he was called by Henry the Eighth). He also started the Oxford Reform Movement, which supported the teaching of Greek and other reforms. But the Reformation was started by Martin Luther, composer of the oratorio *Erwache durch Freud* ("Awake and Read Joyce"). Luther officiated at Finnegan's Wake. Wanting to get if not a *summa* at least a *magna,* he wrote a thesis which he then had to pin on the door of the church; as he explained later, *"Ich kann nicht anders"* ("I couldn't get it under"). This thesis would have been banned from the mails but for a memorable legal decision by Cardinal Wolsey.

The Seventeenth Century stands halfway between the Medieval period and the Modern period, and is thus exceedingly transitional. It was memorable for the Rise of Science and for John Donne, a kind of seventeenth-century T. S. Eliot. Though he was not interested in Science and spelled badly ("Noe Manne is an Iland"), Donne was made vector of St. Paul's and became a kind of seventeenth-century Norman Vincent Peale. The Seventeenth Century is thus exactly like the Twentieth Century and all centuries in between may be skipped. During the Twentieth Century, Western Thought became confused with Eastern Thought, as a result of *The Meeting of Northrop and Southrop*, and has thus come to an End. It is also memorable for neo-Protestantism ("Love thy Niebuhr"), or Rockefeller Plaza Orthodoxy (*Luce et Vanitas*).

Second Semester: Science

Science was invented by the Greeks, who were the first people to realize that it was a Good Thing. It was also invented by Galileo, who leaned against the Tower of Pisa to see if it would move (*eppur si muove*). Later on, science was re-invented by Descartes. After losing a bet with Pascal, he was forced to live in a stove ("*j'ai faim, donc je cuis*"). The bet resulted from a balloon ascension by Robert Montgomery, which in turn gave rise to the cinematic theory of gases, or Gauss (plural: *gassendi*).

The most memorable branch of science is physics. Some people think that physics was invented by Sir Francis Bacon, who was hit by an apple when he was sitting under a tree one day writing Shakespeare. This is not true. It was *Roger* Bacon, and it wasn't Shakespeare; it was Christopher Marlowe. Later physics was taken up by Isaac Newton, who invented the Second Law of Thermodynamics (there is no *First* Law of Thermodynamics). Newton also discovered that the straightest distance between two points is inversely proportional, though he did not say to what. This was left to Einstein. Einstein is chiefly memorable for being smarter than Newton.

Astronomy was independently discovered by Copernicus and Kepler, who sent the news to each other (*de nova stella*) by sidereal messenger. This was very slow, since astronomers measure time in light-years, or the amount of light in a year. Some astronomers like to find stars by themselves, like Hershey, the famous discoverer of the Milky Way and the Mars Bar; others prefer to go around in a Cepheid cluster, or

Magellanic cloud. A memorable contest once took place in astronomy between the Red Giants and the White Dwarfs, refereed by Hubble, the inventor of the Red Shift. Ever since, all games in astronomy have been played according to Hoyle.

Another memorable branch of science is electronics, which is the science of amplifying messages by putting them through a degenerative circuit. Electronics can handily be demonstrated in the home by filling a Leyden Jar full of formaldehyde and turning on the radio. Through the magic of modern communications, electronics reminds us of such famous communicators as Wiener, Weaver, Faraday, and Ohm ("Be it ever so faraday, there's no place like ohm"). Originally electronics inventions were named after people (Lee the Forest, Jennie the Transformer, etc.) but they are now named after Polish patriots—Edvac, Eniac, Cosmotron, and Radar. The reason for this is to embarrass the Russians, in the hope that they will turn a non-compatible color.

We come now to the social sciences, which are divided into sociology, anthropology, cultural anthropology, anthropological sociology, sociological anthropology, psychology, dynamic psychology, group dynamics, palmistry, and statistics (optional). The most memorable thing about the social sciences is the principle of *anomie*, or autonomy, which holds that people tend to behave like each other. This helps to explain such phenomena as the in-group, the out-group, the peer-group, and Margaret Mead. For best results, advanced field work in the social sciences should be conducted among the Mountain Arapesh, who are a pretty lonely crowd.

Biology is especially memorable because of evolution. This was the subject of a maternity suit (the Stopes trial) between William Lane Bryant and the famous lawyer, Clarence Darwin. Darwin believed in the survival of the best fit, but Bryant won, which was the origin of demography, or populism. In disgust, Darwin joined the navy as an enzyme and was sent around the world on a beagle. Evolution might have been forgotten, had it not been for Julian Huxley, who attended the trial and wrote a famous book about it, called *Natural Selection without Glasses, or Eyeless in Gaza.*

Included under biology should also be the history of medicine, which is most memorable when it is psychosomatic. This branch of medicine was invented by the famous physician, Peristalsis, who also invented nutrition (*"Mann ist was Mann isst"*). Nutrition teaches the importance of getting plenty of protein and chlorophyll, both of which are contained in black-strap molasses (G. Hauser Wienerschnitzel, Yogurt, and Strap Iron Co., Mfgrs., *Advt.*). Psychosomatic medicine is difficult to practice without an Orgone Box, which is guaranteed to make you feel Jung and to last for 1,000 years (*tausend-jahrende Reich*). Psychosomatic medicine is not to be confused with extra-sensory perception, which most doctors reject and keep a sharp watch on (*die Wacht am Rhine*), nor with psychiatry, which is concerned with the psyche (soma). Since psychiatry was originally invented by the Greeks ("Oedipus, schmedipus, so long he loves his mother"), it is the end of the course.

Final Examination

(1) Name a great idea.

RALPH McGILL

The Merciful Tenderizer

On a recent visit to Colombia, South America, a charming lady gave me a cooking secret which I would like to pass on. We were consuming an especially tender piece of roast chicken which had arrived at our table in an earthen dish succulently bedded in yellow rice. I remarked that the chicken was very good indeed, and my hostess said that without doubt it had been killed in a fashion which made the meat more tender.

"You mean there is such a method?" I asked.

"To be sure," she said. "When a chicken is seized to be killed, it becomes hysterical with fear and tenses its muscles. The blood is diffused into the muscles, and the glands become active just as they do in human beings and other animals when danger is at hand. A chicken killed in that condition is not good to eat."

This sounded logical.

"So," she said, "when we plan to kill a fowl, we give it two teaspoons of rum. Some housewives hold that one spoonful of rum and one of vinegar are better, but the majority stick to two of rum. For turkeys we use three or four, depending on size."

"Then what happens?" I asked.

"Then," she said, "we let the chicken go. Soon it is flopping and careening about, entirely unconcerned with its impending doom.

When picked up, it squawks happily, relaxes, and hangs limp. It is, in fact, anesthetized and may be dispatched without difficulty. There is no flexing of muscles, no pumping of the adrenal glands. And the meat is much more tender to eat."

While considering this, I had a second helping of chicken. It was very tender.

The next day, while driving from Cartegena to Barranquilla, I asked the driver if all chickens in Colombia were killed in this fashion.

"No, *señor*," he said sadly, "not by all, though it is the recommended manner."

"Why not all?"

"Many cannot afford both rum and chickens, *señor*," he said. "And even for some who can, they are likely to look at the rum and at the chicken, and to decide that if they drink the rum themselves, they will not notice if the chicken is a bit tough."

"Does your wife employ the rum?"

"*Señor*," he said, "she will tonight if the gratuity for this ride is sufficient."

It cheered me, later in the evening, to know that the family of Raphael Rodrigues were eating tender, relaxed drumsticks. Yet I had a slight doubt. Raphael Rodrigues' wistful look suggested thirst rather than hunger, and I wondered if his chicken had got its tot.

STEPHEN LEACOCK

My Discovery
of
England

For some years past a rising tide of lecturers and literary men from England has washed upon the shores of this continent. They come over to us traveling in great simplicity, and they return in the ducal suite of the *Aquitania*. They carry away with them their impressions of America, and when they reach England they sell them. This irregular and one-sided traffic has now assumed such great proportions that we are compelled to ask whether it is right to allow these people to carry away from us impressions of the very highest commercial value without giving us any pecuniary compensation whatever. English lecturers have been known to land in New York, pass the customs, drive uptown in a closed taxi, and then forward to England *from the closed taxi itself* ten dollars' worth of impressions of American national character. I have myself seen an English literary man sitting in the corridor of a fashionable New York hotel and looking gloomily into his hat, and then *from his very hat* produce an estimate of the genius of America at twenty cents a word. The nice question as to whose twenty cents that was never seems to have occurred to him.

I am not writing in the faintest spirit of jealousy. I quite admit the extraordinary ability that is involved in this peculiar susceptibility to impressions. But I do feel that somehow these impressions are inadequate and fail to depict us as we really are.

Let me illustrate what I mean. Here are some of the impressions of New York, gathered from various visitors' discoveries of America, and reproduced, not, perhaps, word for word, but as closely as I can remember them. "New York," writes one, "nestling at the foot of the Hudson, gave me an impression of coziness, of tiny graciousness; in short, of weeness." But compare this: "New York," according to another discoverer of America, "gave me an impression of size, of vastness; there seemed to me a bigness about it not found in smaller places." A third visitor writes, "New York struck me as hard, cruel, almost inhuman." This, I think, was because his taxi driver had charged him three dollars.

Nor is it only the impressions of the metropolis that seem to fall short of reality. Let me quote a few others taken at random here and there over the continent.

"I took from Pittsburgh," says an English visitor, "an impression of something that I could hardly define—an atmosphere rather than an idea."

All very well. But, after all, had he the right to take it? Granted that Pittsburgh has an atmosphere rather than an idea, the attempt to carry away this atmosphere surely borders on rapacity. . . .

"Chicago," according to another book of discovery, "struck me as a large city. Situated as it is and where it is, it seems destined to be a place of great importance."

Or here, again, is a form of "impression" that recurs again and again, "At Cleveland I felt a distinct note of optimism in the air."

This same note of optimism is found also at Toledo, at Toronto— in short, I believe it indicates nothing more than that somebody gave the visitor a cigar. . . .

In the course of time a considerable public feeling was aroused in the United States and Canada over this state of affairs. The lack of reciprocity in it seemed unfair. It was felt (or at least I felt) that the time had come when some one ought to go over and take some impressions off England. The choice of such a person (my choice) fell upon myself. By an arrangement with the Geographical Society of America, acting in conjunction with the Royal Geographic Society of England (to both of which I communicated my project), I went at my own expense. . . .

I pass over the details of my pleasant voyage from New York to Liverpool. During the last fifty years so many travelers have made the voyage across the Atlantic that it is now impossible to obtain from the ocean any impressions of the slightest commercial

value. . . . I will content myself with chronicling the fact that during
the voyage we passed two dolphins, one whale, and one iceberg
(none of them moving very fast at the time). . . .

I pass over also the incidents of my landing at Liverpool, except,
perhaps, to comment upon the extraordinary behavior of the English
customs officials. Without wishing in any way to disturb international
relations, one cannot help commenting on the brutal and inquisitorial
methods of the English customs men as compared with the gentle
and affectionate ways of the American officials at New York. The
two trunks which I brought with me were dragged brutally into an
open shed; the strap of one of them was rudely unbuckled, while
the lid of the other was actually lifted at least four inches. The trunks
were then roughly scrawled with chalk, the lids slammed to, and
that was all. Not one of the officials seemed to care to look at my
things or to have the politeness to pretend to want to. I had arranged
my dress suit and my pajamas so as to make as effective a display as
possible; a New York customs officer would have been delighted with
it. Here they simply passed it over.

"Do open this trunk," I asked one of the officials, "and see my
pajamas."

"I don't think it is necessary, sir," the man answered.

There was a coldness about it that cut me to the quick.

But bad as is the conduct of the English customs men, the immigration officials are even worse. I could not help also being struck
by the dreadful carelessness with which people are admitted into
England. There is, it is true, a group of officials said to be in charge of
immigration, but they know nothing of the discriminating care exer-
cised on the other side of the Atlantic.

"Do you want to know," I asked of one of them, "whether I am
a polygamist?"

"No, sir," he said, very quietly.

"Would you like me to tell you whether I am fundamentally opposed to any and every system of government?"

The man seemed mystified. "No, sir," he said, "I don't know that
I would."

"Don't you care?" I asked.

"Well, not particularly, sir," he answered.

I was determined to arouse him from his lethargy.

"Let me tell you, then," I said, "that I am an anarchistic polygamist, that I am opposed to all forms of government, that I object to
any kind of revealed religion, that I regard the state and property and

marriage as the mere tyranny of the bourgeoisie, and that I want to see class hatred carried to the point where it forces everyone into brotherly love. Now do I get in?"

The official looked puzzled for a minute. "You are not Irish, are you, sir?" he said.

"No."

"Then I think you can come in all right," he answered.

The journey from Liverpool to London is like all other English journeys, in short. This is due to the fact that England is a small country; it contains only 50,000 square miles, whereas the United States, as everyone knows, contains three and a half billion. I mentioned this fact to an English fellow passenger on the train, together with a provisional estimate of the American corn crop for 1922; but he only drew his rug about his knees, took a sip of brandy from his traveling flask, and sank into a state resembling death. I contented myself with jotting down an impression of incivility and lack of generosity as two phases of English character, and paid no further attention to my fellow traveler other than to read the labels on his luggage and to peruse the headings of his newspaper by peeping over his shoulder.

It was my first experience of traveling with a fellow passenger in a compartment of an English train, and I admit now that I was as yet ignorant of the proper method of conduct. Later on I became fully conversant with the rules of travel as understood in England. I should have known, of course, that I must on no account speak to the man. But I should have let down the window a little bit and in such a way as to make a strong draught on his ear. Had this failed to break down his reserve, I should have placed a heavy valise in the rack over his head, so balanced that it might fall on him at any moment. Failing this again, I could have blown rings of smoke at him or stepped on his feet under a pretense of looking out of the window. Under the English rule, as long as he bears this in silence you are not supposed to know him. In fact, he is not supposed to be there. You and he each presume the other to be a mere piece of empty space. But let him once be driven to say: "Oh, I beg your pardon! I wonder if you would mind my closing the window," and he is lost. After that you are entitled to tell him anything about the corn crop that you care to.

But in the present case I knew nothing of this, and after three hours of charming silence I found myself in London.

London, the name of which is already known to millions of readers of this magazine, is beautifully situated on the river Thames, which here sweeps in a wide curve and has much the same breadth and majesty as the St. Jo River at South Bend, Indiana. London, like South Bend itself, is a city of clean streets and admirable sidewalks, and has an excellent water supply. One is at once struck by the number of excellent and well-appointed motor cars that one sees on every hand, the neatness of the shops, and the cleanliness and cheerfulness of the faces of the people. In short, as an English visitor said of Peterborough, Ontario, there is a distinct note of optimism in the air. . . .

These, however, are but superficial pictures of London, gathered by the eye of the tourist. A far deeper meaning is found in the examination of the great historic monuments of the city. The principal ones of these are the Tower of London (just mentioned), the British Museum, and Westminster Abbey. No visitor to London should fail to see these. Indeed, he ought to feel that his visit to England is wasted unless he has seen them. I speak strongly on the point because I feel strongly on it. To my mind there is something about the grim fascination of the historic Tower, the cloistered quiet of the Museum, and the majesty of the ancient Abbey, which will make it the regret of my life that I didn't see any one of the three. I fully meant to, but I failed; and I can only hope that the circumstances of my failure may be helpful to other visitors.

The Tower of London I most certainly intended to inspect. Each day, after the fashion of every tourist, I wrote for myself a little list of things to do, and I always put the Tower of London on it. No doubt the reader knows the kind of little list that I mean. It runs:

1. Go to bank.
2. Buy a shirt.
3. National Picture Gallery.
4. Razor blades.
5. Tower of London.
6. Soap.

The itinerary, I regret to say, was never carried out in full. I was able at times both to go to the bank and to buy a shirt in a single morning; at other times I was able to buy razor blades and almost to find the National Picture Gallery. Meantime I was urged on all sides by my London acquaintances not to fail to see the Tower. "There's a grim fascination about the place," they said; "you mustn't miss it." I am quite certain that in due course of time I should have made my way to the Tower but for the fact that I made a fatal discovery. I found out that the London people who urged me to go and see the Tower had never seen it themselves. It appears they never go near it. One night at a dinner a man next to me said:

"Have you seen the Tower? You really ought to. There's a grim fascination about it."

I looked him in the face. "Have you seen it yourself?" I asked.

"Oh, yes," he answered, "I've seen it."

"When?" I asked.

The man hesitated. "When I was just a boy," he said. "My father took me there."

"How long ago is that?" I inquired.

"About forty years ago," he answered. "I always mean to go again, but I don't somehow seem to get the time."

After this I got to understand that when a Londoner says, "Have you seen the Tower of London?" the answer is, "No, and neither have you."

Take the parallel case of the British Museum. Here is a place that is a veritable treasure house, a repository of some of the most priceless historical relics to be found upon the earth. It contains, for instance, the famous Papyrus Manuscript of Thotmes II of the first Egyptian dynasty—a thing known to scholars all over the world as the oldest extant specimen of what can be called writing. . . . The first time I went by it in a taxi I felt quite a thrill. "Inside those walls," I thought to myself, "is the Manuscript of Thotmes II." The next time I actually stopped the taxi.

"Is that the British Museum?" I asked the driver.

"I think it is something of the sort, sir," he said.

I hesitated. "Drive me," I said, "to where I can buy safety-razor blades."

After that I was able to drive past the Museum with the quiet assurance of a Londoner, and to take part in dinner-table discussions as to whether the British Museum or the Louvre contains the greater treasures. . . .

The Abbey, I admit, is indeed majestic. I did not intend to miss going into it. But I felt, as so many tourists have, that I wanted to enter it in the proper frame of mind. I never got into the frame of mind; at least not when near the Abbey itself. I have been in exactly that frame of mind when on State Street, Chicago, or on King Street, Toronto, or anywhere three thousand miles away from the Abbey. But by bad luck I never struck both the frame of mind and the Abbey at the same time. . . .

But for the ordinary visitor to London the greatest interest of all attaches to the spacious and magnificent Parliament Buildings. The House of Commons is commodiously situated beside the river Thames. The principal features of the House are the large lunch room on the western side and the tea room on the terrace on the eastern. A series of smaller luncheon rooms extends (apparently) all round about the premises, while a commodious bar offers a ready access to the members at all hours of the day. While any members are in the bar a light is kept burning in the tall Clock Tower at one corner of the building, but when the bar is closed the light is turned off by whichever of the Scotch members leaves last. There is a handsome legislative chamber attached to the premises from which—so the antiquarians tell us—the House of Commons took its name. But it is not usual now for the members to sit in the legislative chamber, as the legislation is now all done outside. . . . The House, however, is called together at very frequent intervals to give it an opportunity of hearing the latest legislation and allowing the members to indulge in cheers, groans, sighs, votes, and other expressions of vitality. After having cheered as much as is good for them they go back again to the lunch rooms and go on eating till they are needed again.

The Parliament Buildings are so vast that it is not possible to state with certainty what they do, or do not, contain. But it is generally said that somewhere in the building is the House of Lords. When they meet they are said to come together very quietly shortly before the dinner hour, take a glass of dry sherry and a biscuit (they are all abstemious men), reject whatever bills may be before them at the moment, take another dry sherry, and then adjourn for two years. . . .

No description of London would be complete without a reference, however brief, to the singular salubrity and charm of the London climate. This is seen at its best during the autumn and winter months. The climate of London, and indeed of England generally, is due to the influence of the Gulf Stream. The way it works is this: The Gulf Stream, as it nears the shores of the British Isles and feels the propinquity of Ireland, rises into the air, turns into soup, and comes down on London. At times this soup is thin and is in fact little more than a mist; at other times it has the consistency of a thick *potage St.-Germain*. London people flatter their atmosphere by calling it a fog; but it is not; it is soup.

But the notion that no sunlight ever gets through and that in the London winter people never see the sun, is a ridiculous error, circulated, no doubt, by the jealousy of foreign nations. I have myself seen the sun plainly visible in London, without the aid of glasses, on a

November day in broad daylight; and again one night about four o'clock in the afternoon, I saw the sun distinctly appear through the clouds. The whole subject of daylight in the London winter is, however, one which belongs rather to the technic of astronomy than to a paper of description. In practice daylight is but little used. Electric lights are burned all the time in all private houses, buildings, railway stations, and clubs. This practice, which is now universally observed, is called daylight saving.

But the distinction between day and night during the London winter is still quite obvious to anyone of an observant mind. It is indicated by various signs such as the striking of clocks, the tolling of bells, the closing of the saloons, and the raising of the taxi rates. Expert Londoners are able to tell the difference between day and night almost as easily as we do, and speak of "this evening" and "to-morrow morning" with the greatest accuracy.

It is, however, much less easy to distinguish the technical approach of night in the other cities of England that lie outside the confines, physical and intellectual, of London and live in a continuous gloom. In such places as the great manufacturing cities of Bugginham-under-Smoke or Gloomsburg-on-Ooze night may be said to be perpetual. But of these places I propose to speak in a later paper.

Mr. K*A*P*L*A*N and the Glorious Pest

"Then, amidst a breathless hush," read Mr. Parkhill, amidst a breathless hush, "Patrick Henry took the floor. All eyes turned to the fiery young lawyer, who thereupon delivered the most scathing attack on monarchy yet heard in the Virginia House of Burgesses: 'Caesar had his Brutus, Charles the First his Cromwell, and George the Third'—cries of 'Treason! Treason!' interrupted him—'and George the Third may profit from their example! If this be treason, make the most of it!' "

"Hooray!"

"Vunderful!"

"Dat's da way to talk!"

Mr. Parkhill lowered the text. He felt pleased, not only because the historic words always stirred his senses, but because the beginners' grade, having listened with such intensity of interest, had responded with such amplitude of feeling. "That, class," he sighed, "was one of the most dramatic moments in the history of the thirteen colonies. Ten years later, Patrick Henry delivered another speech, which is even more memorable. It has, indeed, become one of the truly—er—immortal orations in history!" He closed the book. He needed no lifeless text to prompt him in that glorious peroration: " 'Is life so dear, or peace so sweet, as to be purchased at the price of chains and

102

slavery? Forbid it, Almighty God!' " He paused. " 'I know not what course others may take, but as for me—give me liberty or give me death!' "

If his disciples had applauded Patrick Henry on Monarchy, they brought the rafters down for him on Liberty.

"Hoorah!"

"T'ree chiss for Petrick Hanry!"

"Bravo! Bravo!" Miss Caravello was practically on her feet, leading a parade. "Justa like Mazzini!"

"Ha!" The scorn of Hyman Kaplan cracked out like lightning. "How you ken compare a Petrick Hanry to a—vat vass dat name?"

"Mazzini! Greata man. Botha patriot!"

"If in Italy dey had Petrick Hanry bifore, dey vouldn't have Mussolini later!" Mr. Kaplan gazed into space, transported, then flung his hand up in imperial command. " 'Give me liberty—or give me dat!' "

"Good fa you!" cried loyal Gidwitz.

"Hoo ha!" called star-struck Pinsky.

"Keplen, you should absolutel go in politics!"

"Class . . . order, please." Mr. Parkhill had to tap his pointer quite loudly on his desk before he could still his students' ardor. But when the tribute due Patrick Henry was being accorded Hyman Kaplan, who had managed to utter the deathless words as if he were making them up on the spot, it was clearly time to intervene. "I shall now assign your homework."

A happy murmur moved across the ranks. Out came pencils to record, and notebooks to receive, Mr. Parkhill's instructions. As the Spartans before Leonidas at Thermopylae, or the proud French legions before their Corporal at Marengo, so the thirty-odd stalwarts of the beginners' grade of the American Night Preparatory School for Adults hearkened to Mr. Parkhill.

"During this semester," he began, "we have had occasion to discuss many different incidents in American history. We have not done this in—er—chronological order, because I have tried to answer your questions as they arose. Besides, as you all know, American History is taught in Mr. Krout's grade." He did not stress the fact that Mr. Krout lay beyond the forbidding stretches of Miss Higby. "So it is that we discussed Woodrow Wilson, say, before we even mentioned the Monroe Doctrine; or Thomas Paine before some of you even knew about Pocahontas." He smiled; it did sound amusing put that way. "In any event, we have covered quite a bit of ground. And so your assignment, for our next session, is—a composition on any famous figure, or any famous incident, associated with the American Revolution."

"Pssh!" cried Mr. Pinsky, slapping his cheek in a burst of admiration.

"Too hard," said Mr. Scymzak.

"I *lohve* American ravolutions!" announced Olga Tarnova, who hated the Bolsheviki.

Mr. Parkhill's most casual remarks sometimes had this electrifying effect—changing his students into Senators and the classroom into a forum. "A famous figure or incident associated with the American Revolution" elicited such a concatenation of approval and doubt, such cries of courage and premonitions of despair, that Mr. Parkhill felt as if he had not so much assigned an exercise as called a plebiscite.

"Foist-class assignment!" beamed Mr. Kaplan.

"Too hard," Mr. Scymzak repeated.

"Hod but good!" rejoined Mr. Kaplan sternly. "Who vants izzy lassons. Izzy is for slowboats!"

" 'Slow*pokes*,' Mr. Kaplan."

A heartrending wail escaped from Mrs. Moskowitz. "Which figures American Revolution? Which accidents?"

" '*Incidents*,' Mrs. Moskowitz, not '*accidents*,' " said Mr. Parkhill quickly. With Mrs. Moskowitz pedagogy was best practiced as if it were surgery: delay could be fatal.

"My mind is blenk about *in*cidents also," mourned Mrs. Moskowitz. "Please—give alraddy exemples."

A band of gallant friends rushed to give her succor.

"Try crossing the Delaware!"

"Take maybe Benjamin Frenklin?"

"Liberty Bells!"

Mrs. Moskowitz shook her many jowls and groaned, wandering in Cimmerian darkness.

"Maybe John Hencock?" called Reuben Plonsky.

"Spilling tea in Boston Hobber?"

"Don't shoot till their eyes toin white!"

Neither heroes nor events nor historic sayings could lift Mrs. Moskowitz out of the boundless mire.

"Mrs. Moskowitz," Mr. Parkhill began, "perhaps you—"

"Moskovitz, you not tryink!" cried Mr. Kaplan.

"Vat *am* I doing—svimming?"

"You holdink beck de cless!"

"So go on witout me," howled Mrs. Moskowitz.

"You sebotagink our morals."

" 'Mor*ale*,' Mr. Kaplan, not 'morals,' " said Mr. Parkhill anxiously. "Mrs. Moskowitz, I'm sure the assignment is not quite as difficult as you think." He gave her a smile intended to infuse confidence. "I'm sure that after you get home, when you have time to think about it, or review your notes, you will get *many*—er—ideas." He was not at all sure that Mrs. Moskowitz would get any, much less "many," ideas; if any idea was to become part of Mrs. Moskowitz' universe it would be because it found a way of taking possession of her, and not the other way around.

The hand of Barney Kesselman waggled in the air. "How long should be this composition?"

Mr. Parkhill weighed his next words carefully. "I do *not* want a long or—er—elaborate effort, class. Let's say, oh, not more than a page in length."

He glanced at the clock on the wall, that third face between Washington's, from which he often drew resolution, and Lincoln's, to which he often repaired for condolence. It was two minutes to ten. "That is all for tonight."

Now, two nights later, in the welcome solitude of his apartment, red marking pencil in hand, Mr. Parkhill was correcting their offerings. He did not know whether to feel pleased or disappointed. The prose of his novitiates was always full of surprises—some good, some bad; but this batch of papers contained so many surprises that it was difficult to think of them as either good *or* bad; they were just surprising. American history seemed to have plunged his fledglings into the most extraordinary *personal* involvements.

Take Sam Pinsky, for example. Mr. Pinsky, a devoted but run-of-the-mill student, ordinarily did not let his reach exceed his grasp. This time, either inspired or intoxicated, Mr. Pinsky had thrown discretion to the winds. He had undertaken nothing less than a critique of the entire colonial policy of eighteenth-century England, and had become so incensed by what he called British "cold-heartiness" that he had soared into most untypical rhetoric:

> Colonists were starving, frizzing from cold, suffering like flys. But did British care??? No! What they did? They made taxis.
>
> Taxis, taxis, taxis. On food. On tea. On sending even a postal card to a dying mother.
>
> Oh, how foolish was Georgie III.

That was not at all the way Mr. Pinsky usually wrote.

Or take Mrs. Rodriguez. For some reason Mrs. Rodriguez had taken personal offense at General Cornwallis; for apart from making him the blackest villain of the War for Independence, she blamed him for not surrendering to Washington *soon* enough. Her composition was not so much an essay as an ultimatum, and Mr. Parkhill could not tell whether it had been designed to be descriptive of, or delivered to, the unfortunate Cornwallis.

Or take Reuben Plonsky. Mr. Plonsky had penned a vitriolic essay on the Tories, whom he accused of crimes too heinous to be described, or, if described, to be spelled correctly. (It was hardly fair, for instance, to blame the Tories for "encouraging violins" when the worst that could be said about them was that they sometimes met persecution with vio*lence*.)

Or take Mrs. Tomasic, whose Balkan forebears had survived oppressions beside which the Stamp Acts seem philanthropic. Tiny Mrs. Tomasic had paid moving respect to that peerless seaman, "Admirable Grandpa Jones." Mr. Parkhill could see how a neophyte might confuse Admiral with "admirable," but how Mrs. Tomasic had alchemized "John Paul" into "Grandpa" he simply could not fathom.

After these erratic excursions into history, Rose Mitnick's measured words came as both a pleasure and a relief. Her composition was entitled "A Hero: Nathan Hale" and contained this moving passage:

> They tied his hands behind to hang Nathan. But brave,
> with his bare head he made that wonderful speech, simple
> and also poetical. "I regret I have only one life to give for the
> country." He was not maybe so important as Washington,
> but he is my hero. I admire.

Why, save for the occasional omission of a pronoun, that paragraph might have done credit to a veteran of Miss Higby's grade.

Mr. Matsoukas' paper, which he next assayed, had puzzled Mr. Parkhill. It had sung the praise of John Hancock, whose aid to the cause of freedom, wrote Gus Matsoukas, no red-blooded American would ever "forge." It took quite a while for Mr. Parkhill to realize that Mr. Matsoukas had simply been careless; only a "t" separated "forge" from "forget."

Miss Ziev, from whom Mr. Parkhill had not expected to get any homework at all, had come through with this perplexing paean:

TO MINUTE MEN

Farm men with long rifles. Always ready to fight. Did.

Famous battel, with 1 shot whole world heard, was Battel of Grand Concourse.

Good work, Minute Men!

The only way Mr. Parkhill could explain how Concord had become "Grand Concourse" was that some friend of Miss Ziev who resided on that broad thoroughfare had helped her with her homework.

Mr. Studniczka—Mr. Parkhill sighed. Peter Studniczka had submitted yet another of his cryptic substitutions for prose:

1776

Best man — G. Washington
Bad man — King and reps.
Trators — Ben & Dick Arnold
Patroit — PULASKI FROM POLAND!

Mr. Parkhill was not happy about that paper. Something in Mr. Studniczka's mental processes seemed to make him approach English vertically. Whether it was because he actually *thought* in columns (which Mr. Parkhill might understand were Mr. Studniczka, say, Chinese), or whether he suffered from some sort of phobia about whole, horizontal sentences, with a subject, verb, and predicate, Mr. Parkhill did not know. He sighed again. Mr. Studniczka had a long way to go—a long, *long* way to go. He corrected "trators" and "patroit," and in the margin of Mr. Studniczka's inventory wrote: "This is not a *composition*, Mr. S. Please try whole sentences next time." He started to put the paper aside, remembered something, and added: "Ben*edict* Arnold. One man, not two." Then he picked up the next composition.

Pellets of color popped before his eyes. They came not from a pang of migraine, nor from retinal hallucinations; they came off the paper itself, from the title, which glittered with phosphorescent pride:

HAMILTON VERSES JEFFERSON
A play!
By

H*Y*M*A*N   K*A*P*L*A*N

The irrepressible author had, of course, sought to immortalize his name by printing the letters in red, outlining them in blue, and distributing gay green stars between. Mr. Parkhill put the paper down and took a drink of water. He sharpened his marking pencil thoughtfully before picking up Mr. Kaplan's "A play!" again. This is what his startled eyes beheld:

Hamilton: "The government should be strong!"
Jefferson: "No! Be ware strong government. *People* must decide."
Hamilton: "*People?* Ha, ha, ha, ha. Don't trust people."
Jefferson: "I TRUST! Also, U. S. mottol, saying 'God trusts.' O.K. *How's about you?*"
Hamilton: "You are a dreamy. Don't be so nave."
Jefferson: "Better to be dreamy. You are against MAN!"

At this point Mr. Kaplan, tiring under the weight of Anglo-Saxon nomenclature, had dropped into abbreviations which may have lessened the strain on his fingers but assigned disastrous connotations to his protagonists:

Ham: "Every business needs a boss!"
Jeff: "From bosses come Kings! Don't forget!"
Ham: "That's my last offer, Tom S. Jefferson!"
Jeff: "Same to you, L. X. Hamilton."

Mr. Parkhill felt a sharp pain in his head. He removed his spectacles and rubbed his eyes. Something would *have* to be done about Mr. Kaplan—about his spelling, at least; a student simply could not be permitted to wander around replacing hallowed names with outlandish phonetic approximations. "Tom S. Jefferson" indeed! "L. X. Hamilton . . ." The colored flashes now were not occasioned by Mr. Kaplan's crayons.

"Good evening, class," said Mr. Parkhill pleasantly. "I shall return your homework, first. Each paper has been corrected and—er—evaluated. Please study the red pencilings carefully. You can probably learn more from your own mistakes than from almost any other exercise."

Mr. Kaplan raised his hand; Mr. Parkhill braced himself. "Y-yes?"

"You *liked* de homevoik, Mr. Pockheel?"

"Well," said Mr. Parkhill cautiously, "I think all of you *tried* very hard. There were, of course, many errors—too many, I fear. I shall now distribute—"

"Still, *som* homevoik maybe gave you a big soprise," suggested Mr. Kaplan confidentially.

Mr. Parkhill averted his gaze. He knew perfectly well what Mr. Kaplan was driving at. Mr. Kaplan was trying to lure Mr. Parkhill into some compliment to the effect that imagination was more important than error, that one student had risen above his pedestrian fellows by soaring into the empyrean of drama. Mr. Kaplan's pious expression even hinted that he would understand it if the public praises due such a genius omitted his actual name, which might incur the ire of the envious.

"Mr. Kaplan," said Mr. Parkhill firmly, looking his most faithful and difficult apostle straight in the eye, "the purpose of homework is not to 'surprise.' In fact, the best homework is the kind that, containing no errors, causes me no surprises whatsoever!" And with that *tu quoque*, Mr. Parkhill briskly proceeded to distribute the homework. "Miss Pomeranz . . . Mr. Trabish . . ."

Mr. Kaplan looked crushed. How, looking crushed, he also managed to convey the untarnished pride of one who has scaled Parnassus, albeit in vain, was something Mr. Parkhill would never understand.

"Miss Kipnis . . . Mr. Wilkomirski."

As the compositions streamed back to their creators, the sounds of illumination rewarded Mr. Parkhill for his labors.

"I spalled wrong 'Philadelphia'?"

"George is not Georgie . . ."

"Psssh! Was I wrong!" The resonance of a self-administered slap on the cheek told Mr. Parkhill that a dazzling light had dawned on Sam Pinsky.

"Examine the corrections carefully, class. If you have a question, just raise your hand." Mr. Parkhill strolled down the aisle. There was a world of difference, pedagogically, between sitting at the desk and strolling down the aisle: The one was judiciary, the other egalitarian; the one enforced decorum, the other encouraged relaxation.

The next hour went so swiftly that the bell rang before anyone suspected it was time for recess.

And then, during the very closing minutes of the night, that crafty demon who confounds the plans of teachers no less than those of mice and men sent his seneschals among the innocent. Mr. Parkhill was conducting a spelling drill which he had himself devised, and of which he felt rather proud: twenty words containing "e-i-g-h-t" (from "freight" to "weight" *via* "height"), and twenty containing "o-u-g-h" (from "cough" through "rough" to "through").

He had just announced "Bought . . . thought . . . enough" when Mrs. Moskowitz gave a cry of defeat, flung down her pen, and piteously appealed to Miss Kipnis beside her: " 'Enough'? Enough! Why dey dun't put in 'f' when is pronounced ffff? A mind *crecks* from soch torture, Cookie!"

"You got to be *patient*," sighed Cookie Kipnis.

"Learning takes *time*," pleaded Miss Mitnick.

They had reckoned without the defender of the faith.

"Ha!" scoffed Hyman Kaplan. "U. S. vasn't fonded by sissies!"

"I dun't want to fond; I want to spall!" protested Sadie Moskowitz.

"Class—"

"Nottink good is izzy!" declaimed Hyman Kaplan.

"Eating is planty good, and planty easy!"

"You compare spallink to ittink?" Mr. Kaplan's expression set a new high for amazement. "You tritt English like lemb chops?"

"The way *you* talk, it's chop suey!" snapped Mr. Plonsky, and his cohorts burst into laughter.

"Class, *class*," said Mr. Parkhill. "We are engaged in a spelling drill, not a debate!" He waited for the echoes of combat to die away, then addressed Mrs. Moskowitz sympathetically. "I can well understand how someone from another land must feel when confronted by some of the—er—peculiar ways in which our English words are spelled."

"I am fromm anodder lend," said Mr. Kaplan promptly, "an' still don't holler 'Halp!'"

"Mr. Kaplan," said Mr. Parkhill testily, "English *is* a difficult language. And many of our words *are* spelled in most unreasonable—"

"Moskowitz can still make a good profit fromm odder pipple's semples," exclaimed Hyman Kaplan.

Mr. Parkhill looked up. What on earth was that? He frowned. "I beg your pardon."

Mr. Kaplan looked as blank as an oyster.

"I thought," said Mr. Parkhill, "I heard you say that Mrs. Moskowitz could—er—'make a good profit—'"

Mr. Kaplan nodded. "I mant like de Fonding Fodders."

This was too much for Miss Mitnick, who twisted her handkerchief and beseeched him, "What have Fonding Fathers to do with Mrs. Moskowitz?"

"It's obvious," said Mr. Kaplan carelessly.

"Ob—"

"*Mr.* Kaplan," Mr. Parkhill cut in drily, "your comment is as unclear to me as it is to Miss Mitnick! I suggest you explain—no, no, you need *not* go to the front of—"

The admonition came too late. (Where Mr. Kaplan was concerned any admonition seemed to come too late.) The bard of the beginners' grade was midway between his seat and his goal, that frontal zone to which some homing instinct irresistibly propelled him. He stopped, turned, and fixed Mrs. Moskowitz with narrowed eyes. "De

Pilgrim Fodders didn't go beck to England becawss dey had to spall 'enough'!" he cried, then transferred his scorn to Miss Mitnick. "Dey had beeger trobbles. Indians, messecres—"

"Mr. Kap—"

"—spyink fromm de Franch, poisicutions fromm de British—"

"Professor Kaplen, stop giving a lecture in American history!" howled Mr. Plonsky, smiting his forehead.

"Stick to Mrs. Moskowitz!" shouted Mr. Blattberg.

Mr. Kaplan, a Triton among minnows, was deaf to their protestations. "An' ven de time came for de Amarican Ravolution, brave men like John Edems, Tom Spain, James Medicine—"

"It's Thomas *Paine*, Mr.—"

"—knew vas still missink a slogan, a *spok!* So along came Petrick Hanry." Mr. Kaplan's eyes went dreamy. "Dat vas a man. . . . A tong like silver to kepture de messes!"

" '*Masses*,' Mr. Kaplan, not—"

"An' Petrick Hanry vent into de Virginia House of Poichases—"

" '*Burgesses*'—"

"—an' at vunce vas qviet, like de gomment districk on Chrissmis Iv. So Petrick Hanry got don on de floor—"

" '*Took* the floor'!" said Mr. Parkhill in alarm.

"*Took* de floor—denk you—an' in beauriful voids, parful voids which comm don de santuries for all Amaricans who got true blood, he sad—"

" '*True-blooded*'—" Mr. Parkhill was getting desperate.

" 'Julius Scissor had his Brutis, Cholly de Foist had his Cornvall, an' if Kink Judge got a bren in his had he vill make a profit from soch a semple!' "

Mr. Parkhill sank into his seat.

"Dat," Mr. Kaplan concluded, "also epplies to Moskovitz!"

"Omigott!" someone exclaimed.

"All I sad was 'enough' should have in it vun little 'f'!" wailed poor Mrs. Moskowitz.

"Koplon, you mad!" fumed Gus Matsoukas.

"This mon will change the heestory single-honded." That, perhaps the truest thought yet uttered, came from Olga Tarnova.

"I hoid enough," Mr. Plonsky groaned, and put his head between his hands.

"Mr. Kaplan . . ." Mr. Parkhill began. But he scarcely knew where to begin, so he began again. "Mr. Kaplan, I have rarely heard so *many* mispronunciations in so short a span of time." He knew he was being severe, but he did not shrink before stringent measures. "Charles the First is *not* 'Charley the—er—Foist.' Cromwell is *not* 'Cornwall.' And what Patrick Henry said was most certainly *not* what you quoted! There is a world of difference between 'George the Third *may profit from their example*' and 'George the Third can make a profit out of such a sample'!" Indeed the enormity of the difference washed out of Mr. Parkhill's conscience the slightest vestiges of remorse for his tone. "Do you understand, Mr. Kaplan?"

Mr. Kaplan murmured, "My!" cocked his head, signifying attention, closed his eyes, indicating cerebration, opened one eye, denoting illumination, and said "Aha!", proclaiming conversion. Then, with a rueful yet noble sigh, he started for his seat. "Still, I vill alvays edmire de glorious pest."

Miss Mitnick, who was getting more pale and more resolute by the moment, promptly protested: "Mistake! In pronunciation. '*Past*' is not '*pest*'!"

Mr. Blattberg laughed, Mr. Wilkomirski guffawed, Miss Tarnova choked.

"Tonight is averybody an axpert?" Mr. Kaplan inquired caustically.

Tonight Miss Mitnick summoned all her courage to rejoin, "You don't have to be expert to know 'past' from 'pest'!"

A camel playing the bagpipe would have caused no greater sensation. The room rocked with merriment.

"Good for you, Miss Mitnick!"

"*Bravissimo!*" cried Carmen Caravello.

"You got Kaplen!"

"Et lest!"

Mr. Kaplan ignored the petty barbs and puny arrows, and turned to the one who had been foolhardy enough to give him the challenge direct. "Mitnick," he said pityingly, "you vould be corract, in usual soicomstences. But dis time, no. *You* are talkink abot prononcink; *I* am talkink abot history."

"'Past' *means* history!" Miss Mitnick said tearfully. "You said 'glorious pest'."

"Kaplen, give op!" crowed Mr. Blattberg.

"Keplan, sit down!" brayed Mr. Plonsky.

"Koplan wrong, wrong!" exultant Miss Tarnova crooned.

"Mr. Kaplan," intervened Mr. Parkhill crisply, "Miss Mitnick is absolutely right. 'Past' refers to what has gone by. 'Pest,' on the other hand, refers to a—" He never finished; some ominous bell tolled a note of warning in his brain; an awful premonition congealed before his mind's eye; too late, too late. He did not need to hear Mr. Kaplan's next words to recognize the trap into which he, like poor Miss Mitnick, had so gullibly fallen.

"To a tyrant like Kink Judge," declaimed Hyman Kaplan, "vat else vas Petrick Hanry excapt a glorious pest!"

After that, twenty words with "o-u-g-h" seemed an inglorious nuisance.

JAMES THURBER

The Darlings
at the

Top of
the Stairs

Childhood used to end with the discovery that there is no Santa Claus. Nowadays, it too often ends when the child gets his first adult, the way Hemingway got his first rhino, with the difference that the rhino was charging Hemingway, whereas the adult is usually running from the child. This has brought about a change in the folklore and mythology of the American home, and of the homes of other offspring-beleaguered countries. The dark at the top of the stairs once shrouded imaginary bears that lay in wait for tiny tots, but now parents, grandparents, and other grown relatives are afraid there may be a little darling lurking in the shadows, with blackjack, golf club, or .32-caliber automatic.

The worried psychologists, sociologists, anthropologists, and other ologists, who jump at the sound of every backfire or slammed door, have called our present jeopardy a "child-centered culture." Every seven seconds a baby is born in the United States, which means that we produce, every two hours, approximately five companies of infantry. I would say this amounts to a child-overwhelmed culture, but I am one of those who do not intend to surrender meekly and unconditionally. There must be a bright side to this menacing state of civilization, and if somebody will snap on his flashlight, we'll take a look around for it.

More has been written about the child than about any other age of man, and it is perhaps fortunate that the literature is now so extensive a child would have become twenty-one before its parents could get through half the books on how to bring it up. The trouble with the "child expert" is that he is so often a dedicated, or desiccated, expository writer and lecturer, and the tiny creative talents he attempts to cope with are beyond him. Margaret Mead, the American anthropologist, is an exception, for she realizes the dangers inherent in twisting infantile creativity into the patterns of adult propriety, politeness, and conformity. Let us glance at a few brief examples of creative literature in the very young, for which they should have been encouraged, not admonished.

The small girl critic who wrote, "This book tells me more about penguins than I wanted to know," has a technique of clarity and directness that might well be studied by the so-called mature critics of England and the United States, whose tendency, in dealing with books about penguins or anything else, is to write long autobiographical rambles.

Then there was the little American girl who was asked by her teacher to write a short story about her family. She managed it in a single true and provocative sentence: "Last night my daddy didn't come home at all." I told this to a five-year-old moppet I know and asked her if she could do as well, and she said, "Yes," and she did. Her short story, in its entirety, went like this: "My daddy doesn't take anything with him when he goes away except a nightie and whiskey."

I am known to parents as a disruptive force, if not indeed a naughty influence, upon my small colleagues in the field of imaginative writing. When Mandy, aged four, told me, "I want to be a ghost," her mother said quickly, "No, you don't," and I said, "Yes, she does. Let her be a ghost. Maybe she will become another W. E. Henley who wrote, 'And the world's a ghost that gleams, flickers, vanishes away.' "

"Who is W. E. Henley?" the child's mother asked uneasily.

"Wilhelmina Ernestine Henley," I explained. "A poet who became a ghost."

Her mother said she didn't want Mandy to become a poet or a ghost, but a good wife and mother.

Finally, there was Lisa, aged five, whose mother asked her to thank my wife for the peas we had sent them the day before from our garden. "I thought the peas were awful, I wish you and Mrs. Thurber was dead, and I hate trees," said Lisa, thus conjoining in one creative splurge the nursery rhyme about pease porridge cold, the basic plot sense of James M. Cain, and Birnam wood moving upon Dunsinane. Lisa and I were the only unhorrified persons in the room when she brought this out. We knew that her desire to get rid of her mother and my wife at one fell swoop was a pure device of creative literature. As I explained to the two doomed ladies later, it is important to let your little daughters and sons kill you off figuratively, because this is a natural infantile urge that cannot safely be channeled into amenity or what Henry James called "the twaddle of graciousness." The child that is scolded or punished for its natural human desire to destroy is likely to turn later to the blackjack, the golf club, or the .32-caliber automatic.

The tiny twaddler of ungraciousness has my blessing, as you can see. You can also see that I am mainly concerned with the incipient, or burgeoning, creativity of the female child. This is because I am more interested in Thurber's theory of Elaine Vital, the female life force, than in Bergson's theory of Elan Vital, the masculine life force, which it seems to me is all he isolated. Elaine Vital, if properly directed—that is, let alone—may become the hope of the future. God knows we have enough women writers (at least one too many, if you ask me), but I believe they are the product of a confined and constrained infantile creativity. Being females, they have turned to the pen and the typewriter, instead of the blackjack, golf club, and .32-caliber automatic.

Boys are perhaps beyond the range of anybody's sure understanding, at least when they are between the ages of eighteen months and ninety years. They have got us into the human quandary, dilemma, plight, predicament, pickle, mess, pretty pass, and kettle of fish in which we now find ourselves. Little boys are much too much for me at my age, for it is they who have taken over the American home, physically. They are in charge of running everything, usually into the ground.

Most American parents will not answer the telephone when it rings, but will let a little boy do it. Telephone operators, I have been informed, now frequently say to a mumbling toddler, "Is there anyone older than you in the house?" Many of the tradespeople and artisans I deal with, or try to, in my part of Connecticut, go in for this form of evasionism. A small male child will pick up the receiver and burble into the transmitter. In this way urgency, or even crisis, is met with baby talk, or prattle tattle. The fact that my plumbing has let go or a ceiling is falling down is reduced, in this new system of non-communication, to a tiny, halting, almost inaudible recital of what happened to a teddy bear, or why cereal is not good with sliced bananas and should be thrown at Daddy. The tradesman or artisan and his wife are spared the knowledge of a larger disaster at the expense of the nerves and mental balance of the caller. I shall set down here an exasperating personal experience in this area of obfuscation.

"Oo tiss?" a tiny voice demanded when I called the plumber one day.

"This is Tanta Twaus," I said, "and Tanta Twaus won't give you any Twissmass pwesents this Twissmus if you do not put Mummy or Daddy on the other end of this doddam apparatus."

"Appawana?" asked the tiny voice. At this point his mother, like a woman in transport and on her third martini, grabbed up the receiver.

"He said, 'Appomattox,' didn't he?" she cried. "Isn't that wonderful?"

"Madam," I said, chilling the word, "the answer to the question I just put to your son is Waterloo, not Appomattox. The next voice you hear will be that of me, dying in the flood of broken pipes and the rubble of fallen ceilings." And I slammed up the receiver.

Ours is indeed a child-centered culture in the sense that the little boys have got me squarely centered in their gun sights. I shall continue to urge on the little girls who hate trees, are indifferent to penguins, envy Banquo, wish Mother were with the angels, and can read Daddy like a book. What you are going to do, I don't know, but I advise you to keep glancing over your shoulder, and look out for the darlings at the top of the stairs.

SUMNER LOCKE ELLIOTT

The
Cracked
Lens

Late in November of last year, I was approached by the production firm of Talent Associates Ltd. to write the script of a television documentary to be known as "Hedda Hopper's Hollywood." It was to be video-taped in Hollywood for a Sunday night airing on a national network in opposition to the Ed Sullivan show and the hostess was to be Miss Hedda Hopper, who, it seemed, had declared herself ready to produce almost any motion picture personality not safely embedded in Forest Lawn Cemetery.

Furthermore I was assured by Alfred Levy, the president of Talent Associates and the executive producer of the show, that the approach to this hour-long excursion would be an analysis of the vast changes which have taken place in the industry and that consequently all the facilities of the motion-picture studios would be available to us.

When he added that we would make visits to many celebrated estates, to chatelaines such as Marion Davies and Mary Pickford, and to some historic sets still in existence, I was trapped. I was brought up in Australia on the Saturday afternoon treat of the "pictures," and anything to do with the older, more gilded days of Hollywood holds an atavistic fascination for me. The following capsule of events has been compounded from scraps of notes that I made during a three-week period which I shall not easily forget.

December 15: The vanguard of our production staff, which arrived in Hollywood today, consisted of Michael Abbott, a young producer for Talent Associates, William Corrigan, a director skilled in the documentary approach, and myself. After checking in at the Beverly Hills Hotel, we drove immediately to Hedda's charming little house nearby, where she welcomed us with enthusiasm and a list of more than thirty stars who she declared not only were essential but had given her their solemn word that they would appear. Michael Abbott pointed out that, minus commercial time, we would only have forty-six minutes to include everything. Hedda was unperturbed.

"Some of them," she said, "will only wave."

I said that as we were envisaging a serious documentary we would need to involve the points of view of other workers in the industry such as designers, cameramen, and directors. Hedda nodded.

"I can get you King Vidor," she said. "He plays the banjo quite well and it would be very cute."

Some of Hedda's suggestions were a little bizarre. Did we know, for instance, that Mervyn Le Roy could do a very cute little tap dance? And that Mae West was a deeply religious girl? We might show her coming out of church accompanied by choir boys singing. In the silence that greeted this I said that, charming though the idea was, might it not be misconstrued as comedy in questionable taste. Michael came to my rescue.

"After all, Hedda," he said, "it *is* a Sunday evening program and I'm sure the drug people would prefer us to keep well away from religion. . . ." Hedda relented.

After dinner, I read the rough outline which we had assembled in New York and which we hoped would document the transformations of Hollywood life—Cecil B. de Mille's mansion compared to a typical present-day home; glamour from Gloria Swanson to Debbie Reynolds; Gary Cooper watching a television Western star of today; and so on.

Hedda said that it needed more astringency and we agreed. Bill Corrigan said that we needed an explosive start—someone who would not pull punches about what is wrong with Hollywood. Someone like Bette Davis. Hedda said, "Bette's in Laguna Beach with the children and she'll do it." She handed me a list of names and private telephone numbers.

"Now, these are the people I've already contacted and who are waiting for you to call them and tell them what they're to do."

I glanced at the list. It contained thirty-six names.

December 16: By noon I had developed a pretzel-like shape, owing
to a case of telephone crouch, but very little result. I had spoken to
Bette Davis' sister, Gary Cooper's secretary, Marion Davies' housekeeper, and other nameless minions and relatives who were charming
and experienced at delaying tactics. The greats of filmdom all seemed
to be out with the children, in Detroit at a wedding, in Palm Springs
for a few days, or "lying down and would call me back." Finally I
struck oil. Gloria Swanson was at home and came to the phone. Her
attitude hardly coincided with Hedda's assurance that they were all
"clamoring to be on the show."

"Why do you want to do it in the first place?" asked Miss Swanson. "It's too boring for words, all that old Mack Sennett stuff.
I'm the only one of them who hasn't written a book and don't intend to."

She was adamant. I said, "Miss Swanson, we can't do a treatise on
Hollywood without *you!* You represent a period of glamour that the
movies have never recaptured."

"Glamour! I detest that word. It's like everything else in this town,
immature. Only the French know real glamour. All they care about
here is the ghastly American worship of youth and that's why there
is no place for the mature actress on the screen today. Oh, the men
are still around but those aging Romeos are playing opposite *children*
and I think it's nauseating. What adult woman wants to see that?
How can she identify herself with some *child?*"

When she finally drew breath I said, "Miss Swanson, would you
care to say just that?"

"I would adore to!"

I said that I would outline a speech on those lines for her to deliver with what I hoped would be as much acerbity. It was just the
kind of thing we wanted.

"Is there a fee attached to this?"

I referred her to Michael Abbott. The fee agreed upon for everybody is the minimum possible for any speaking performer—$210, or
what is known in the business as "scale." Interviewing disembodied
stars on the telephone is nerve-racking enough without having to
discuss this bewildering news with them.

December 18: Yesterday teemed with setbacks. Twentieth Century-
Fox has forbidden us the use of their back lot because we are working
with video tape, which—to quote an executive—"We are fighting with
our lives." Mary Pickford is out with a broken collarbone. The studio
where we are to tape the interiors is where they filmed the original

"Jazz Singer" and looks as though it has not been swept out since. I spoke to Bette Davis' sister again on the phone and later got Francis X. Bushman to discuss the original chariot race in the silent "Ben Hur."

In the afternoon, Bill Corrigan and I visited the mansion of the late Cecil B. de Mille with the crew. We were met by a charming lady who described herself as a newcomer, having only worked with Mr. de Mille for eight years, but introduced us to Florence Cole who had served with the great man for over thirty. Both ladies spoke in tones of great dedication and awe about the treasures of the library, the multitudinous awards, the collections of Bibles in every size from every country in the world, and the relics from Mr. de Mille's countless productions. Tireless, they ran up and down stairs, and presented us with the Crown of Thorns from the "King of Kings" and horses' headdresses from the silent version of "The Ten Commandments." Reverently they placed in our hands the original screenplay of "The Squaw Man"—the first feature-length picture ever made in Hollywood complete with Mr. de Mille's own notes in pencil. The keepers of Mr. de Mille's castle generally refer to him in the present tense. "Mr. de Mille always likes . . . Here is the chair where Mr. de Mille sits when he is watching the daily rushes." After a time, the impression that Mr. de Mille will appear around a corner is overwhelming.

"And here are the Ten Commandments," said one of the ladies, touching two stone tablets resting in a red velvet case. Then she added thoughtfully, "They're *copies* of course. The *originals* are in the Paramount commissary."

December 19: I finally made contact with a few of the people on the telephone list. One of them was Anthony Perkins who talked so fast and intricately that my notes read like E. E. Cummings. On the other hand, communion with Gary Cooper was punctuated with silences and heavy breathing. He admitted that he liked to make a Western every two years and after a little more desultory conversation we let it go at that. Even without a point of view, Mr. Cooper's monosyllabic charm comes across like radiant heat.

After I had wrestled for some hours with Tony Perkins' speech, he arrived at the studio with his own. He said, in effect, "When a young performer attempts to individualize himself, he is instantly branded by Hollywood as an ungrateful publicity seeker and so it takes a lot of nerve to say this is what I believe, this is how I'm going to behave and that's the way it's going to be." (This may not sound earth-shaking but it was progress for me. I have been witnessing today the reality

I have been reading about for years—that most Hollywood people retreat like sand crabs when called on to repeat publicly an uncomplimentary opinion they have voiced privately. Fear runs through the movie colony like a virus, most of all the fear of offending.)

Michael Abbott said to me, "Now get a good explosive statement from Bette Davis to precede this and we're off to a good start for the opening of the show."

I was banished to the hotel to try again to snare Miss Davis on the phone. Her sister said that she was out with the children. It was like trying to reach Judge Crater.

December 20: Jacqueline Babbin, another producer for Talent Associates, has arrived to help co-ordinate the script. Miss Babbin is a handsome brisk girl who could organize an armada. On the plane she had mapped out a synopsis.

"Now everything will work if we group the people into subjects," she said. "We open with your idea of Hedda standing on a mountaintop looking down on Hollywood and then—wham—we go to Bette Davis!"

I said, "Or her sister!"

Jacqueline was assuming that everyone would co-operate from Mae West to the weather. "For instance," she said, "if you can get Gary Cooper to mention de Mille at the end of his speech, that would take us immediately to the de Mille mansion without Hedda's voice over it. Then, get a director like King Vidor to talk about making pictures in Rome and that would get us automatically to Charlton Heston and the 'Ben Hur' boys."

I said, "King Vidor has just made 'Solomon and Sheba' and you won't get that kind of co-operation for $210."

Jacqueline was not to be defeated. "But maybe he could mention the effect of crime pictures on children and that could get us to Walt Disney." We coined a new phrase, "with Vidor co-operation, with Swanson co-operation," and went on planning a script that I knew by then could only be written after everyone had been taped. Michael burst into the room.

"We have to cancel the show," he announced. It seemed the best news since VJ-Day.

It seemed that the American Federation of Television and Radio Artists known as "AFTRA" had insisted that the stars appearing were "performers" and must be paid their regular salaries. Even with dropouts the cost would exceed a million dollars. I left Michael and Jacqueline arguing with Al Levy. I had an appointment with Marion

Davies and, show or no show, I was not going to be cheated out of that.

I waited in a high-arched hallway lined with full-length portraits of Marion Davies in many of her famous roles. My appointment had been for twelve-thirty, but it was nearly one before the lady of the por- traits came downstairs leaning on the arm of a very attractively dressed younger woman. Miss Davies came toward me slowly, a wistful mem- ory of Miss Phoebe in "Quality Street," which hung nearby. She put out her hand and apologized sweetly for keeping me waiting, but, "You television people are such early birds." As we went down some steps to the huge library she murmured the other woman's name, which seemed to be "Mrs. Girdle," and they continued their conver- sation concerning Mrs. Girdle's visit that morning to a friend hospi- talized for a major operation. Delicate as bone china to the eye, Miss Davies proved herself capable of firing an angry salvo.

"Everyone I know is being cut up," she announced as we settled on satin divans and drinks were served. "Those damn doctors had *me* pegged for dead for two years." The conversation continued ani- matedly about the untrustworthiness of the medical profession until I nerved myself to break in.

"Miss Davies, we're all so excited at the thought of having you on the show."

The other woman looked at me sharply. "What show?"

"Hedda's show," I said, putting the blame on her. Without any conviction I began extolling the advantages of appearing in "Hedda Hopper's Hollywood" and ended by saying that the way it was shaping up it was likely to be highly unusual. That, I knew, was certainly not an overstatement.

Into the limp silence that followed, Miss Davies fired another salvo. "What makes me good and mad," she announced with the slight stammer I had always heard about, "is that if you retire they think you're a has-been. I retired because I was good and god-damn bored with the whole thing and I gave up two million dollars to do it."

"That's right, darling," echoed Mrs. Girdle, crossing with me to light Miss Davies' cigarette and beating me to it. "But you don't want to say that on television."

Miss Davies looked at me with a child's blue eyes. "I've never been on television, you know, and I'll be very nervous."

I said there was no need to be. We had a wonderful director and a marvelous crew (did we?); they were experts with lighting and camera.

Miss Davies, who had taken my hand, withdrew suddenly. "No close-ups," she said. "I've been going to the dentist and he hasn't finished capping me."

"You'll be marvelous, don't worry," I said.

"You're very sweet."

"And the public wants to see you again."

"I don't know what the hell for."

"What would Marion have to do?" the other woman asked.

We had been ruminating on this for weeks. Hedda had simply stated flatly that Marion must appear on the show. Miss Davies and her friend were waiting. I mumbled that we were bringing the crew to photograph the impressive grounds and pool and that possibly at the end we could discover Miss Davies seated in the library and that she might say a few words about the legendary parties she had given. Had she not entertained both Churchill and Shaw?

"Show Mr. Elliott the picture of me and GBS at Ocean House," she said.

As I was admiring the photographs—Shaw and Marion in yachting caps—Miss Davies' friend said in a quick undertone, "I don't think Marion ought to do this, she's nervous of appearing on a screen after so long."

Miss Davies beckoned me to see a picture of herself at sixteen and repeated that she was very nervous.

I said that Hedda could do all the talking about the famous parties and that Miss Davies need only say at the end, "Thank you for coming to my house."

She nodded, "I'll wear a simple sweater and skirt."

"Oh, no, darling," said Mrs. Girdle. "They want to see you in the full regalia—ice-blue satin ballgown with the ermine and wearing your rubies."

"The rubies photograph black. We always had trouble with them."

"Then wear your diamonds," said Mrs. Girdle.

"We'll give you a screen credit as technical adviser," I said to the friend.

"My husband would hit me over the head. He hates television because he doesn't get a dime for all those old movies."

Miss Davies smiled at me. "Stay to lunch because Clark's coming."

Mrs. Girdle! I was about to explain to Mrs. Clark Gable that I had not caught her name when another luncheon guest entered with Captain Horace Brown, Miss Davies' husband. Mrs. Gable introduced me as something like Havelock Ellis and I rose to go. I told Miss Davies not to be nervous, that we all loved her for doing it.

"Thank you for coming to my house," said Miss Davies by way of rehearsal.

December 24: We are suffering from fall-out. Mae West, Tuesday Weld, and Mickey Rooney have defected. We have Mickey's son but the scene I had written for the two of them to be taped on the Andy Hardy set at MGM is now useless. Late yesterday afternoon, Michael Abbott and Bill Corrigan returned from the Marion Davies house and reported that the sequence had gone very well. Gene Hibbs, the make-up specialist, had transformed Hedda and Marion into radiant ingenues and Marion wanted a close-up.

Later I had the opportunity of watching Mr. Hibbs—a chunky ex-football player—at his Faustian task of rejuvenating the female face. Two adhesive strips of fine net containing little hooks are glued to each side of the temple; then rubber bands are secured to the hooks and tied tightly on the top of the head, lifting up the face until not a nuance of a dewlap remains. Then the hair is arranged so as to hide the adhesives.

Today, at my urging, Hedda telephoned Bette Davis but the phone remained unanswered. During the long delays between takes, she landed Joan Crawford in New York. Miss Crawford would be delighted to appear but could not come to California. I left Al Levy and Michael frantically calling the New York office to arrange a second unit to tape Miss Crawford in the East and found Hedda ad-libbing to the camera.

"Every morning when I get up," she was saying, "I thank the good Lord I'm still alive and living in Hollywood."

December 25: Christmas Day on the deserted stages of a motion picture studio is cheerless indeed. We had risen at 5:00 A.M. and spent the morning taping Hedda on top of a mountain overlooking Hollywood in the teeth of an arctic gale. An annoying beep had developed in the sound recording and it had been some hours before it had been detected as an FM station interfering through a nearby radar tower. Hedda had remained uncomplaining on a fence in the wind while the trouble had been rectified. Seven times she had leaned back toward a perilous drop and said, "This is my town. There's no town like it in the world for its business is entertainment."

In the afternoon we huddled like the Hundred Neediest Cases on the cavernous set of the Paris Opera House munching stale sandwiches and potato salad. Renée Valente, who had come the day

before from New York to cope with AFTRA, appeared like Florence
Nightingale with a bottle of bourbon which cheered us slightly but,
as its effects wore off and the day wore on with interminable delays,
patience snapped and tempers flared. The sequence recalling the days
of Lon Chaney and John Barrymore was somewhat marred by the
inclusion of a dismal plug for a current television series—a sop to a
local producing company. As I was watching the chaos surrounding
us, Michael came up with a doleful face and the news that we must
dispense with Joan Crawford. He said, "They've just discovered in
New York that we are YOTSY."

"We're *what?*" Whatever it was, it sounded offensive.

"YOTSY. IATSE. International Alliance of Theatrical Stage Em-
ployees," Michael explained. "We ought to be NABET."

"The hell we ought. What's NABET?"

"National Association of Broadcast Engineers and Technicians."

"Oh, the crew, you mean."

"Certainly, the crew. If we tape Crawford in New York with a
NABET crew, then our boys will walk off the show because they're
a YOTSY bunch."

The news that Miss Crawford had been torpedoed and sunk by
the unions was relayed to Hedda.

"Merry Christmas," said Hedda.

December 28: Bette Davis finally telephoned yesterday. She is in
bed with a towering cold and will be replaced by Bob Cummings.

Debbie Reynolds gave me a forthright point of view by phone. She
said, among other things, "I have to remember that I only have about
five workable years left. Once you lose the leading lady face, you're
cooked, and I'd rather quit than stay around until they don't want
me any more."

I wrote her speech around this refreshingly frank statement. An
hour or so later she was out of the show owing to a clause in her television contract with the American Broadcasting Company which
forbade her appearance on a rival network.

Hedda was alerted on the set and she marched off bristling, to telephone Miss Reynolds. She returned smiling. "Debbie will be here
tomorrow," she said. Bill Corrigan said to me, "How does Hedda do
it?" I suggested that we change the title of the show to "Friendly
Persuasion."

December 29: This was Black Tuesday. It began at 7:00 A.M. in a
freezing studio with Debbie Reynolds and her publicity aide, a young

man with a crew cut and a forceful air who read the speech I had written, and frowned.

"I don't think this is good for you, Debbie; it's too downbeat, it isn't what people want of you. They expect you to be lively and pert because you love your work."

"I don't this morning," said Miss Reynolds. "I'm pretty tired. I've just made five pictures in a row."

"*Say* that," said Crew-cut, "and say you're just starting another, plus your new television show, and you're very happy because you *love* your work."

I protested that the original speech made a lot of sense; wouldn't Miss Reynolds please say what she had said on the phone.

"I don't mind saying it, Jimmy."

"You can't say you only have five years left!"

"Well, I could say pictures are made too fast today. I think television is too fast."

"Uh-uh, better not say that," said Crew-cut. He was crossing out the guts of the speech.

Debbie yawned. "What I really need is a vacation," she said.

"You could say *that*," said Crew-cut.

"Yes, and then I could say, 'Has anyone got a spare room? You have? Miami? I'll be right there.'"

"That's cute," said Crew-cut, writing.

Debbie's prettified speech was being taped when Michael burst in with newspapers. Ed Sullivan had begun a feud with Hedda and the unions, claiming unfair competition. Having paid Charlton Heston a fee of $10,000 for reading an excerpt from the Bible on his program, Mr. Sullivan was burning about the fact that everyone was appearing in "Hedda Hopper's Hollywood" (Mr. Heston included) for a minimum scale. Mr. Sullivan charged that our show was a grievous form of "payola" in which stars were being compensated for their appearance by flattering comments in Hedda's column. All the newspapers bore banner headlines and Hedda thundered back in print: "He's a liar! He's scared to death I'm going to knock him off the air."

Mr. Sullivan had shot back that Hedda had established a reign of terror in Hollywood. Michael was crowing. "You couldn't *buy* this kind of publicity," he said. His smile faded somewhat when a secretary handed him a note informing us that Charlton Heston, who was due at the studio in the afternoon to tape his sequence about "Ben Hur," would not be able to appear on the show because of further

Bible-reading commitments with Ed Sullivan. Tension mounted in spirals as Mr. Heston refused to speak to Hedda on the phone and relayed the excuse that he thought our show was only to be a local network presentation. Hedda snorted.

"What would I be doing on a *local* show? What would Gary Cooper be doing on a *local* show?"

After Sol Siegel, a powerful force at MGM, had attempted to reach Mr. Heston in vain, Hedda put down the phone.

"We'll do it without Heston," she said firmly. "We don't *need* him."

Now we had a "Ben Hur" discussion without Ben Hur. I went back to the set to await Gloria Swanson. Promptly at two o'clock the other people concerned in the "Ben Hur" sequence arrived. Stephen Boyd from the current production and Ramon Novarro and Francis X. Bushman from the silent version. I explained that Mr. Heston would not be with us and apologized that I would have to keep them waiting as Miss Swanson had to be taped first and was late. They stood around shivering in the cold and I found a seat for them on the only available piece of furniture, a grubby couch. It was necessary to rewrite the sequence on the spot eliminating Heston and while I was doing this, Miss Swanson arrived. She was carrying a gold silk dress on a hanger and looked annoyed.

I apologized for the cold studio and she said, without smiling, "I have a telephone. Someone could have called to tell me. I was supposed to have been sent a speech but it never arrived."

I said I was sorry, there must have been some secretarial error, and read her the speech I had written.

She nodded. "That's more or less what I said on the phone but let's work on it. Where is my set? Where is the director?"

I took her over to the set. "Take that chair away. I'll stand to do it." It was removed. Miss Swanson smiled graciously at the crew.

"Hello, boys, hello." She checked the lighting with Bill Corrigan while I held the gold silk dress. Then she turned back to me. "Now where do I change into my dress?"

A dressing-room, hitherto unused, had been put up in a corner of the stage. It was merely wooden slats with gauze stretched across them and without a light or any carpet. It was bare of furniture except for a mirror stuck on a rickety table, and the temperature inside was sub-zero. His enemies would have thought twice before putting Dreyfus in it. Miss Swanson looked in the door.

"This?"

She is a small woman, but in moments of displeasure she can add inches to her height and she was growing taller by the minute. When she spoke it was in the chilling tones of a Tsarina giving orders for a flogging.

"I shall want a carpet on the floor and an easy chair and something clean to put down on that table and I'll wait in the car while you fix it up."

She went off and I found our stage manager who said that the only furniture available was the dirty couch on which the "Ben Hur" characters were sitting like frozen mounds, still waiting. I told the stage manager to find a comfortable chair and a strip of carpet and fast, and he went off with a face that said, "Easy chairs, carpet? What next?" Clearly this local television station was ill-equipped to accommodate a star for whom Paramount had once built a studio in Long Island. Miss Swanson sat in her car and took most of the sting out of her speech with a blunt pencil and then disappeared to change while I hurried back to remind the abandoned "Ben Hurs" that this too would pass.

Hedda caught hold of me coming across the set and said, "I've just had a call from Joan Crawford in New York and *nobody* has bothered to tell her that she can't be used. I think that some apology is in order." I agreed and went to find Michael who was too elated with the Sullivan feud to listen. He had just heard that the New York *Journal-American* had run a long front-page story on it that evening. "It's the greatest thing that's ever happened in television," he said. "Everyone in America will be watching us." I remarked that I hoped the results would warrant it because not a word of script had yet been written to link together the widely disparate interviews and sequences that we had taped.

Several exhausting hours later, after Gloria Swanson and the "Ben Hurs" had finally been taped, we all watched the footage that had been shot and Bill Corrigan echoed my sentiments. Whatever point of view we had envisioned had bogged down into a series of fatuous plugs and amorphous reminiscence. The best things by far were some superb shots Bill had made of the Harold Lloyd estate and of the charming street built for the film "Meet Me in St. Louis" on the MGM back lot. Marion Davies, radiant and charming, was on and off in a flash and the rest was a jumbled hodge-podge that would require enormous ingenuity to put into some semblance of continuity. Hedda watched the screening with us and didn't seem at all perturbed.

"It's a gasser!" she said. "My God, I look forty!"

January 2: Ed Sullivan triumphantly announced yesterday that besides Mr. Heston, we had now been deserted by Mae West, Bette Davis, Mickey Rooney, and others who fled weeks ago. Much more exasperating is the news that—even without Gary Cooper and Bob Hope, who are to be taped today (our last day of shooting)—the show is way too long. Even with ruthless cuts I will be left in many instances with only seconds of narration to lead in and out of the twenty-eight sequences. Instead of luminous witty prose I have been driven to such desperate devices as having Hedda say, "Westerns have always been a permanent feature of Hollywood and so are the Westmore brothers."

January 3: Gary Cooper delivered the speech I had written for him today, word for word, while I stood by abysmally ashamed of it and wishing I had been able to wheedle more out of him on the phone. He remained monosyllabic until after the second take had been pronounced a perfect one; but then he relaxed and suddenly grew loquacious, telling us story after story of the greener days of motion pictures. As he talked on, I reflected dismally that now would be the time to scrap everything we had done and begin again with the knowledge we now possessed, too late. We had had a gold mine of personalities and data available to us and had mined it for pebbles. Behind the inane show we had jammed together in three weeks there was an image of something infinitely more penetrating. Hindsight is the stable door of television. But then suppose we had actually been able to uncover some of the buried reality of Hollywood, who would have paid for and produced such a show?

Al Levy and Michael did not share my gloom. Al said, "Hedda has done a magnificent job." I comforted myself by remembering a remark with which the actor and folk-singer Theodore Bikel had reassured a nervous actress: "There are four hundred million Chinese who will neither know nor care."

January 5: Hedda dubbed in the narrations sitting in an airless booth with me for seven hours, and the production of "Hedda Hopper's Hollywood" was completed. She said, "It's great—but never again." We kissed on it. Bill Corrigan and I left on a night jet for New York. Owing to a breakdown in the galley no coffee was served and as we alighted at Idlewild on a clear bright winter morning water was pouring through the front lounge of the plane.

"How could it be raining *inside* the plane?" I asked Bill.

He said wearily, "Don't you think it's par for the course?"

January 11: "Hedda Hopper's Hollywood" went on the air last night at eight o'clock. I watched it with friends who were not visibly impressed. Nor were the critics. In audience rating it tied almost evenly with Mr. Ed Sullivan, who failed to appear on his own show because of a heavy cold. Early this morning a friend called me to say that she had missed seeing the show. In fact, she said apologetically, she had not known it was to be on. Neither had four hundred million Chinese.

JOHN UPDIKE

A Wooden
 # Darning
Egg

The carpentered hen
unhinges her wings,
abandons her nest
of splinters, and sings.

    The egg she has laid
    is maple and hard
    as a tenpenny nail
    and smooth as a board.

The grain of the wood
embraces the shape
as brown feathers do
the rooster's round nape.

    Pressured by pride,
    her sandpapered throat
    unwarps when she cries
    Cross-cut! ka-ross-cut!

Beginning to brood
she tests with a level
the angle, sits down,
and coos *Bevel bevel.*

My Father
 and His
Pastors

A man who accepts a religion without being religious lets himself in for more hardships than one would suppose. My father persisted most manfully in going to church; and he usually started around there at peace with the world, and settled himself down contentedly in his end seat; but somehow before very long his expression would darken, as his hopes of hearing a sensible service little by little were dashed; and he came out in an inflamed state of mind that could not have been good for him.

The Episcopal service in general he didn't criticize—it was stately and quiet; but the sermon, being different every Sunday was a very bad gamble. And once in a while there would be an impromptu prayer that he would take great offense at. Sometimes he disliked its subject or sentiments—if he chanced to be listening. Sometimes he decided it was too long or its tone too lugubrious. I remember seeing him so restive during a prayer of that kind, that—although the entire congregation was kneeling in reverence—he suddenly gave a loud snort, sat up straight in his pew, and glared at the minister's back as though planning to kick it.

I glanced over at Mother. She had been sailing along devoutly, as best she could, in the full tide of prayer, with the lovely rapt look that would come at such times on her face; but she had also begun to watch Father out of one eye—for whenever a prayer was longer than usual she feared its effect on him—and now here he was sitting up, and she had to stop praying and turn away from God to this obstinate, obstinate man. "Put your head down," she whispered fiercely; and then, when he wouldn't, she felt so furious at him, and so impotent, and so guilty for having such feelings, and so torn between her yearning to sink back again into the sweet peace of prayer and her hot determination to make the bad boy in Father behave, that she sent him a look like a flash of lightning, shooting out through quick tears; indignant to the very roots of her red hair, and as hurt as a child. This sank into him. He never would at any time kneel in church—she had given up struggling for that—but at last with a deep angry growl he once more bent stiffly down.

Toward the latter part of his life Father found a minister whose sermons he liked. This was the Reverend Mr. Henshaw of Rye, where he lived in the summer. Mr. Henshaw wasn't "one of these pious fellows," Father said, with approval—though why piety was so unsuited to the clergy he never explained. And some years before this, one summer on the Hudson near Tarrytown, there was a Mr. Wenke, an earnest young cleric, who also found favor. But this was mostly because one of the vestry, old Mr. John Rutland, was very strict with Mr. Wenke about the length of his sermons. Mr. Rutland had got it into his head that all sermons should end at twelve, sharp; and if he saw Mr. Wenke being carried away by his own eloquence, he would take out his watch and stare ominously, first at him, then at it. Pretty soon Mr. Wenke's roving eye would be caught and held by this sight. He would falter or sometimes almost choke in the midst of his flow, then lamely end his remarks, and get out of the pulpit.

In the city at this same later period Father went to St. Bartholomew's, and there too the various clergymen suited him, though not quite so well. He liked St. Bartholomew's. The church itself was comfortable, and the congregation were all the right sort. There was Mr. Edward J. Stuyvesant, who was president of three different coal mines, and Admiral Prentice, who had commanded the Fleet, and old Mr. Johns of the *Times*; and bank directors and doctors and judges—solid men of affairs. The place was like a good club. And the sermon was like a strong editorial in a conservative newspaper. It did not nag at Father, it attacked the opposition instead; it gave all wrong-headed persons a sound trouncing, just the way Father would have.

Mother didn't enjoy these attacks. Denunciations upset her. She took almost all denouncing personally, as directed at her, and it made her feel so full of faults that she trembled inside, though she looked straight back up at the preacher, round-eyed and scared but defiant. She preferred something healing, and restful, some dear old tale from the Bible. But denunciations satisfied Father. He liked something vigorous. And in general he instinctively took to the Established Church pattern—a church managed like a department of a gentleman's government. He liked such a church's strong tory flavor, and its recognition of castes. He liked its deference to sound able persons who knew how to run things and its confidence in their integrity and right point of view. In effect, it put such men on their honor, without foolishly saying so. No other approach would have found a way into their hearts.

But nothing is perfect. After Father had made himself at home in this reliable temple he discovered too late that even here a man wasn't safe. The rector began talking about the need for what he called a New Edifice. He said the church had a leak in the roof, and the neighborhood was changing to business, and that they had received a good offer for the property and had better move elsewhere. This gave Father an unsettled feeling. He wished to stay put. But the rector kept stirring things up until he at last got his way.

Committees were appointed, and active teams of workers were organized, who began to collect large subscriptions from every parishioner. Father paid no attention to all this. It was no plan of his. If they insisted on having better quarters, he would try to enjoy them, but except from this effort the rest of it was not this affair. It was only when he was made to see that he, too, would have to subscribe, that Father became roused and startled. This had never occurred to him. He said he might have known it was just a damn scheme to get money.

He was still more upset when Mother told him what sum was expected of him. He had imagined that they would want fifty dollars, or even a hundred; and that was enough to depress him. But she said that, since he had bought a good pew, they would expect him to give several thousand. This was like an earthquake. Father in fact took it as some wild cataclysm of nature, some unheard-of violent destruction of an honest citizen's peace. After roaring out that the rector and his Christian workers could all go to hell, he barricaded himself every evening in his cyclone cellar—the library—and declared he wouldn't see any callers. This lasted a week. Then when he had cooled down a little, Mother had a long talk with him and told him who were on the committee—some men whom he liked. She said he would really have to subscribe. He'd at least have to see them.

He waited, fretful and uneasy, for the attack to begin. One night when Mother was sitting in her room there were sounds of talk in the library. She hurried down the passageway, clutching her needle and mending, and listened at the door. Father was doing all the talking, it seemed. He was stating his sentiments in his usual round tones, strong and full. He got more and more shouty. Mother began to fear the committee mightn't like being scolded. But when she opened the door on a crack and peeked in, there was no one in there but Father. He was in his easy chair, talking away, with his face all puckered up, and he was thumping his hand with a hammer-like beat on his newspaper. "In ordinary circumstances," he was saying to the imaginary committeemen, "in ordinary circumstances I should have expected to subscribe to this project. But during the past few years my investments" (thump, thump, on the newspaper) "have shown me heavy losses." Here he thought of the New Haven Railroad and groaned. "*Damned* heavy losses!" he roared, and flung the paper aside. "Who the devil's that? Oh, it's you, Vinnie. Come in, dear Vinnie. I'm lonely."

I don't recall how much he gave in the end, but I think it was a thousand dollars. The reason Mother thought that he would probably have to give more, was that our pew was way up in front; it was—so to speak—in a fine section. All our neighbors were prominent. There may have been plenty of ordinary Christians in other parts of the building, but I did not see them. Furthermore this pew, though a small one, had cost Father five thousand dollars, and parishioners were being asked to give as much as the cost of their pews. Father had hated to invest all that money in a mere place to sit, but he could sell out again some day, and meanwhile he had a good pew. He rented the one in Rye for a hundred and twenty dollars a year; but a family that wanted a good pew at St. Bartholomew's in those old days used to buy it. They went to the sexton or somebody, and told him what size and so forth, and after a while he would negotiate a purchase for them from some other parishioner. Pews were like seats on the stock exchange. Nobody speculated in pews, of course, and they rarely changed hands; but they went up and down in price, naturally, as the demand rose or fell; and after Father had bought his—most unwillingly—from old Mr. Baggs, he used to ask Mother periodically for the current quotation. Mother disliked to get this. It obliged her to ask the sexton, who was dignified, and who didn't like to quote pews; and another objection was that after Father bought they went down in value. When she came home with the news that the last sale had been for thirty-two hundred, Father said she had led him into this against his own better judgment, and now the bottom was dropping out of the market, and he never would get his money back. "Old Baggs, *he* knew. He was a shrewd one," he declared. "Egad, yes! He knew when to sell." And he swore that if that damn pew ever went up again he would unload it on somebody.

When the church moved away from its old quarters, Father wouldn't go with them. After having had to help build a New Edifice which he had not wanted, he felt he'd enough of such experiences and needed a rest; and he stopped going to church altogether, except in the country.

All during my childhood, before our St. Bartholomew period started, we went to a more homelike church that was less rich and fashionable. It was squeezed in between some old houses on Fifth Avenue near Tyson's Market, and it had a choir of men and boys in surplices, who sang mellow chants, and a narrow but high vaulted roof that rang with the organ music, and stained glass with deep colors; and best of all I thought was Mr. Dryden, the sexton, who had extraordinarily long pointed whiskers that waved in the air when he was in a hurry—a pair of thin curly streamers. He nearly always was in a hurry, and I liked attending this church.

Nowadays there is an office building there, as tall as a dozen such churches, the air is full of gasoline, and the avenue is shut in and darkened; and the powerful traffic throbs by with a tense, roaring hum. But when I was a boy the low houses were set back from broad sidewalks; there was fresh air and plenty of room and window-boxes of flowers, and a bit of green here and there, trees or ivy, and a wide field of sky.

I suppose that the reason we went to this church that I speak of, the Church of the Peace Everlasting, was because it stood near our home. Its name, at least so far as Father was concerned, was a mockery, for he suffered most cruelly there. Yet he went there for years. Yes, and he kept right on going without any question of changing. He disliked change more than he did suffering. In the end he burst out and bought his liberty along with Mr. Baggs' pew—so the latter was cheap after all: but he lost the best years of his life at the Peace Everlasting.

The clergyman there was the Reverend Dr. Owen Lloyd Garden.

He was a plump, bustling man, very goodhearted and pleasant; though in spite of his goodheartedness and kindness I never felt at ease with him. He never seemed to speak to me personally, but to a thing called My Child. He was more at home speaking to a large audience than to a small boy, however. He had warm and sympathetic feelings toward people *en masse*. The congregation responded to this quality in him and liked him; and he not only kept the pews filled but he sometimes attracted such crowds that Mr. Dryden would scurry by, with his whiskers flying straight out behind him, putting chairs in the aisle.

Doctor Garden had come over to New York from England, but by descent he was Welsh. He had a broad red face, thick black hair, and a square blue-black beard. His robes were red, black, and white. His strong English accent was a point in his favor in an Episcopal church; it seemed to go well with the service. But owing, we understood, to his Welsh descent, he was very emotional, and he used to plead with us at times in his sermons in a sort of high mellow howl. My father disliked this. In the first place he heartily detested having anyone plead with him; in the second place Doctor Garden seldom could plead without crying. It wasn't put on at all; he was deeply moved by his own words. The atmosphere became tense and still when he leaned from his pulpit and stretched out his arms yearningly to us and sobbed, "Oh, my people." The whole church was hushed. At such moments Father would testily stir in his seat. "The damned Welshman, there he goes sniveling again," he would mutter.

This would horrify Mother. From her end of the pew she would signal him that he must stop. If he didn't notice she would tell my small brothers to pass word along to me that I must make Father keep still. It was like expecting a boy to make the jungle behave. The most I felt up to was to get him to see Mother's signals, and that meant that I had to pull myself together and poke him. This was nervous work. He was a muscular, full-barreled man; there was nothing soft in him to poke; and he had a fiery way even of sitting still. It was like poking a stallion. When he became aware that he was being prodded by my small, timid finger, he would turn fiercely upon me, and I would hastily gesture toward Mother. Mother would whisper, "Clare! You mustn't!" and he would reply, "Bah!"

"Oh, Clare!"

"I know, Vinnie; but I can't stand that damned—"

"Sh—sh! Oh, hush!"

Another thing he detested was the picture Doctor Garden drew, sometimes, of a businessman sitting in his office at the close of his day. Doctor Garden didn't cry over this, to be sure, but he grew gentle and solemn—he spoke as though he himself were standing at that businessman's side, like an unseen Presence, a loving Good Influence, evoking the man's better self. He apparently had only the haziest ideas of a business office, but he drew on his imagination freely to fill in the picture. He would describe how this hard-headed man sat there, surrounded by ledgers, and how after studying them closely and harshly for hours he would chance to look out of his window at the light in God's sky, and then it would come to him that money and ledgers were dross. Whereat, as the gathering twilight spread over the city, this strange waxwork figure of a businessman would bow his head, and with streaming eyes resolve to devote his life to Far Higher Things.

"Oh, damn," Father would burst out, so explosively that the man across the aisle jumped, and I would hear old Mrs. Tillotson, in the second pew behind, titter.

Aside from the wild untruth of such pictures of business, from Father's point of view the whole attitude involved was pernicious. Anyone dreamy enough to think of money as "dross" was bound to get himself in hot water; that went without saying; it was a sign both of ignorance of, and of disrespect for, finance. Father had more respect for finance than he had for the church. When he left the financial district behind him to visit the church, he felt as I suppose Moses felt coming down from the mountain. Moses found people blind to his mountain and worshiping a calf idiotically, and Father found Doctor Garden capering around something he called Higher Things. Well, let him caper if he wanted to—that was all he was good for. My father was a more charitable Moses who expected no better. But this flighty parson went farther—he wanted Moses to join him! Betray finance for this stuff and nonsense! It was enough to make a man sick.

It was Father's custom to put one dollar in the contribution plate weekly, no more and no less. When Mr. Gregg brought the plate to our pew, Father would first pass it on to us, and we boys would each thump in a nickel, trying to produce a loud ringing sound, as though it were a quarter; and Mother would quietly slip in her offering in a tight little roll, more than she could afford to give probably, and saved up God knows how. Then Father would hand the plate back to Mr. Gregg, who would patiently wait while Father took out and unfolded a crisp new dollar bill, and drew it through his fingers so as to make a little crease in it, lengthwise, and laid it out flat on top of everything else, large or small.

This dollar was apt to become the subject of a debate on our way home. Mother felt there were Sundays when such a sum was not enough. It bothered her dreadfully after a sermon that had described some great need to see Father, absolutely unmoved, put in only his dollar.

Father's first gun in reply was that a dollar was a good handsome sum, and that it would be better for Mother if she could learn this. He had a great deal to say on this point. His second gun, which he would then fire off at her with still more enjoyment, was that any money he gave to the church would be wasted—it would be spent by a pack of visionary enthusiasts in some crazy way. "Sending red-flannel weskits and moral pocket handkerchiefs to the heathen," he quoted.

But after a while Mother found a counterargument which actually beat both of his: she made him feel that it was beneath his own dignity not to put in more, sometimes. Even then he didn't surrender; he compromised instead on this method: before starting for church he put his usual dollar in his right-hand waistcoat pocket, but in the left-hand pocket he put a new five-dollar bill; and he stated that from now on he would make a handsome offer to Garden: let him preach a decent sermon for once, and he would give him the five.

This made every sermon a sporting event in our pew. When Doctor Garden entered the pulpit we boys watched with a thrill, as though he were a racehorse at the barrier, jockeying for a good start. He looked rather fat for a racehorse, but he was impressive and confident, and it was kind of awe-inspiring to see him go down every time to defeat. He always either robbed himself of the prize in the very first lap by getting off on the wrong foot—a wrong key of some sort—or else, in spite of a blameless beginning, he would fail later on: he would, as it were, run clear off the course that Father had in silence marked out for him, and gallop away steadily and unconsciously in some other direction. It gave a boy a sobering sense of the grimness of fate.

"I don't see what the matter was today," Mother would declare, going home. "You should have given more than a dollar today, Clare. It was a very nice sermon." But Father would merely say with a twinkle that Garden ought to get a new barrelful.

The only time I saw Father tested was one Sunday in Lent. It was remarkable enough that he should have been present that Sunday, for the one thing he always gave up in Lent was going to church. Doctor Garden's flow of grief in that season was more than he could stomach. But on this particular morning, to our surprise, Father went without question. It turned out afterward he didn't know it was Lent—he had "thought the damn thing was over." And as luck would have it, Doctor Garden was absent, ill in bed with a cold; and the substitute clergyman who took his place won Father's approval. He was a man who showed no emotions, he was plain and matter of fact, and his subject was the needs of some lumber country in the Northwest. He had worked there, he knew the men, knew the business, and he described it in detail. I listened a while, but there were no bears in it or cowboys; it was mostly business statistics; and I was studying a picture on the wall of an angel who looked like Mr. Gregg—a large, droopy angel with wrinkled garments, only he had no mustache—when my brother George secretly nudged me and pointed at Father. Father was listening closely. We glued our eyes on him. His face was keen and set; he had his arms folded; he was taking in every word. But we couldn't tell whether he liked it. The sermon went on a few minutes; and then, before we thought the man was half through, he stopped. He had finished.

The organist began playing the offertory. There was a rustling of skirts, a stray cough. Imagine our excitement as we waited for the plate to come round. It seemed to take Mr. Gregg hours to get up the aisle, he stood so long, stooping and bulgy, at the end of each pew. "He wouldn't even hurry to see a fire-engine," George whispered indignantly. At last he got to the Hamiltons' pew in front of us—and then he stood at ours. We were all watching Father. But he hardly noticed Mr. Gregg, he was thinking about something else, and his thumb and finger slid automatically into his one-dollar pocket.

We let out our breaths and relaxed from the strain, disappointed. But just as we were slumping dejectedly down, Father paused; he put the one-dollar bill back, and decisively took out the five.

We could barely help cheering aloud at that substitute clergyman's triumph. And yet he himself never realized what he had done—he stepped quietly out of the pulpit and went back to obscurity. This man had won a victory that none of his profession had gained, but nobody knew it except the Recording Angel and the four little Day boys.

A Lecturer at Large

Reflection on the Vernacular

In cooking *petits pois,* or lesser peas,
Some use receipts and some use recipes.
In spite of opposition warm,
I choose to use the former form.
In fact, though you may think me gossipy,
I plan to settle near Lake Ossipee
When my arrangements are complete
To change its name to Lake Osseipt.

Maybe You Can't Take It With You, but, Look What Happens When You Leave It Behind

As American towns and cities I wander through,
One landmark is constant everywhere I roam;
The house that the banker built in nineteen-two,
Dim neon tells me is now a funeral home.

WILLIAM M. WOOLLETT

 Old Homes

 Made

New

Whether a dwelling should be remodeled or not is often an open question, and it is safe to say that under two circumstances only should this be done—one in which the building, in its construction and material, is of such a solid and substantial character as to render its destruction inadvisable; and, again, when, although perhaps in a dilapidated condition, its preservation is in the highest degree desirable, owing to the associations of the family, its peculiar phase or style of architecture, or the historical interest that may attach itself to it. . . . The writer believes that the same general principles that would apply to new work, in this class of buildings, will apply equally to the work of alterations.

First. That the convenience of the plan, its best distribution and adaptation to the wants of the particular individuals by whom it is to be occupied, and the site on which it is to be placed, should in all cases be the paramount consideration. . . .

Second. That the exterior should grow naturally from the plan, its outline being fixed and determined by that; and whether it shall possess qualities, worthy of admiration or pleasure in general, de-

The text and pictures herewith are excerpts from the book *Old Homes Made New* by William M. Woollett, published in New York in 1878.

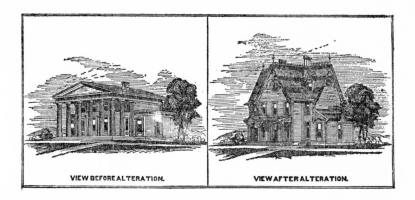

VIEW BEFORE ALTERATION.   VIEW AFTER ALTERATION.

pends upon the skill of the designer; that it should also be a consistent following out of the proper and natural uses of the materials of which it is built; each material being fully acknowledged.

Third. That the architectural effect should be obtained by the natural combinations and workings of the constructive portions of the structure, and not by adding or planting on of these features: and again by the natural variety of the outline rather than by the richness and variety of the detail.

Fourth. That the proportionately greatest work of art in architecture is that which produces the most effective result at the least expenditure of labor and detail in design, which, in the practical mind of the American, is also money.

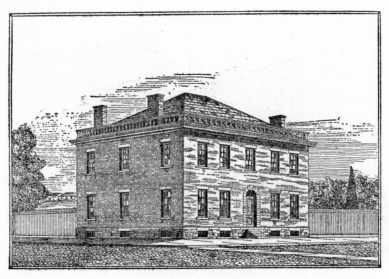

VIEW BEFORE ALTERATION.

The client desired a "French roof," but the views of the client were met and our own sense of right saved from outrage by the roof shown. . . . The roof is one of the most important features of the building, and is one of the few means at the disposal of the designer, by which he is enabled to remove a rectangular structure from the commonly expressed likeness to a "box.". . . The windows are enlarged with new caps, sills, and sash; a bay window placed over the

VIEW AFTER ALTERATION.

entrance doorway at the end of the second story hallway, and another on the side projecting from the dining-room. These changes give quite a different appearance to the building, and are all countenanced by utility and increased comfort of the interior. Where wood has been used in the gables, cornices and dormers, the material is fully acknowledged, and its forms and details are those of wood construction.

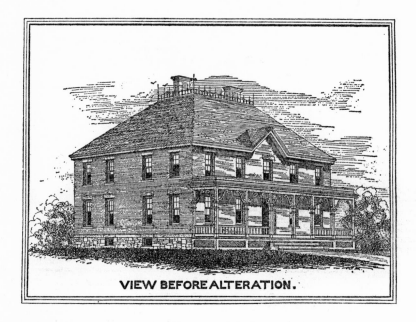

VIEW BEFORE ALTERATION.

This house . . . coming into client's possession by purchase, was found to be a substantial brick edifice. The plan was modified so as to present an attractive home for a small family. . . . On the exterior, the plan being rectangular, the effort to overcome this has been made by the breaking up of the features of the roof, and in conjunction with the brickwork, wood and shingle work have been freely introduced. . . . The introduction of new piazzas on the front and rear

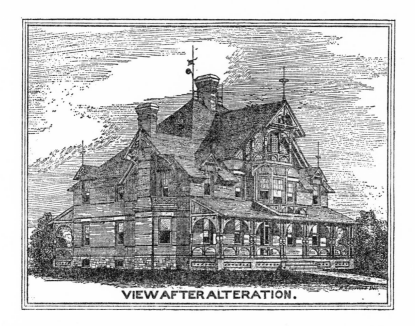

VIEW AFTER ALTERATION.

give breadth to the exterior. A bay at the end of the hallway over the piazza and balcony formed in front of same; and balcony canopied, again corbeled out over the bay, help to remove this centre gable from the ordinary. The chimney at the end of the bay is carried up full height with a portion of the gable on the side brought out to meet and support it, supplying at the same time a cover to the balcony over the bay.

INTERIOR OF DINING ROOM.

Some sketches of the appearance of the more important portions of the interior as altered; it being now a generally accepted belief that this portion of the work should receive as much consideration from the designer as the exterior, and that, by a little variety in the grouping and piquancy in the detail, the rooms of a house may become sources of enjoyment rather than places merely to be endured. . . .

This room [above] before alteration was a plain rectangular one, with coupled windows at the end, as shown. The desire was to finish and furnish it with more pretension and comfort, and (if so fortunate) with more taste than formerly. . . .

VIEW IN HALLWAY AFTER ALTERATION.

In this interior [above] the endeavor of the designer has been to gain whatever effect there may be, not through elaborate work or carving, but in the variety in forms and outline; the detail in this and other designs being kept simple and subservient.

My Career
 as a
Lawbreaker

To a writer the word "euphoria" tends to mean the brief period when the last hundred pages of a book are writing themselves. In the summer of 1931 it had that meaning for me and another one as well. A friend of mine had lent me his summer place in northern Vermont. It was too big for my family needs and luxurious above our station, but we soon found that we needed all its facilities. For it had an additional feature which brought my Cambridge friends up in numbers that kept the several guest houses full and sometimes had an overflow sleeping in the woodlot: it was just twenty minutes from the Canadian border.

Regularly at four o'clock every afternoon I put the manuscript of *Mark Twain's America* aside and got into my car. At 4:20 I reached Derby Line, a Vermont village whose main street, in fact its only one, straightway crossed a brook that was the international boundary and became the main street of Rock Island, Province of Quebec.

Parking just inside the United States, I walked across the bridge and at 4:22 entered the village tavern and ordered a bottle of the Canadian ale that still seems to my nostalgic palate the best brew made on this continent.

The tavern was in the basement of a small hotel. It hummed with geniality in two languages but its principal fascination was a breed of loungers of wildly unconvincing appearance but great narrative skill. Some day the scholars of the American Folklore Society will get round to the Prohibition story. They will find all the sagas, cycles, variants, and modulations that they keep turning up in other sectors of popular belief, the same culture heroes, the same Sinbads and Paul Bunyans. I heard all the stories at the tavern, where for the price of another bottle of beer, which I remember as thirty cents for a twenty-ounce pint, I could take my pick of flight, chase, cunning, bribery, the Inspector Outwitted, the Fox Confuted, in fact anything except murder. For the folk artist was a borderer after all, a Vermonter or a Canadian, and on the border rum-running was a good deal more genteel than it was on Cape Cod.

I assume now that everything I heard was art, not history, but during Prohibition, our national fantasy, it was both pious and patriotic to believe anything you were told about rum-running. And of course great quantities of liquor *were* run across the border, by automobile on woods roads and by boat up Lake Champlain. Long before 1931 an originally competitive business had been organized and most of the traffic was monopolized by two groups. They did sometimes feud with each other but in a fraternal way and the casualties seldom amounted to more than a black eye or a ducking in the lake. Nor did the revenuers of the saga, the Border Patrol, offer more than a formal dissent. The honorable tradition of smuggling in these parts is older than the United States. Not only its skills but its loyalties have been developing for two centuries. No one wants to get a neighbor into trouble, still less to shoot at him.

A visit to the tavern was the first item on the program of entertainment which I devised for people whose affection for me was so warm that they would drive the nearly three hundred miles from Cambridge prepared to stay indefinitely. There were some good effects too, as on the afternoon of July 4, when the place filled with thirsty men in uniforms more splendid than any you would see at the Governor-General's ball in Ottawa. They were the American Legion of Newport, Vermont, ten miles away at the head of Lake Memphremagog. They had spent several hot hours parading to celebrate the birth of freedom, and now they had crossed over for a glass of beer.

The second item on my program was a picnic. The nearest Quebec Liquor Commission store was at Sherbrooke and we would arrive there just before noon. We bought French bread a few minutes out of the oven, butter, the cheese called Oka that is made by Quebec Trappists, and an appropriate amount of wine, justly estimated at one bottle per person and one for the pot. Well, one extra per automobile. Then we repaired to the shore of some neighboring lake, where for some hours the afternoon had more blue and gold in it than could be seen on the Vermont side.

But a compulsion which Prohibition had produced showed itself when an American entered a store where he could legally buy whiskey —and could be sure that the whiskey he bought was what the label said it was. Such a novelty could be intoxicating in itself. Going in search of a poet or a professor of English who seemed to have dropped out of our party, I was likely to find him sitting on the curb, brandishing a bottle of Haig & Haig which he had not yet bothered to open, and singing loudly, to the scandal of Sherbrooke and the shame of his fellow-slaves.

No one wanted to drink whiskey on such an occasion but no one intended to leave it in Quebec, either. Besides, it was judicious to build up a reserve in Vermont, lest illness or the weather keep us home some day. Finally, a citizen must do what he could to end our national disgrace. So we joined the company of patriots who in all countries and all ages have fought despotisms by smuggling. Whenever I went to Sherbrooke I brought back a couple of bottles of whiskey. It would have been perfectly feasible to put them in the glove compartment, or for that matter to leave them unwrapped on the rear seat. The Derby Line customs officials never searched my car; to do so would have marred the friendship that had sprung up between us on my daily visits to the tavern.

But everyone was an actor in the Prohibition drama, the make-believe forced on us by the mores of the time. Coming back from a picnic, we would stop a mile short of Rock Island and spend up to an hour putting into effect whatever expedients had been worked out at a staff conference the evening before. Once the inspiration ran to jacking up a car, half-removing the splashpan, and laying fifteen dollars' worth of Scotch on it before bolting it back, a job that would have cost fifteen dollars at a garage. When I was alone, I used a complicated harness of twine which would hoist a couple of bottles behind the cushion of the rear seat, where no inspector would find them unless he ran his hand over the cushion or stooped to look up.

The customs officials, of course, knew by heart every device a tourist could invent to outwit them. It was always pleasant to spend half an hour watching them work, with several pints of ale making me tolerant at the end of an afternoon. Usually they waved cars on after a glance at the first suitcase but occasionally they gave one the works. The embarrassment of freeborn and defiant Americans caught striking a blow for freedom was intense out of all proportion to either the offense or the penalty, which amounted merely to confiscation of the liquor. One day a U. S. Senator who was a bellowing Dry came through. The whole force forsook everyone else and let cars line up bumper to bumper for fifteen minutes while they all but took the upholstery off his Cadillac. They were practicing caste discrimination, for I am sure that at least two of them saw the Senator's chauffeur hand me a bottle for safekeeping when he got out of the car.

Thus the mantel and sideboard of my borrowed summer estate soon carried a display of fine liquors. This richness led to the establishment of an importing firm that was to become the admiration of Cambridge, or at any rate of my rapidly expanding circle there. One evening a friend whose identity I am not concealing when I call him Emery and whose patriotism had been warmed by the best Scotch he had drunk in years—Emery and I fell to lamenting that we could not assure ourselves for the coming winter such comfort as we were experiencing at the moment.

I remind you that such talk was extraordinary realism: it recognized a truth which one was duty-bound to deny. The fantasy of Prohibition required everyone to believe that he was one man who knew how to get honest, uncut liquor. His bootlegger employed Pullman porters to bring Real Old McCoy down from Canada, or personally supervised its transportation from the Cape Cod beach where it was landed, or had an in with enforcement agents and so got his pick from confiscated stock. The pretense did not extend to gin, which we were not obliged to regard as anything but what it was. One Dedham bootlegger was widely approved for using a printed label on which his name appeared above the legend "High Grade Bathtub Gin."

Emery and I laid our problem before a farmer who lived down the road a piece. He had a name so typical of Vermont that it could serve as the title of a Walter Hard poem: call him Eli. Having kept an eye on our activity, Eli had an answer already worked out. He converted a canvas hunting coat into a vest with fourteen pockets, each capable of holding an imperial (forty-ounce) quart. His wife drove him to Sherbrooke in the family Model T. He bought the fourteen quarts that he reckoned to be his optimum load, and she drove him back to a curve in the road about three miles north of the border. Here he entered the only vestige of the Great North Woods remaining in the area and his wife went on to wait for him at a rendezvous about four miles below the border on the Vermont side. . . .

For toting fourteen forty-ounce quarts through seven miles of forest, Eli set a fee of one dollar per bottle. (On one trip he fell and broke a bottle; since an honest man must guarantee delivery, he refused the fee for that one.) When Emery went home—he lives in Andover—he took with him a selection of QLC spirits. At the end of the summer I took to Cambridge all that my car would hold. At intervals thereafter, and they tended to grow shorter, Emery and I sent Eli a check covering three or four trips across the border, forty-two or fifty-six imperial quarts, and a list of what we wanted. A week or so later we received a postcard saying that there had lately been a lot of rain in Vermont or that Eli's setter had had pups. Thereupon we drove to Rock Island and spent an evening in the tavern, or went on to Sherbrooke for a better dinner and some wine. The next day we returned to Vermont, stopped at Eli's house for our cargo, and drove home.

The whole QLC list was ours to choose from but, though we were glad to drink well beyond our means, there were limits. So we stuck mostly to $3.50 or $4 Scotches and the $4 cognac. Nowadays, repentance would swiftly come upon me if I were to drink brandy and soda very often, but I was twenty-two years younger then—and, besides, any genuine spirits were more emollient than the liquors we had been hardened to. We never brought in gin; it would have been pointless without vermouth and the importation of low-proof goods would have been an economic waste. We did buy a few collectors' items, simply for swank and vainglory. A bottle of Greek brandy or *eau-de-vie de Marc,* even one of Benedictine, suggested to the Cambridge hedonists that any whim could be gratified at my house. An expensive Scotch, say Grant's Best Procurable, made a fine gift, being reverenced far beyond its cost. Eli, however, refused to transport mere frivolities. Arriving at his place on one occasion, I found that he had not brought a bottle of champagne which I had ordered for a friend's birthday. He said that he would not help me spend my way to the town poor farm.

Our importing firm stayed in operation till good liquor came on the market following Repeal, which, the elders among you will remember, took some time. Ethical men both, Emery and I retained our amateur purity: we never sold a bottle to a friend. But our cellars and our connoisseurship gave us a popularity we could not afford, and we were forced to abate it by occasionally letting some intimates club together and order a load. They invariably refused to bring the liquor down themselves, convinced that the traffic was hazardous to an extreme. At least their cars would be confiscated, beyond that there were jail sentences, and who knew but that they might be forced into bribery, assault, or even gunfire? They thought of us as professionals, with spectral cutlasses between our teeth and a wad of protection money in our wallets—just such characters as spent their leisure in the hall of heroes at the Rock Island tavern. We could not see that the illusion did them any harm.

And in fact the best part of an exhilarating experience was that drive south from Eli's house. I suppose the only risk we ran was the unlikely one that we might have a collision in the presence of a city cop. Even that would have had to occur in circumstances which required the cop to be censorious rather than sympathetic about a lot of spilled whiskey. But the dramatic fantasy of Prohibition had us driving U.S. 3, 4, and 5 with the certainty that every quarter-mile was hazardous. At any moment a pursuit car might overtake us, round every curve we might be stopped by a road block. I often drive those highways now and the landscape remains beautiful but it has lost its zest. No revenuers are chasing me.

On the evening of December 5, 1933, my wife and I went to the Parker House for the ceremonies befitting the return of legal liquor. The legislature of my native Utah was selling out its Mormon teetotalism for the publicity that would attend its becoming the thirty-sixth and decisive state to ratify the Twenty-first Amendment. The flash came through about 11:00 P.M. and at once our waiter brought us a now legal bottle of Rhine wine in a now legal ice bucket, an insipid Liebfraumilch—all the good wines in Boston were locked up in closed, dispirited speakeasies. But a newspaper photographer made a flash of it and us, and next morning's *Herald* ennobled it as the first champagne sold legally in Boston since 1920.

During the last war Canada diluted its whiskeys and enormously raised the tax on them. It has neglected to abate either evil and now the smuggling through the Derby Line and Rock Island custom houses runs north. Thrifty folk come down from Quebec to buy good, cheap liquor at Vermont state stores and hoist it up behind the rear cushion with a harness of twine. And a little while back I remarked to some young person, "I was a bootlegger once." The appalling lack of sociological understanding that characterizes the modern young showed in his bewildered question, "Whatever for?" At that, I was bragging like a tavern lounger. I was never a bootlegger, I was not even a rum-runner. Eli was the rum-runner: I was merely in the carrying trade.

Dictionary

of

Charlestonese

Although, as everyone knows, Charlestonians speak perfect English, residents of many other sections of the United States unfortunately do not. Ironically, these sloppy talkers from elsewhere complain sometimes, while visiting the Holy City, that they cannot understand the pure and clear accents of Charlestonians. To remedy this deplorable situation, here is a list of important examples of the local English, selected from *Lord Ashley Cooper's Dictionary of Charlestonese:* [1]

ABODE—Wooden plank.
A BOOT—Approximately.
BALKS—A container, such as a match balks.
BECKON—Meat from a pig, often eaten with a-igs for brake-fuss.
BONE—Blessed event, i.e., "I was bone a Charlestonian." (A *very* blessed event, in the minds of all Charlestonians.)
BUN—Consume by heat, i.e., "When you make toe-est, don't bun the braid."
BUS—Upper part of the human body.
COAT—Where they got that jedge an' all, i.e., "Stannup for hizzoner, coat's in session."
CONDUIT—Impossible of accomplishment.

FAINTS—A barricade of wood or brick.

FAMINE—Tilling the soil, i.e., "I've been famine all my life."

FRUSTRATE—Tops; initial ranking.

HAIL—The abode of integrationists, some damyankees, and other evil spirits.

HEPCAT—Act of giving assistance to a feline.

HOMINY—What number?

ICE COOL—The institution of learning which stands midway between grammar school and college.

LACK—Enjoy, i.e., "I lack fried chicken."

LAYMAN—A fruit from which layman-ade is made, i.e., "Is that your layman-ade?" "No, that's Pappa's-zone." "Well, poet back in the pitcher, 'cause Pappa's now drinking bare."

LOIN—Storying. Not telling the trut'.

MEAN—A gathering of people, as a committee mean.

MINUET—You and I have dined.

PASSÉ—Father has spoken.

PASTOR—Field where cows graze.

PAUNCH—Blow struck with the fist.

POACH—A verandah.

POET—To transfer a liquid, i.e., "Poet from the pitcher to the glass."

POLICE—Term of polite request. A person desiring to maneuver a car to the curb might ask a pool-lease-man, "Cain I police pack hair?" To which the pool-lease-man would doubtless respond, "No, you cain not."

RAH CHAIR—Where you are at.

SANE—Speaking, i.e., "I cane hardly hair what he's sane."

SEX—One less than seven, two less than eh-et, three less than noine, foe less than tin.

TARRED—Weary.

TIN SIN STOW—The foive and doyme.

TON—To swerve. To ton around.

TRAFFIC—Something stupendous, like a movie that is beyond colossal or epic.

VERSION—The kind of Queen that Queen Elizabeth I was.

VERTIGO—What happened to HIM?

YUK COME—Someone approaches, i.e., "Yuk come Romeo."

MAX STEELE

Forget
 the
Geraniums

We were sitting as usual that summer on the terrace of the Café Mona, around the corner from the Odéon and straight down from the Comédie Française. Now it was late August and the streets were deserted. Thousands of Parisians had gone south on their annual holidays and the only creature about was the street-cleaner with his broom of bound twigs.

Benito Rapello—an American artist studying on the GI Bill—and I were alone on the terrace that morning. The fact is he had sent me a *pneumatique* asking me to meet him here. The note was rather puzzling because I did not really know him that well: I had seen him several times in an evening sketching class and later had gone with Daphne, a mutual friend, to the opening of his third exhibit, which was even more successful (the French liked it, that is) than the first two; and I had talked with him maybe ten times in passing on the street.

He was about thirty, extremely clean-cut and perhaps too good-looking in a Latin way: teeth too regular and white, eyes too dark and soft, a strong jaw too square, complete in every way, even down to the cleft chin and jaw muscle which rolled and dimpled when he chewed or talked. Sometimes he was with a strikingly beautiful woman but I think there was nothing to that because she was living with a sculptor in Montparnasse.

Usually he was alone and always in a hurry, which was understandable considering the fact that he had over sixty paintings in each show and all three in a period of four years. Solid clean water colors of the Seine, quite simple and nice and unpretentious; and even more solid oils which were of Paris too, places one knew quite well, such as the bridge at St. Martin or the *quais* along the Île St. Louis, but which in his pictures were the most desolate places in the world, filled with a solemn green light which one might expect to see in the sky in advance of a hurricane or maybe thirty minutes after an atomic blast. It was this strange, impending, doomed light and the complete bareness and lack of hope, that the French liked and not the admirable draftsmanship which they looked upon with contempt as at anything outdated in the fields of fashion and ideas. The other American GI students were guardedly quite proud of him, in spite of a certain envy —not of his paintings, they let you know—but of his ability to work, and work hard and stay out of café life. As a result there were rumors about him of various sorts, so contradictory that if you considered them all together they seemed rather ridiculous. If he were aware of these rumors one could never know: he was always very pleasant, though extremely serious, polite, correct, even a little formal. Certainly he dressed more like a bright young man just out of Harvard than like a Left Bank artist or an American student in Paris.

Well then, he was sitting at the Café Mona that morning when I arrived at ten o'clock. The place was naturally deserted at that early hour, it being mainly a nighttime hangout for the odd assortment of strange Americans and their tobacco-hungry, occasional admirers. His blue-black beard, more like a thick paste than like a stubble, would have been surely an affectation, a rather silly source of pride for a vain man, but he stroked it immediately and apologized for it by saying that he had been up all night and had not been home to shave. Otherwise he looked, as always, quite neat and healthy. He ordered a coffee and *croissant* for me but wanted nothing himself. During the time Pierre had gone to fetch the coffee and bun I said without too much curiosity: "I haven't seen you around in a long time. Not since the beginning of summer, isn't it?"

"Yes," he said. "At least two months." He paused as though that would be all, then wet his thin lips, which were already wet, with the tip of his tongue and let them curl ironically. "I've been crucifying Christ."

"Crucifying Christ," I said as though it might be a well-known expression or joke, if it were a joke.

"No, quite seriously. I've been nailing Christ to the Cross."

"For two months?" I asked. "Is it a painting?"

"No. I had to get a job. My GI Bill ran out in June and I went down to a foundry a French friend works summers in—where they're casting those warhorses for Perón, as a matter of fact—and got a job nailing Christ to the cross. I had to have work." He explained that they made every size crucifix. From pocket size to cathedral size. Stacks and stacks of them. All day long. He sighed suddenly and all the irony drained from his face, leaving his eyes unusually dark. "Well, it's over now."

"Uh-oh," I thought warily. "He wants to borrow money. Why else a *pneumatique* at nine in the morning?" All the broke Americans assumed they could borrow money from anyone who still wore a tie and socks.

He may have seen the close, guarded look on my face for he added: "I quit."

That did not make the possibility of a loan less likely. But then he said, flatly, in exactly the same tone as before: "I'm going to kill myself."

"I beg your pardon," I said. It was probably another expression, like Crucifying Christ, which too would have a perfectly plausible, unalarming explanation.

He looked up from the water running along the curb and for a second his face tightened so that he did not need to add another word for emphasis; but he did, nevertheless, calmly and flatly as before: "I'm going to kill myself."

It would have been too dramatic, indeed burlesque, to set the coffee cup down noisily on the saucer, so I took a long sip while trying to think. When I could delay no longer and it was obvious that he had nothing more to say, I asked: "Do you know why?"

He knew why. That was a little after ten o'clock and at a little after three he was still orating why. He was not sad. It was no momentary depression. It was something he had been considering sanely for some time, even before coming to Europe. It was not love, money, or success. It was not the lack of any of these three. He could have anything he wanted. He wanted nothing. "Everything is a farce," he kept saying in summation. No matter what we talked about he concluded that it was a farce.

Even so, to me after a night of sleep, that did not seem reason enough for suicide. It could as easily be the reason for trying to stay alive as long as possible. But I listened not so much to his words as to the flat tone in his voice and knew that he was not merely playing. Once you have heard that note, calm, beyond despair, you heed it when you hear it again a second time. In college I had known an un-humorous lad who said in that matter-of-fact voice that he was going to kill himself and who had gone straightway unheeded (it was dur-ing a football broadcast) to his room, poured lighter fluid over his clothes, set them on fire, cut his throat with a razor blade, and jumped out of the third floor of the dormitory onto the cement service plat-form. An ambulance could not be got so he had to be half-carried, half-walked, wrapped in a blanket, across the campus to the in-firmary where he went into shock and died almost immediately. So here at the Café Mona I listened without alarm but with real respect to Benito Rapello's undramatic words which were convincing be-cause of the complete lack of emotion with which he recited them.

One thing I kept in mind while he spoke: "He wants to be talked out of it, he wants to be persuaded. Otherwise he would have done it last night. Otherwise he would not have waited alone until the post office opened to send the note." I would have hoped for someone else to join us to aid, but we had only one friend in common, Daphne, and she was now in North Africa. Each time he stopped talking I would ask a question, for when the silence became too long and deep he always ended it by extending his hand and saying thanks for listening and moved in his chair as though about to leave. It didn't seem a good idea to be persuading him constantly to stay or to live because if he kept pretending or threatening he would have both to leave and to kill himself for his own distorted pride.

"But your painting?" I said tentatively, knowing that it sounded fatuous to a man who had been up all night and got himself into such a state.

"To hell with it," he said.

"But the reviews were excellent. Even Bernard Mérimée's."

"Exactly," he said. "But what does it mean? I can paint. I know that. I can go on and on and paint more and more pictures and better and better and better ones and the critics will say more and more decent things and stupid people will start buying them and paying more and more. But what does it come to? Nothing. It's a farce. A great big farce like everything else." We talked about painting for almost forty minutes: the young painters who were being pushed by the right critics; those who had real talent who were building respectable reputations; those who were phonies who were getting there on exploitable personalities; those who were arriving by affording chic galleries; those who had once had talent but who now, having nothing more to say, were turning out slick phony junk and becoming even more the rage; those who were willing to pay actual money to critics. All these people arriving, getting there, some through merit, some not, but all arriving. And where was there? It was a great big farce; that's what it was, a farce.

"What about going back to the States?" I offered. But no, he had left the States with exactly this same sense of futility, not as acute and debilitating as now because then he had believed that the fault lay not within himself but in the essentially materialistic, essentially anti-intellectual philosophy of the Americans. Now he knew that was not true. Their ambitions were simply different, their goals perhaps more obvious and less admirable (to own a Packard rather than a Picasso), their means more direct and open. But even so, here or there it was a farce.

For a while, his first year abroad, he had not understood America and had been in constant revolt against its mania for cleanliness and against its puritanism. He had grown a beard, gone dirty, worn clothes that hung like rags. He had slept with so many that he sometimes did not recognize them any longer on the street. All in meaningless revolt against a meaningless system. Farce in reaction to farce.

"Women," he said. "I've had more women in two years here than I would have thought possible. Sometimes serious affairs too, but they always end the same way: boredom. No, seriously," he said when he saw my quizzical brow. "After a while anything becomes boring and I don't think I'm capable of any real, deep, sustaining emotion, except in painting." He paused a long time, then said without any vanity but as a statement of ordinary fact: "You can't look like me," he indicated his face with a flare of his hand, "and have a straight back, strong chest, no hips, and good legs without attracting more women than you know what to do with. And men. And I've tried that but it's ridiculous." He had tried, it evolved, beer, wine, reefers, cognac, complete celibacy, and every other vice, and having a completely detached approach was not at all interested in what anyone said. "Those petty little gossipers see all those things, like drunkenness and lustings, as ends in themselves rather than as ways toward something real: as a way out of oneself." But now he was tired of experimenting, tired of trying to break through his isolation.

During these long discourses I was trying to remember articles on suicide I had read since the night the stunned boy had been found on the dormitory step and led dazed and pleading to the infirmary. ("No one believed me," he kept saying, his eyes wide and wild, "no one believed me." And then lying on the floor in the hall of the infirmary whispering from his torn-looking mouth: "If you only knew what it is I'm afraid of." What it was he never revealed.) More people, I remembered, kill themselves in daytime than at night, more on sunny than on dark days, more on Sundays and holidays than during workdays. None of this was encouraging for here we sat in the middle of a bright sunny afternoon while half of Paris was away on holidays. People rarely kill themselves, the book had said, on a full stomach, but Benito Rapello refused any invitation to go around the corner to a restaurant. He had a cup of tea before him only because Pierre, the waiter, insisted that he could not sit there all day without ordering. The fragrance of geraniums, a professor had said, was known to have an exhilarating effect upon depressed patients, but he had not explained how to lead the patient to a geranium.

Finally I asked what I had been wondering since receiving his note: "Why me? Why did you decide to talk first to me?" It sounded blunt and even accusing, but he did not seem to notice.

"Because," he said, "Daphne told me that you tried to commit suicide."

"Did she?" I was astonished. I could not even remember having confided such information to her. Actually I was annoyed.

"Yes," he continued. "Oh, it was nothing. I'd merely mentioned that you, more than most people here, seemed to know what you were doing and apparently enjoyed being alive. She said maybe so but you'd poured lighter fluid on yourself in college and jumped from a window."

"That was somebody else." I reddened disagreeably. "A boy I knew."

He watched the red which would not subside and half-relenting, half-persisting said: "Maybe I got the story wrong. But you have tried?"

He had no right to be asking, but then under the circumstances I had no right to refuse him any knowledge that might change his mind.

"I suppose most people have. Or have thought about it."

"But you almost succeeded." He obviously believed I was the lad with the lighter fluid.

"Yes," I said and felt, under his gaze, that I should lean casually over and turn the water on the table before us into wine. Such desperate faith he had in me now: how could I admit that I had merely swallowed forty-four of what were supposed to be powerful sleeping-pills and then had (for fifteen dollars) rushed myself to the hospital in an ambulance to have them pumped out? Or about the laughter of the intern who discovered, in such a loud voice, that it had been only milk of magnesia tablets? Under Benito's admiring gaze I sat discreetly trying to look like one who had been burned, slashed, and hurled from a third-floor window.

"What made you change your mind?" he asked. "You seem happy enough now."

I shrugged my shoulders and pouted like a Frenchman. Such a complex question that any answer would be silly, incomplete, and untruthful. "Analysis, I suppose."

"Psychoanalysis!" He spit the word out as though it were fat meat.

I admitted reluctantly yes, wondering, with annoyance, why in hell some people can't kill themselves without having to ask personal questions.

He began a tremendous, offensive tirade against analysis, so bitter that I knew he was extremely interested. I said nothing and made no defense for it. In fact I agreed with him on many points: it was painfully expensive, and did certainly take time, sometimes years; yes, some people seemed not to benefit outwardly from it, though you couldn't be sure they were dismissed. The only positive point I insisted on was that it was a wiser choice than suicide. He argued on and on but always we came back to the fact which I established with authority: it was a wiser choice than suicide. Finally and quite suddenly he agreed by saying: "Do you know of any psychiatrist here? One who speaks English."

"If I do, will you go?"

He thought for several minutes. "For how long?"

"For even one hour."

Again he reflected: "Yes, for one hour."

"You'll wait here?" I asked without stressing the question. "While I phone."

He said sure.

I phoned the American Hospital and asked for a list of psychiatrists who spoke English. The girl there explained that many of the doctors were out of town during the holidays. Couldn't I telephone back in September? When I told her my predicament she let me speak at once to a neurologist on duty who said I didn't want to get in touch

with an analyst but with a psychiatrist and gave me immediately the
name and address of one with whom he had talked only five minutes
before and who fortunately lived not ten minutes' walk from the
Café Mona, three minutes by cab. He himself would telephone the
man that we were on the way. Well, naturally he couldn't say but he
didn't think Rapello would do anything drastic, not if he had been
sitting talking rationally all day, but he shouldn't go, in such a state,
alone through another night without sleep.

We walked. Rapello wanted to buy cigarettes. He considered, too,
going to his room to shave which could have been a hopeful sign or
merely a ruse, so we went on without stopping. All the way he became more nervous: "What am I going to say to the man?"

"Just what you've been saying to me."

"Just that?" He stopped. "What's the use of going?"

"He may ask you a few questions. May ask you something which
will open up whole new fields of thinking, whole new ways of looking
at yourself and at the world."

Rapello was not convinced but he followed and as we rang the bell
to the heavy door he whispered like a child: "All that I said this morning to you?"

"Whatever you like," I whispered back.

Suddenly he drew away. "About the money. I don't have any with
me. How much is this going to cost?"

"He won't ask for money. If he does I have some."

The doctor himself opened the door and the girl at the desk in the
reception room did not even look up from her typing. A rather ele-
gantly dressed lady sat nervously pretending to read a magazine which
she had obviously just picked up. The doctor regarded us and could
not make up his mind. Had my mask of sanity slipped?

"This is Benito Rapello," I said hastily in introduction. "The
American Hospital called you about an appointment, didn't
they?"

"Yes, yes," he said kindly but rather vaguely. "Fortunately I have
some minutes." He had a very heavy accent, clearly not French, perhaps German or farther east even. He chose his words with careful
deliberation, like a nearsighted typesetter, as though he were not sure
they were the words he wanted.

Rapello disappeared with him into the tremendous Louis Quinze
living room beyond the sliding doors. The nervous patient glanced at
her watch and said in a torrent of French that she could not sit here
like this, that she would come back in thirty minutes, in an hour,

never if she felt like it. The girl did not look up from her typing during the outpour or when the door slammed shut.

Beyond the sliding doors Benito Rapello's steady voice droned on, five minutes, ten, fifteen, a half an hour, forty-five minutes. During this time I went over all that he had said that morning and hoped the wise-looking old doctor could find a more appropriate comment than I had found. ("But I'm simple," I had said lamely, yet sincerely. "I like farce.") Near the end of the hour the girl asked Rapello's name, address, and ability to pay which she typed onto a card.

When the sliding doors finally opened and the two came into the room, Rapello's eyes were as happy and bright as a child's but the doctor's face was as before: calm, sage, and inscrutable. Rapello thanked the doctor and as he did so his face broke into an amused smile, the sparkle and sincerity of which completely startled me. He was almost laughing. When the old doctor opened the door, Rapello burst out, and, most unlike him, galloped down the steps. He raced through the hall below too fast for me to keep up.

"Wait. Hey, wait up!" For a moment I didn't know whether to follow or go back and call for the doctor. When I caught up with him at the corner he turned, as though still unaware of me, toward the Seine.

"What did he say?"

But Benito was across the street and off again toward the river. We were almost running now and when I came abreast of him his eyes were still bright and his thin lips were twitching to hold back a grin. "Let's go get a beer," he said. "I'll buy you one."

Near the Beaux Arts we sat in front of a café looking out across at the Louvre. We were both breathing hard and Benito had not yet decided to relate what had happened in the conference room. He merely sat shaking his head from side to side and the smile was growing into a broad grin.

"Well," I said when the waiter had placed the beers before us and left.

"I talked for an hour . . ." Rapello began chuckling. "I talked for an hour . . ." Handsome people rarely give themselves over to any emotion so disfeaturing and contorting as open laughter; but for a second Benito Rapello threatened to. Long habit though straightened his face and smoothed his features again. "I told him just what I told you this morning: everything is a farce."

"Yes?" I said in mock-sobriety.

"He just sat there listening." Benito's lips began stretching into an elastic grin that would not stay the same size. "Not saying a word. Only listening. And nodding his head in agreement."

Benito drank off half his beer as though he were just back from a three-day desert journey. "He didn't say a word. Not until the end of the hour."

"What then?"

For a moment Benito could do nothing with the grin. But finally he said: "At the end of the hour, he reached for an English dictionary on his desk and said: 'This word: *farce*. What does it mean?' "

That was almost a year ago. Now when Benito Rapello and I meet on the street or see each other on the terrace of the Café Mona he says: "This word, farce." And I say: "What does it mean, Lazarus?"

The Case
for the
 # Red Smith
Irregulars

It is considerably easier to say that Red Smith is the best sports writer in the business than to prove that Walter Wellesley Smith is a sports writer at all. The by-line of Walter (Red) Smith—the most widely syndicated in its field—emerges, painfully at times, from the type-writer of a small-boned, quiet man who has the look about him of one who would not be caught dead at a sporting event, even if he could get a ticket. What is more, as a contributor to a field of journalism that frequently seems ordained to be read with the lips, Smith is commandingly literate.

The effect of this vast anomaly is that the Smith column "Views of Sport," which appears in the New York *Herald Tribune* and about sixty other newspapers, has acquired a dedicated following of some four or five million daily readers, many of them certified eggheads. They read Smith as much for turn of phrase as for subject matter. No one else, they reason, is likely to cover a dog show and come away writing about "a Boston terrier in a crimson turtle-neck sweater, look-ing like the Harvard captain of '97." Of the pilgrims aboard a special Princeton football train en route to the Yale game, Smith wrote,

"There were so many crew haircuts that the tweedy passengers looked like a clipped privet hedge." Once, when fellow-columnist Jimmy Cannon quoted some Florida waitresses who said that fishermen as a breed were both abusive and poor tippers, fishing enthusiast Smith rose for the defense. "If Mr. Cannon says he has done research with waitresses," he wrote, "nobody has the right to dispute him. But if he talked fishing with 'em, it was the biggest form reversal since Jim Dandy won the Travers."

Although a good deal of his time is taken with the Big Four of American sports—baseball, football, horse racing, and boxing—Smith's columns, which appeared in book form so successfully in 1950 that a second compendium was published last year, have ranged from cock-fighting and Finnish sauna baths to duck-billed platypuses and the question of octogenarian delinquency in St. Petersburg, Florida. On one occasion, Smith devoted two columns hand-running to the eerie assertion that Sherlock Holmes was "a horse player of degenerate principles who thought nothing of fixing a race and probably had his syringe in the veins of more than one thoroughbred saddled by his mysterious acquaintance, 'Wilson, the notorious canary trainer.'" An excerpt from this unnerving thesis is here in point.

> Immediately after the Wessex [Smith wrote], Holmes gave further evidence of his insatiable lust for gambling. Silver Blaze's owner, Colonel Ross, was howling for information about his horse, but the detective cut him off with: "As I stand to win a little on this next race, I shall defer a lengthy explanation." Note those words: "I stand to win a little." Not: "I am risking a trifle on the next race." Holmes knew there was no risk. At the track he left nothing to chance.
>
> As best he was able, the discreet Watson suppressed reference to his idol's nefarious activities on the turf. For example, he alluded only obliquely to Holmes's connection with "Wilson, the notorious canary trainer." But Watson's very reticence is in itself revealing. How could a canary trainer become notorious if he stayed with canaries? There is absolutely nothing whatsoever in any way, shape, or form notorious about canaries. A bird trainer, however, can branch out, as Hirsch Jacobs has demonstrated in our day; Mr. Jacobs began with pigeons and went on to become America's leading horse trainer in eleven of twelve consecutive years.

This unearthly inquiry, which Smith abandoned only after hinting broadly that Holmes also had a hand in rigging the Oxford-Cambridge Rugby match, was printed just before Smith attended, by invitation, the annual banquet of the Baker Street Irregulars. The name of this group—which is essentially a highbrow Sherlock Holmes fan club—is peculiarly suggestive; it might not be inappropriate to make a case for another organization known collectively as the Red Smith Irregulars. It seems a fair way to describe Smith's admirers, who originate at all points of the social compass.

The ranks of dyed-in-the-wool Smith fans have included Robert E. Sherwood, Shirley Jackson, Rocky Graziano, Mark Van Doren, Ernest Hemingway, and—though it rests uneasy upon Smith's mind —Beau Jack, the former lightweight champion of the world. Smith learned of Jack's devotion through one of a series of subway and commuter-train advertisements the *Herald Tribune* ran some years back, in which famous figures were depicted praising the newspaper's reporters in their fields. In the field of sports, it was Beau Jack saying, "I like Red Smith's column!" Beau Jack was nationally famous for being able neither to read nor write.

No such allegation can be leveled, of course, at Miss Jackson, who said in the *New York Times* that reading Smith's first book, *Out of the Red,* was "like looking into Chapman's Homer"; nor, for that matter, at Mr. Hemingway, whose own fondness for Smith's writings was expressed by the dispirited colonel in *Across the River and into the Trees.* At Columbia, Professor Van Doren has used Smith's columns as textual standards in his journalism classes. In being voted the sports-writing award of the National Headliners' Club, Smith was hailed as a throwback to the golden age of sports, the 'twenties, which produced not only their Tildens, Granges, and Ruths but sports writers to match. The names of Grantland Rice, Ring Lardner, Damon Runyon, Paul Gallico, Davis Walsh, Bill McGeehan, and Hype Igoe tripped as easily off the tongues of sports fanciers as did those of the athletes themselves.

With the death of Rice, Red Smith became, statistically in terms of syndication, the number one sports writer in the country. He was at the time forty-nine years of age, with an annual income of $30,000, a home in Stamford, Connecticut, and the assurance that no sports event of any consequence, anywhere, was complete without him. All of these were relatively late acquisitions; ten years before, Smith was a sports writer in Philadelphia, beset by that commonest of sports-writing ambitions—to get to New York. Indeed, when the call did come, it was not from a New York paper but from the Brooklyn *Eagle* instead. Smith reasoned, not inexpertly, that Brooklyn was farther away from New York than Philadelphia was. He remained where he was, and betimes Stanley Woodward, then sports editor of the *Herald Tribune*, signed him up.

Smith already had, of course, a sizable reputation in the trade. His newspaper career, including general-news and copy-desk work, had taken him from the Milwaukee *Sentinel*, to the St. Louis *Star*, to the Philadelphia *Record*. It turned him into a sports writer when, in St. Louis, the management of the *Star* fired the whole sports staff and threw Smith into the breach. Perhaps it was this casual approach to his specialty, coupled with the sane conviction that when all is said and done the field of sports is essentially fun and games, that helped keep Smith from joining the ranks of the breathless, or Golly Moses, school of sports reporting. Smith's style of writing is essentially sparse: it prefers the verb to the noun and the noun to the adjective. He is bemused by the creations of some of his colleagues, especially sports broadcasters. "Suppose," he once wrote thoughtfully in a column discussing the tribulations of the typical sportscaster, "—maybe it's an outlandish hypothesis, but after all, we're just supposing—he should lapse into English."

Smith's writings frequently display wonderment, but never awe. His own athletic career was limited to a lone one-mile race as a member of the track team at Notre Dame. He came in last. Slight of build, he has worn eyeglasses, for the correction of nearsightedness, since his boyhood in Green Bay, Wisconsin. His nickname derives from a now-thinning stand of red hair, which, receding from an already high forehead, has left in his long oval face and clear blue eyes a look of sheer scholarship. His brow is ribbed by furrows which do not increase in number when he concentrates, which is often, or frowns, which is seldom.

"It's a good thing Red don't get mad," a Brownsville admirer has said. "If he did, how could you tell?"

Probably the maddest that Smith ever got in print was in 1947, when a report reached his ears that Happy Chandler, the then-unhappy commissioner of baseball, was claiming that a junta of leading sports writers, Smith included, was conspiring to do him in. "And I wouldn't be surprised," Chandler was reported as alleging further, "if there's a lot of money behind it."

With infrequent exception, Smith favors the third-person style in his columns, but he made a point of departure here.

"I wish to state, using the first person," he wrote, "that if I can get paid for thinking Happy Chandler has performed like a clown and a mountebank, then I want all that kind of money I can get. Ordinarily I have to work for mine."

When, some four years later, Chandler was ousted as commissioner, Smith could be heard to murmur that, "Nothing that Happy Chandler did in his six unquiet years as baseball commissioner became him so well as his leave-taking. . . . Not many men can achieve an air of perfect nonchalance when they have been publicly divested of their pants."

It is a rule with Smith that he seldom rides to battle, and then only against the high and the mighty, such as the multimillionaire management of the New York Yankees. Once, when the entire sporting world was up in arms over a close play at the plate in a vital pennant game at Yankee Stadium, Smith, eyes trained on the play, delivered his verdict.

"Only an idiot," he wrote, "would base an opinion on what he could see from the Black Hole of Calcutta that serves as a press box in Yankee Stadium. On a big day it is all anyone can do to cover a game from that slum, let alone umpire it."

Another time, when the Yankees established separate dining and club quarters underneath the stands for moneyed patrons, Smith observed that almost all of the members of this society were listed "in either the Social Register or the telephone directory."

Unlike some of his colleagues, however, Smith has not sought to establish himself as a branch official of the Better Business Bureau. He delights in the twilight world of sports, the fringe area where gather the six-day bicycle riders, the punch-drunk sparring partners, the channel swimmers, and the seriocomic athletic directors of our great universities.

"Views of Sport" is peopled with characters. One of these, who appears frequently in the column simply as "Butch," is a Brooklyn clothing salesman named Feldman who is old in the ways of what is known in the city streets as "action"—policy, numbers, horses, dice, cards.

"The cop on the beat says why don't we go play in a cellar somewheres and he won't bother us," Smith quotes Butch as saying. "What he don't understand is if five guys go to play in a cellar, why, there's only five guys in the game. But if you play on a corner a couple of truck-drivers come down out of their trucks and maybe a Department of Sanitation guy gets in it and maybe even a cop will stop by for a pass or two. On the corner there is fresh money all the time."

Smith has what is known in the trade as a photographic ear. "You listen for that key line," he has said. "You want to interview someone so that next day, when it comes out in the column, a third person who was there at the interview will say, 'Look at that! They talked for an hour, the guy never took a note, and here it all is, word for word.' Actually, it isn't word for word, of course. You've just listened for that typical expression, and that makes the whole thing read like a verbatim transcript."

Smith's reluctance to take notes during an interview amounts almost to an obsession. Once, he talked with an Australian jockey for upwards of an hour.

"'e never took a note," the horseman reported afterward, in awe. "Not till just before the very end, when I give 'im the names of three of me mounts. 'e wrote them down, but 'e apologized for it. Said 'e could never remember the names of 'orses."

"If you could get mad at Red for anything," a friend has said, "it's that note-taking business. Once I gave him some stuff for a column, over a lunch table, and there were a couple of guys whose names were part of the story. I spelled the names for him, and then I wrote them out on the back of an envelope and handed it to him. He said thanks, and next day there was the whole column—except for those two names."

Smith is wide open to suggestions for column material. A phone call to him at the *Herald Tribune* usually gets him direct, and the most outrageous ideas of a penny-ante huckster may stir him to action. "You get so you sense what will make a column and what won't," Smith said not long ago. "You walk around with antennae that quiver when a column is there."

Once he is on to something, however, he does it all himself—from the leg-work down to writing the four cross-lines, one of which will be used to caption his column and the others to separate paragraphs. His concern with the question of taking notes (he feels that it hampers the flow of conversation during an interview) is heightened by the fact that he does so much interview work. Nowadays, it is only at rare intervals that Smith actually spot-covers an event. That task is generally left to another member of the *Herald Tribune* sports staff; a situation which Smith does not find unpleasant, for both out of habit and preference, he is a slow worker.

"I have always taken a dim view," he reports, "of those sports writers who were supposed to be at their best 'under the guns'—you know, going against that deadline, half drunk."

His late, dear friend Joe H. Palmer, whom Smith described, in the dedication to his latest book V*iews of Sport,* as "the best writer I ever knew," was, Smith thinks, one of the few exceptions. Palmer, who covered horse racing for the *Herald Tribune,* was a former professor of English. "He not only wrote fast," Smith said, "but he used the touch system. It used to get me mad as hell. His stuff not only was effortless, it even *looked* effortless. And it was beautiful.". . .

Smith writing a column is something to behold. "Every day," he has said, "you bleed a little." He adopted a policy of agonizing reappraisal long before John Foster Dulles. Sometimes he will dwell for half an hour on a single word. Among other things, he has to fight off the strong writer's weakness for puns. Fortunately for his readers, he is not always successful in holding off. Covering the Olympic Games at Helsinki in 1952, he expressed doubt as to the reliability of Soviet track and field records.

"Western skeptics," he wrote, describing the background of a Red runner named Kazantsev, "suspected the Russian had been clocked by a *Pravda* copyreader while running down a flight of steppes."

One time in New York, when second baseman Junior Gilliam of the Dodgers had had a big night in a game against the Giants, Smith began his column with: "There is no balm in Gilliam for the Giants." Then he added, "And that'll be enough of that," and went on to discuss another subject.

Baseball is one of Smith's favorite sports to cover. There are two others—boxing and horse racing. "I used to be a nut on football," he recounts. "I couldn't get enough of it. In Philadelphia, I'd cover Villanova or Temple Friday night, Penn on Saturday, the pro game on Sunday, and then the high-school city championship. But it sort of faded on me after the two-platoon system came in; and besides, all the press boxes at football fields seem to be a lot higher than they used to."

When asked to select his favorite columns, however, Smith is wont to point to the ones that concern horses, his Brooklyn buddy Butch, and fishing. Smith gets in a good deal of trout and bass fishing (he has described the black bass as a "derby-wearing, cigar-smoking fish to whom a hook in the mouth is no worse than a bad cold") when he vacations each summer at the home of his parents in Sturgeon Bay, Wisconsin, a fishing paradise. The period just before vacation each year is the only time at which Smith attempts to get a few columns ahead. Ordinarily, his is a day-to-day effort. He knew a fellow columnist in Philadelphia who at one point was one hundred and five columns ahead.

"My God," Smith said to him, "what if you should drop dead tomorrow? That's half a year's work for nothing."

"Red couldn't write ahead if he wanted to," a friend has said. "He's not a machine. He's *human*."

Red Smith does provide warm, attentive company. He is hardly offended by the Saxon vocabulary of the sports world, and a tolerance for Scotch and cigarettes proves helpful. Some of his closest friends are sports people, like columnist Frank Graham of the New York *Journal-American*. But even though he has a strictly newspaper background—he majored in journalism at Notre Dame, and his brother Art is a rewrite man on the New York *Daily News*—Smith has exceeded the boundary lines of his profession. The following paragraph, taken from a Smith column depicting a bass-fishing excursion, is offered in illustration.

> There should have been a vast and congested bass population alongside the patches of water hyacinth in the rushes, just off the tough, elephant-eared weeds they call "bonnets," and around the roots and knees of the big cypress trees that stand out in the water like bathers. The lures splashed and popped and jiggled on the surface. Nothing else happened.

To use a word that Red Smith never uses, Wow.

JOHN FISCHER

How to
 Cure
Bird-Watchers

One of our readers—a young woman living in Sacramento—has writ·
ten to ask whether there is any known cure for bird-watching. Her
father, she says, keeps gawking around the neighborhood with field
glasses, often at unseemly hours. This causes embarrassment to her
and her friends. Only last week a couple parked in a quiet lane was
startled by the old gentleman at an unfortunate moment, and matters
weren't helped much by his explanation that he was only looking for
a spiny-toed nightingale.

The lady has come to the right place. This is a service magazine,
in a soulful kind of way. We aim to help with the spiritual problems
of our readers, just as *McCall's* takes care of the grosser human needs
by printing all those articles about forty-three new ways to cook hamburger. Besides I have been plagued by birds for years, and while I
can't say that I've learned to cope with them I at least know how to
give them a good fight.

It is true that I have never suffered myself from bird-watching.
Since childhood, when I was forced to take care of a herd of malevo-
lent chickens, I have regarded all varieties of *Aves Neognathae* as
smelly, noisy, feather-brained, hysterical little beasts, from which any
sensitive man naturally averts his eyes. Nevertheless at a tender age I

stumbled by accident on a sure-fire remedy for the affliction. The only difficulty is that the young woman will have to persuade her father to do his bird-watching, at least once, barefooted and along the banks of some southern stream. The Suwannee River would serve. Or Dead Man's Bayou.

My own discovery was made on Sweetwater Creek in northern Texas. I was after catfish, using a No. 6 hook baited with boiled potato. (This method is neither as sporting nor as efficient as dynamite, but my parents—who had never heard of Dr. Spock and permissive child-raising—discouraged me from playing with explosives.) So I was ambling along barefoot, brooding over parental tyranny and looking hard for one of those muddy backwaters where catfish hold their committee meetings.

All of a sudden my left foot came down on something unpleasant. I had never stepped on a water moccasin before, but somehow I knew right off what to do. The moccasin is a fat and sluggish snake, and before he knew what was squushing him I was ten feet in the air; and by the time he got his fangs cleared for action, I had hit the ground about five yards off in a high lope.

Ever since I have been a compulsive snake-watcher. Anyone, I believe, who has felt the coils of a water moccasin under his toes will thereafter keep his eyes firmly on the ground. Never again is he likely to be bothered with the sight of birds, aside from sandpipers and those little squinch owls that live in prairie-dog holes.

Even a reformed bird-watcher, however, is by no means out of the woods. With any decent animal—a grizzly, for instance—you can be reasonably sure that if you don't bother him, he won't bother you. But not birds; they seek out their victims with the vindictive persistence of the Kremlin's secret police. If you go to earth, so to speak, on the twenty-fourth floor of a Manhattan apartment, a posse of pigeons is sure to turn up at six the next morning to hoot and sneer at you from the window sill. Starlings will build a nest in the intake of your air conditioner. Or you will find, as one inoffensive New Yorker did recently, that something of the order *Columbiformes* has flown right inside and laid an egg on your bedspread.

Take the case of George and Helen Papashvily, sculptor and writer, who sought tranquility in the upper fastnesses of Bucks County. They had hardly got the plumbing into their old stone farmhouse when they were beset by a retarded cardinal.

Like so many of his genus, he was belligerent as well as stupid. For weeks he carried on a running battle with his own reflection in the dining-room window—swooping into the pane like a *kamikaze* pilot, beating it with his wings, and pecking at it till his beak dripped blood. The round ended when he had knocked himself out or collapsed on the grass in exhaustion.

At this point the Papashvilys—who are kindly to the verge of simple-mindedness and constantly imposed upon by man and beast—would rise wearily from their dining-table and rescue the dope. After they had trickled brandy down his throat with an eye dropper, plied him with smelling salts, and pressed cold towels to his forehead, he usually revived enough for another assault.

This might have kept up indefinitely, or anyhow until the brandy ran out, if a she-cardinal hadn't come along one day and diverted him to other interests. They are now, presumably, populating the thickets of northern Pennsylvania with generation after generation of half-witted *Richmondena*.

Smart birds are even worse. Everything that wears feathers is a criminal at heart—as Dr. A. C. Bent demonstrated in his classic fourteen-volume *Life Histories of North American Birds*—but the elite of this over-world obviously are the crows. They are as well organized as the Mafia, and more cunning. Nobody has ever rounded up a gang of crows in an Apalachin farmhouse.

The reason is that—unlike Barbara, Genovese & Co.—crows do their conspiring in an open field, with guards posted to cover every approach. These sentries apparently carry binoculars, and are trained not only to spot a gun at five hundred yards but to tell whether it is a rifle or shotgun; and they have learned the range of each. Consequently, as every hunter knows, they are about the most elusive game on this continent.

I once tried to beat their system by sneaking up on a crow convention in a station wagon. They know that autos are harmless, and ordinarily pay them no attention. So I pulled up, in an offhand way, beside a pasture where maybe twenty-five of them were plotting their next job.

Sure enough, after one contemptuous glance they went right on with their scheming. I rolled down a window. Still no alarm. Then I reached for the carbine I had hidden under a gunny sack, and started to poke it—slowly and cautiously—over the sill. Not more than an inch of the muzzle was sticking out when the nearest sentry saw it, recognized instantly what it was, and blew the whistle. The whole gang took off, jeering vulgarly, before I could get in a shot.

The only practical way to outwit a crow is with dynamite, the sportsman's best friend on water or land. Here is a tested recipe, bearing the Harper's Seal of Approval:

First you find a thicket of shinnery oaks where crows gather to roost. These scrubby little trees grow in dense clumps all over the Texas Panhandle; they make an ideal lair for crows, as they once did for horse thieves and train robbers. As many as five thousand birds may infest a single clump.

At daybreak they leave in small bands, scattering over miles of countryside on their criminal pursuits—stealing pheasant eggs, devastating grain fields, pecking the eyes out of newborn calves. As soon as you are sure they are all gone, you slip into the shinnery and start stringing up your dynamite. Half-sticks will do, tied to branches at about head height and spaced roughly five yards apart all through the thicket. Their detonators all have to be connected to a single wire, which runs to a hiding place a safe distance away—usually a neighboring patch of brush. There you wait, beside your storage battery and switch, until the enemy comes home at sundown.

This is the crucial moment. You have to lie well-ambushed and absolutely still; for if an advance patrol spots you, it will warn the whole flock—which at once will line out for another roost miles away. If you escape detection, however, you simply bide your time until the whole colony is assembled; then close the switch. The results are gratifying. A rain of black feathers, shinnery leaves, and crows' feet will cover the landscape for acres around.

In our struggle with the birds, the most dangerous chink in man's armor is sentimentality. They are alert for any sign of this weakness; and, as we have seen in The Papashvily Case, they know how to take instant advantage of it.

My aunt Annie was, I guess, the softest-hearted woman in Comanche County, Oklahoma. For many years she lived on a homestead there, keeping house for her widower father. One Christmas a neighbor gave her a jar of brandied cherries and—though Annie disapproved of liquor even in semi-solid form—the guests at dinner that night managed to put away the whole quart.

In her thrifty way, Annie saved the pits and fed them next morning to her flock of hens. This was meant in the kindliest spirit—Annie felt that even Plymouth Rocks deserved a Christmas treat—but it turned out to be a mistake. When Annie went out at noon to collect the eggs, she found every one of the chickens lying stone cold dead with its claws sticking up stiff in the air.

Crushed by grief as she was, she didn't mean to let those chickens go to waste. Annie couldn't bring herself to chop off their heads—that was man's work anyhow, and could wait till her father came in from plowing the northeast forty—but she could at least begin to get them ready for the cold-storage locker. With tears sliding down her nose, and muttering prayers against the evil of drink, she plucked them all —carefully saving the feathers for pillow-stuffing. Then she laid the corpses in a row along the shady side of the barn to await the ax.

Trouble was, they didn't stay dead. When her father brought in the team at supper time, he encountered a spectacle which, he said, beat anything he had seen since the night when a Kiowa war party scalped the whole village of Chillicothe. Twenty-three hens were staggering around the barnyard—over-hung, shivering, and naked as September Morn.

The sight so scandalized the mules—a high-strung pair at best—that it took him twenty minutes to get off the harness.

Annie worked all night, cutting up old burlap bags and sewing them into hen chemises, while her outraged flock huddled squawking behind the stove. By morning they were the best-dressed chickens in Oklahoma; but they didn't seem to appreciate it. For the next six weeks, while they were growing a new crop of feathers, they wore their smocks with a look both sheepish and hang-dog—which, for chickens, is quite a trick. I am willing to grant (grudgingly) that they, anyhow, must have been birds worth watching.

ROBERT GRAVES

 Catkind

Through my window,
Listening carefully,
I overheard a low
Moonlight murmur from an olive-tree—
Three cats rehearsed the virtues of catkind:
Catkind's silky tread and devious mind,
Catkind's quiet economy
(Cleansing itself with wash of its own body),
Catkind's nonchalance,
Catkind's persistence,
Catkind's circumambulance,
Its fealty to the Queen of Cats above—
"But when we love," they wailed, "alas,
    we LOVE!"

MILTON MAYER

The Girl

 from

Sewickley, Pa.

Like (I suppose) most people, I don't get to Pittsburgh much. As a matter of fact, I never get there, except for a lecture every second year or so, and then—the way one does on a lecture tour, in a town where he isn't closely acquainted—I bounce in and out. I was there a while back, en route from Columbus to Erie, and on the way in from the Pittsburgh airport I saw a sign which read:

SEWICKLEY 2

Sewickley, Sewickley. Come, now—where and when and how had I had to do with Sewickley? I couldn't think, and I let it go. I had an hour to wait for the train to Erie and I killed it looking in the windows of the secondhand stores across the bridge from the P. & L. E. station. I got a copy of the *Post-Gazette* and got on the train and got something to eat in the diner. When I came back to my seat it was dark and the lighting was bad, so I watched what little there was to watch out the window.

And then I remembered. I remembered Aix-les-Bains and Dorking Town and Sewickley.

I remembered a day in the summer of 1927, a quarter-century ago.

I was nineteen. We were traveling, my mother and father and my older brother and I, from Rome on the *petit grand tour Américain,* and they got on the train at Aix, twenty American college girls jabbering English. Of course they saw me from the platform. I was sitting at the window, my chin on my folded hands (and my folded hands on the pearl handle of my Malacca stick), staring emptily out, above and beyond the jabbering crowd on the platform, into the empty distance. Of course they saw me: a man still young in years but worn with unutterable sophistication.

Of course they saw me, because they came rollicking through the train to their seats in the car behind us and rollicking back, a little later, to the dining-car ahead. I was still staring emptily out, in my pearl-gray spats, and my pearl-gray suit, and my pearl-gray hat, and my stick; Frenchman, likely, but one of those Frenchmen who belong to no country and to whom every country has, to its edification, belonged.

I was aroused by my father, who said, "Get a move on, boy. This is our sitting for lunch. Have you washed your hands?" My hands were encased in pearl-gray gloves.

"He hasn't washed them since he got those gloves," said my brother.

"Wash your hands," said my mother, "and come on. We'll be in the diner. But for pity's sake—hurry."

Beneath the double-breasted jacket of my pearl-gray suit was a pair of red suspenders, purchased in Rome the day before; the whim of a man whom red suspenders and red suspenders alone would move from an ennui begotten of absolutely every other experience. My father, when I bought them, said, "You're crazy, boy." My mother said, "He'll grow up," and my brother said, "When?" They were my first suspenders, and my brother said, "Don't forget to pull them up after you've been to the bathroom."

I washed my hands and went into the dining-car. On my right arm I carried my pearl-gray hat, in my left hand my pearl-gray gloves and my stick, on which I leaned, walking with a loose limp that would hardly deceive anyone who had watched the performance of the dying roué in "The Fool," which had been on the road a season or two before.

The American girls filled almost the whole of the diner, and our table was at the far end. As I entered the car, a falling hush reached my half-consciousness. My face was a pallid mask, my eyes fixed on nothingness—for which the Cinzano advertisement on the farther door of the dining-car sufficed. But the hush was broken by a giggle arising from girl to girl and from table to table after I passed. And the incidence of the giggle, proceeding, even as I proceeded, from the back to the front of the car, was not to be mistaken. The pallid mask of my face turned red.

As I turned around and sat down, my brother whispered to me, "You forgot to pull up your suspenders."

A week later we reached the Hotel Cecil in London, to spend three days before we sailed on the *Mauretania*. With my stick I managed to get up the broad stone steps, and my brother said to the doorman, "You'd better take his arm. He's in the last stages." In the lobby were two of the American girls who had been on the train from Aix. Coming down in the elevator for dinner were two more. They were all staying at the Cecil.

The first day I didn't go out at all. I explained my behavior to my parents as a general lassitude arising, I thought, from a number of worries, "the worst of which," said my brother, "is that pack of girls who laughed at him in the diner." The second day I had breakfast in the room and went downstairs at eleven, when the girls were sure to be out on tour. One of them was alone with me in the elevator. She said, "Hello," and I bowed from the neck.

"How long are you staying?" she said.

I stared at her.—How long did a man like me, in my condition, know he was staying, and where?—She was the first of the lot I had really looked at, or through. She was not the prettiest. She was very tall (like me), spare, knuckly, small-featured. And nice. Really nice. And pretty enough. "Until Thursday," I said.

"So are we," she said. "Are you going back on the *Ile?*"

"No, on the *Mauretania.*"

"Oh," she said, "that's too bad," and then she pulled herself up, the way you do when you might blush, and said, "I mean it's so good to have someone to talk English—American—to," and she laughed a nice laugh compounded of embarrassment and friendliness. I held my stick behind me, and when we got out of the elevator I left it there alongside the car.

We talked some more and she said that the other girls were out on a rubberneck tour but she hadn't felt so well and, besides, she liked to go places alone once in a while, you never had a chance to when you were in a tour. I understood that, and I said so, and we went for a walk, and when we came back she said, "Thanks for coming with me. I don't really like to go *alone,* and I get kind of scared, even when they speak English. But this is the end of the tour and we've all been together seven weeks."

I asked her what she'd be doing tomorrow, and she said it was their last day and she guessed there would be something scheduled and they'd have to pack and all—and I said, "You can pack tomorrow night. So can I. Why don't you say you're not feeling well at breakfast and I'll meet you in the lobby at ten and we'll go somewhere."

"Where?" she said.

"*Really*," I said, and my pearl-gray limp came back, "there are dozens of places out of London—it's your first time over, isn't it?"

She said it was, and didn't ask me if it was mine.

"Well, then," I said, "I'll arrange something, and we'll be back at five."

I hot-footed it to the American Express Company, and one of the clerks, when I asked him where a fellow and his girl ought to go on their last day in England, said, "Why, Dorking."

So we went to Dorking Town.

I don't know, now, what it was like or how we got there. (By train, I suppose.) I remember a buggy, and village lanes, and a teashop, and that's all. And I may as well say that all of the details of this story (except the pearl-gray outfit; there's a snapshot of me in it) are only what the lawyers, when the witness shakes his head, call "your best recollection, if you please." It was a quarter-century ago, and, as bad money drives out good on the market, so bad history, of which we have had a lot this quarter-century, drives out good in the memory.

I remember, as I say, that she was tall and spare. She was dark—at least she wasn't a yellow blonde. I remember that her fingers were long, so I must have held her hand that day—but it may have been only in getting on or off the train. I don't remember what we talked about, except that we didn't talk about the dining-car from Aix. She never once said she'd seen me before—she was that nice—and that, I suppose, is why I fell in love with her in the elevator in the Cecil.

I remember that we got back to London later than we intended to, and we said good-by. I must have promised to call her in New York, or to write her, and we must have exchanged addresses. Well—I had a girl back home and she may have had a boy. I know that we never wrote or saw each other again. I don't remember where she was going to school. I don't remember her name. I remember that she lived in a town I had never heard of—Sewickley, Pa.

And what if I went to Sewickley and found her? I'm forty-eight years old and happily married, and I hope she is, too. Besides, 1956 is not 1927, and, while we lean people wear pretty well, I'm not the blade I was—or pretended to be. And women wear worse than men. Or at least they act as if they do, and like as not she is no longer lean but gaunt.

Sewickley isn't Chicago, either. It's suburban rich (I've learned) and always has been, and I suppose she's solid, maybe shallow, or even country-club, in all her views (there's no reason that I can think of why she shouldn't be: neither of us had any views at all, in Dorking), and I'm a rheumy old radical. I can get myself shined up for occasions, but what in the world would we talk about? If a real love affair is best ended when it ends, how much more so a day that began and ended in Dorking?

And how would I find her if I wanted to? Go from house to house in Sewickley? And is the impossibility (as I suppose) of finding her the reason that I'm afraid that the next time I'm in Pittsburgh I'll try to? I might advertise in the *Post-Gazette* personals, but how would the ad read?—

> DORKING TOWN.—Will yng lady (1927) spent happy day yng man write Box 297?

I'd do better to put my ad in the lost-and-found column:

> LOST.—My 19th yr. Sntmntl. value to loser. Lib. rwrd. of any 10 yrs. since for return of same.

Philosophy
of
Punitive
Action

All my life I have been a thing-smasher. I don't mean by this that I habitually smash things through unintentional clumsiness. I mean that when things—machines, gadgets, cobblestones, sharp corners, low ceilings—fail to function, trip me up, or come into violent contact with me, I give them a good swift poke or kick or otherwise mete out the punishment that the perversity of inanimate objects so richly deserves. On the other hand, I have seldom struck a fellow-being.

This policy has been instinctive with me as far back as I can remember. When I was a boy of seven or eight our house had a mouse pestilence, and my father staked me to some traps and promised me a bounty of five cents for every mouse I caught. I remember distinctly that I had much more trouble with the mousetraps than I ever did with the mice. The mice of course sometimes sprang the traps and escaped with the bait, but, after all, the mice didn't pretend to be on my side of the contest. The traps did, and that was what made me mad. The flat or single mousetrap is a high-tension hair-trigger affair, and it is apt to snap when you are trying to set it. As a rule I was cautious enough to avoid getting my fingers caught when the traps misfired, but the shock of the sudden unexpected *snap!* annoyed me exceedingly.

One day I was careless enough to permit my finger to get caught in one of these sudden misfires. Without delay I rushed out of the pantry, where the mutiny had occurred, ran through the kitchen, disengaging my finger from the trap as I ran, opened the kitchen door, and threw that trap against the stone wall in our back yard as hard as I could throw it. This didn't help the trap any, but it helped me immeasurably. I knew that from that minute on I was the master of that trap and that I could hurl it against the wall whenever I chose. Childishness? Perhaps, but one of the objects in life is to feel good, and whenever I threw a mousetrap I felt simply dandy. Hard on the trap? Well, was I created for the trap's benefit or the trap for mine?

My cousin still marvels at an event that took place in the Allegheny coal country when I was a lad of sixteen and he considerably younger. My family owned an old Model T Ford which I was permitted to drive and in which, on this occasion, he was a passenger. For some reason the car suddenly stalled. I knew it wasn't out of gas. I got out and cranked and cranked until I was nearly exhausted, but the car refused to start.

I wasn't too exhausted to stand up in front of that car and kick its radiator. With each kick I felt calmer, stronger, and more imbued with the sense of accomplishment. It didn't hurt my feet because I had good heavy shoes on, and it didn't damage the car to any extent. It smashed in a little of the radiator fluting, but I always felt that this gave the car character.

When I had kicked to my heart's content I walked to the nearest garage, not in despair but in triumph, and told them to get the car and fix it. I knew nothing about what makes an automobile go, and I still don't; if I had tried to tinker with it I should have got nowhere, and in the end I'd have walked away defeated, not victorious.

Too many people today tinker with perverse inanimate matter instead of punishing it. Most of them aren't qualified to cope with our complicated modern machines and gadgets anyhow, and their tinkering only makes matters worse. If it be objected that violence may also make matters worse, I emphasize that it can't possibly do the machine as much harm as it does good to the person who assaults it. I think tinkering should be left to the professional tinkerers, the repair men, who, goodness knows, need employment in these times.

Moreover, by occasionally damaging things we amateurs can create even more employment. This may not be very good economic reasoning, but it's as good as a lot I've seen in recent years.

No overhead beam or sharp corner or low ceiling has ever got away with hitting me in the head. I hit right back, and I hit harder—not with my head or my fist but with the nearest available weapon. In fact, that is an important rule for revenge on inanimate objects. The inexperienced person is apt to use his fist on heavy beams or brick walls, with unhappy results; I look round for a big stone or stick, a massive book, or something of that nature. True, this takes an instant's reflection, and most people, I am afraid, use this instant to regain their temper and decide not to strike at all.

This is wrong. I take great pains to keep my temper lost, so to speak, while I am looking round for something to retaliate with. I remember once barking my shins on a radiator in the dark. I turned on the lights, looked round for something to smack the radiator with, and couldn't find a thing in the room that would serve my purpose. So I went out to the tool shed, and got a hammer. I don't like to boast, but if I hadn't found a hammer in the tool shed I am certain that I should have had the patience to go and borrow one from a neighbor. If I ever let any object like that radiator get away with a mean act it would be a sign that my spirit had finally been crushed —as too many people's are, I fear—by the world of inert matter. I don't intend ever to let it be.

Most people who disavow punitive action on inanimate objects are the very ones who when misunderstandings arise between them and other people immediately fly off the handle and indulge in harsh language if not actual physical force. This is all wrong. I have said that few people are equipped to tinker successfully with *things*; but anybody with the power of speech and a modicum of intelligence is perfectly capable of reasoning sensibly with his fellow-beings—if only he weren't too lazy and impatient to do so.

Moreover, most of the things in this world were put in it, or at least formed into their present shape, by human beings and for the good of human beings, and are hence of secondary importance to man himself. Human beings have feelings and a sense of pain, whereas inanimate objects have not. So what is the sense of being patient and considerate with inert matter, created for man's betterment, and cruel to the beings who are, presumably, its masters? I think I have a point there too. Moreover, if you hit a human being he may hit you back even harder. I *know* I have a point *there*.

SHIRLEY JACKSON

The

 Third Baby's
the Easiest

Everyone says the third baby is the easiest one to have, and now I know why. It's the easiest because it's the funniest, because you've been there twice, and you know. You know, for instance, how you're going to look in a maternity dress about the seventh month, and you know how to release the footbrake on a baby carriage without fumbling amateurishly, and you know how to tie your shoes before and do knee-chests after, and while you're not exactly casual, you're a little bit off-hand about the whole thing. Sentimental people keep insisting that women go on to have a third baby because they love babies, and cynical people seem to maintain that a woman with two healthy, active children around the house will do *any*thing for ten quiet days in the hospital; my own position is somewhere between the two, but agree that the third is the easiest. The whole event is far too recent for me to be deluded.

Because it *was* my third I was saved a lot of unnecessary discomfort. No one sent me any dainty pink sweaters, for instance. We only received one pair of booties, and those were a pair of rosebud-covered white ones that someone had sent my first child when he was born and which I had given, still in their original pink tissue paper, to a friend when *her* first child was born; she had subsequently sent them to her cousin in Texas for a second baby, and the cousin sent them back East on the occasion of a mutual friend's twins; the mutual friend gave them to me, with a card saying "Love to Baby" and the pink tissue paper hardly ruffled. I have them carefully set aside, because I know someone who is having a baby in June.

I borrowed back my baby carriage from my next-door neighbor, took the crib down out of the attic, washed my way through the chest of baby shirts and woolen shawls, briefed the two incumbent children far enough ahead of time, and spent a loving and pains-taking month packing my suitcase. This time I knew exactly what I was taking with me to the hospital, but assembling it took time and eventually required an emergency trip to New York from our home in Vermont. I packed it, though, finally: a yellow nightgown trimmed with lace, a white nightgown that tied at the throat with a blue bow, two of the fanciest bed-jackets I could find—that was what I went to New York for—and then, two pounds of homemade fudge, as many mystery stories as I could cram in, and a bag of apples. Almost at the last minute I added a box of pralines, a bottle of expensive cologne, and my toothbrush. I have heard of people who take their own satin sheets to the hospital but that has always seemed to me a waste of good suitcase space.

My doctor was very pleasant and my friends were very thoughtful; for the last two weeks before I went to the hospital almost everyone I know called me almost once a day and said, "Haven't you gone *yet?*" My mother- and father-in-law settled on a weekend to visit us when, according to the best astronomical figuring, I should have had a two-weeks-old baby ready to show them; they arrived, were entertained with some restraint on my part, and left, eying me with disfavor and some suspicion. My mother sent me a telegram from California saying, "Is everything all right? Shall I come? Where is baby?" My children were sullen, my husband was embarrassed.

Everything was, as I say, perfectly normal, up to and including the frightful moment when I leaped out of bed at two in the morning as though there had been a pea under the mattress; when I turned on the light my husband said sleepily, "Having baby?"

"I really don't know," I said nervously. I was looking for the clock, which I hide at night so that in the morning when the alarm rings I will have to wake up looking for it. It was hard to find it without the alarm ringing.

"Shall I wake up?" my husband asked without any sign of pleased anticipation.

"I can't find the *clock*," I said.

"Clock?" my husband said. "Clock. Wake me five minutes apart."

I unlocked the suitcase and took out a mystery story, and sat down in the armchair with a blanket over me. After a few minutes the cat, who usually sleeps on the foot of my son's bed, wandered in and settled down on a corner of the blanket by my feet. She slept as peacefully as my husband did most of the night, except that now and then she raised her head to regard me with a look of silent contempt.

Because we live in a small country town and our hospital is five miles away I had an uneasy feeling that I ought to allow plenty of time, particularly since neither of us has ever learned to drive and consequently I must call our local taxi to take me to the hospital. At seven-thirty I called my doctor and we chatted agreeably for a few minutes, and I said I would just give the children their breakfast and wash up the dishes and then run over to the hospital, and he said that would be just fine and he'd plan to meet me later, then; the unspoken conviction between us was that I ought to be back in the fields before sundown.

I went into the kitchen and proceeded methodically to work, humming cheerfully and stopping occasionally to grab the back of a chair and hold my breath. My husband told me later that he found his cup and saucer (the one with "Father" written on it) in the oven, but I am inclined to believe that he was too upset to be a completely reliable reporter. My own recollection is of doing everything the way I have a thousand times before—school-morning short-cuts so familiar that I am hardly aware, usually, of doing them at all. The frying pan, for instance. My single immediate object was a cup of coffee, and I decided to heat up the coffee left from the night before, rather than take the time to make fresh; it seemed brilliantly logical to heat it in the frying pan because anyone knows that a broad shallow container will heat liquid faster than a tall narrow one, like the coffee pot. I will not try to deny, however, that it *looked* funny.

By the time the children came down everything seemed to be moving along handsomely; my son grimly got two glasses and filled them with fruit juice for his sister and himself. He offered me one, but I had no desire to eat, or in fact to do anything which might upset my precarious balance between two, and three, children, or to interrupt my morning's work for more than coffee, which I was still doggedly making in the frying pan. My husband came downstairs, sat in his usual place, said good-morning to the children, accepted the glass of fruit juice my son poured for him, and asked me brightly, "How do you feel?"

"Splendid," I said, making an enormous smile for all of them. "I'm doing wonderfully well."

"Good," he said. "How soon do you think we ought to leave?"

"Around noon, probably," I said. "Everything is fine, really."

My husband asked politely, "May I help you with breakfast?"

"No indeed," I said. I stopped to catch my breath and smiled reassuringly. "I feel *so* well," I said.

"Would you be offended," he said, still very politely, "if I took this egg out of my glass?"

"Certainly not," I said. "I'm sorry, I can't think how it got there."

"It's nothing at all," my husband said. "I was just thirsty."

They were all staring at me oddly, and I kept giving them my reassuring smile; I *did* feel splendid; my months of waiting were nearly over, my careful preparations had finally been brought to a purpose, tomorrow I would be wearing my yellow nightgown. "I'm *so* pleased," I said.

I was slightly dizzy, perhaps. And there *were* pains, but they were authentic ones, not the feeble imitations I had been dreaming up the past few weeks. I patted my son on the head. "Well," I said, in the tone I had used perhaps five hundred times in the last months. "Well, do we want a little boy or a little boy?"

"Won't you sit down?" my husband said. He had the air of a man who expects that an explanation will somehow be given him for a series of extraordinary events in which he is unwillingly involved. "I think you ought to sit down," he added urgently.

It was about then that I realized that he was right. I ought to sit down. As a matter of fact, I ought to go to the hospital, right now, immediately. I dropped my reassuring smile and the fork I had been carrying around with me.

"I'd better hurry," I said inadequately.

My husband called the taxi and brought down my suitcase. The children were going to stay with friends, and one of the things I had planned to do was drop them off on my way to the hospital; now, however, I felt vitally that I had not the time. I began to talk fast.

"You'll have to take care of the children," I told my husband. "See that . . ." I stopped. I remember thinking with incredible clarity and speed. "See that they finish their breakfast," I said. Pajamas on the line, I thought, school, cats, toothbrushes. Milkman. Overalls to be mended; laundry. "I ought to make a list," I said vaguely. "Leave a note for the milkman tomorrow night. Soap, too. We need soap."

"Yes, dear," my husband kept saying. "Yes dear yes dear."

The taxi arrived and suddenly I was saying good-by to the children. "See you later," my son said casually. "Have a good time."

"Bring me a present," my daughter added.

"Don't worry about a thing," my husband said.

"Now, don't you worry," I told him. "There's nothing to worry about."

"Everything will be *fine*," I said. "Don't worry."

I waited for a good moment and then scrambled into the taxi without grace; I did not dare risk my reassuring smile on the taxi driver but I nodded to him briskly.

"I'll be with you in an hour," my husband said nervously. "And don't worry."

"Everything will be fine," I said. "Don't worry."

"Nothing to worry about," the taxi driver said to my husband, and we started off, my husband standing at the curb wringing his hands and the taxi tacking insanely from side to side of the road to avoid even the slightest bump.

I sat very still in the back seat, trying not to breathe. I had one arm lovingly around my suitcase, which held my yellow nightgown, and I tried to light a cigarette without using any muscles except those in my hands and my neck, and still not let go of my suitcase.

"Going to be a beautiful day," I said to the taxi driver at last. We had a twenty-minute trip ahead of us at least—much longer, if he continued his zigzag path. "Pretty warm for the time of year."

"Pretty warm yesterday, too," the taxi driver said.

"It *was* warm yesterday," I conceded, and stopped to catch my breath. The driver, who was obviously avoiding looking at me in the mirror, said a little bit hysterically, "Probably be warm tomorrow, too."

I waited for a minute, and then I was able to say, dubiously, "I don't know as it will stay warm *that* long. Might cool off by tomorrow."

"Well," the taxi driver said, "it was sure warm *yesterday*."

"Yesterday," I said. "Yes, that was a warm day."

"Going to be nice today, too," the taxi driver said. I clutched my suitcase tighter and made some small sound—more like a yelp than anything else—and the taxi veered madly off to the left and then began to pick up speed with enthusiasm.

"Very warm indeed," the driver babbled, leaning forward against the wheel. "Warmest day I ever saw for the time of year. Usually this time of year it's colder. Yesterday it was *terribly*—"

"It was not," I said. "It was freezing. I can see the tower of the hospital."

"I remember thinking how warm it was," the driver said. He turned into the hospital drive. "It was so warm I noticed it right away. 'This is a warm day,' I thought, that's how warm it was."

We pulled up with a magnificent flourish at the hospital entrance, and the driver skittered out of the front seat and came around and opened the door and took my arm.

"My wife had five," he said. "I'll take the suitcase, Miss. Five, and never a minute's trouble with any of them."

He rushed me in through the door and up to the desk. "Here," he said to the desk clerk. "Pay me later," he said to me, and fled.

"Name?" the desk clerk said to me politely, her pencil poised.

"Name," I said vaguely. I remembered, and told her.

"Age?" she asked. "Sex? Occupation?"

"Writer," I said.

"Housewife," she said.

"Writer," I said.

"I'll just put down housewife," she said. "Doctor? How many children?"

"Two," I said. "Up to now."

"Normal pregnancy?" she said. "Blood test? X-ray?"

"Look—" I said.

"Husband's name?" she said. "Address? Occupation?"

"Just put down housewife," I said. "I don't remember *his* name, really."

"Legitimate?"

"What?" I said.

"Is your husband the father of this child? Do you have a husband?"

"Please," I said plaintively, "Can I go on upstairs?"

"Well, *really*," she said, and sniffed. "You're *only* having a baby."

She waved delicately to a nurse, who took me by the same arm everybody else had been using that morning, and in the elevator this nurse was very nice. She asked me twice how I was feeling and said "Maternity?" to me politely as we left the elevator; I was carrying my own suitcase by then.

Two more nurses joined us upstairs; we made light conversation while I got into the hospital nightgown. The nurses had all been to some occupational party the night before and one of them had been simply a riot; she was still being a riot while I undressed, because every now and then one of the two other nurses would turn around to me and say, "Isn't she a riot, honestly?"

I made a few remarks, just to show that I too was lighthearted and not at all nervous; I commented laughingly on the hospital night-gown, and asked with amusement tinged with foreboding what was the apparatus they were wheeling in on the tray.

My doctor arrived about half an hour later; he had obviously had three cups of coffee and a good cigar; he patted me on the shoulder said, "How do we feel?"

"Pretty well," I said, with an uneasy giggle that ended in a squawk. "How long do you suppose it will be before—"

"We don't need to worry about *that* for a while yet," the doctor said. He laughed pleasantly, and nodded to the nurses. They all bore down on me at once. One of them smoothed my pillow, one of them held my hand, and the third one stroked my forehead and said "After all, you're *only* having a baby."

"Call me if you want me," the doctor said to the nurses as he left. "I'll be downstairs in the coffee shop."

"*I'll* call you if I need you," I told him ominously, and one of the nurses said in a honeyed voice, "Now, look, we don't want our husband to get all worried."

I opened one eye; my husband was sitting, suddenly, beside the bed. He looked as though he were trying not to scream. "They *told* me to come in here," he said. "I was trying to find the waiting room."

"The other end of the hall," I told him grimly. I pounded on the bell and the nurse came running. "Get him out of here," I said, waving my head at my husband.

"They *told* me—" my husband began, looking miserably at the nurse.

"It's al-l-l-l-l right," the nurse said. She began to stroke my forehead again. "Hubby belongs right here."

"Either he goes or I go," I said.

The door slammed open and the doctor came in. "Heard you were here," he said jovially, shaking my husband's hand. "Look a little pale."

My husband smiled weakly.

"Never lost a father yet," the doctor said, and slapped him on the back. He turned to me. "How do we feel?" he said.

"Terrible," I said, and the doctor laughed again. "Just on my way downstairs," he said to my husband. "Come along?"

No one seemed, actually, to go or come that morning; I would open my eyes and they were there, open my eyes again and they were gone. This time, when I opened my eyes, a pleasant-faced nurse was standing beside me; she was swabbing my arm with a piece of cotton. Although I am ordinarily timid about hypodermics I welcomed this one with what was almost a genuine echo of my old reassuring smile. "Well, well," I said to the nurse. "Sure glad to see *you.*"

"Sissy," she said distinctly, and jabbed me in the arm.

"How soon will this wear off?" I asked her with deep suspicion; I am always afraid with nurses that they feel that the psychological effect of a hypodermic is enough, and that I am actually being inoculated with some useless, although probably harmless, concoction.

"You won't even notice," she said enigmatically, and left.

The hypodermic hit me suddenly, and I began to giggle about five minutes after she left. I was alone in the room, lying there giggling to myself, when I opened my eyes and there was a woman standing beside the bed. She was human, not a nurse; she was wearing a baggy blue bathrobe. "I'm across the hall," she said. "I been hearing you."

"I was laughing," I said, with vast dignity.

"I heard you," she said. "Tomorrow it might be me, maybe."

"You here for a baby?"

"Someday," she said gloomily. "I was here two weeks ago, I was having pains. I come in the morning and that night they said to me, 'Go home, wait a while longer.' So I went home, and I come again three days later, I was having pains. And they said to me, 'Go home, wait a while longer.' And so yesterday I come again, I was having pains. So far they let me stay."

"That's too bad," I said.

"I got my mother there," she said. "She takes care of everything and sees the meals made, but she's beginning to think I got her there with false pretenses."

"That's too bad," I said. I began to pound the wall with my fists.

"Stop that," she said. "Somebody'll hear you. This is my third. The first two—nothing."

"This is *my* third," I said. "I don't care who hears me."

"My kids," she said. "Every time I come home they say to me, 'Where's the baby?' My mother too. My husband, he keeps driving me over and driving me back."

"They kept telling me the third was the easiest," I said. I began to giggle again.

"There you go," she said. "Laughing your head off. I wish *I* had something to laugh at."

She waved her hand at me and turned and went mournfully through the door. I opened my same weary eye and my husband was sitting comfortably in his chair. "I said," he was saying loudly, "I said, 'Do you mind if I read?' " He had the *New York Times* on his knee.

"Look," I said. "Do I have anything to read? Here I am, with nothing to do and no one to talk to and you sit there and read the *New York Times* right in front of me and here I am, with nothing—"

"How do we feel?" the doctor asked. He was suddenly much taller than before and the walls of the room were rocking distinctly.

"Doctor," I said, and I believe that my voice was a little louder than I intended it should be. "You better give me—"

He patted me on the hand and it was my husband instead of the doctor. "Stop yelling," he said.

"I'm *not* yelling," I said. "I don't like this any more. I've changed my mind, I don't want any baby, I want to go home and forget the whole thing."

"I know *just* how you feel," he said.

My only answer was a word which certainly I knew that I *knew*, although I had never honestly expected to hear it spoken in my own ladylike voice.

"Stop yelling," my husband said urgently. "*Please* stop saying that."

I had the idea that I was perfectly conscious, and I looked at him with dignity. "Who is doing this," I asked. "You or me?"

"It's all right," the doctor said. "We're on our way." The walls were moving along on either side of me and the woman in the blue bathrobe was waving from a doorway.

"She loved me for the dangers I had passed," I said to the doctor, "and I loved her that she did pity them."

"It's all right, I tell you," the doctor said. "Hold your breath."

"Did he finish his *New York Times?*"

"Hours ago," the doctor said.

"What's he reading now?" I asked.

"The *Tribune*," the doctor said. "Hold your breath."

It was so unbelievably bright that I closed my eyes. "Such a lovely time," I said to the doctor. "Thank you so much for asking me, I can't tell you how I've enjoyed it. Next time you must come to our—"

"It's a girl," the doctor said.

"Sarah," I said politely, as though I were introducing them. I still thought I was perfectly conscious, and then I was. My husband was sitting beside the bed, smiling cheerfully.

"What happened to *you?*" I asked him. "No *Wall Street Journal?*"

"It's a girl," he said.

"I know," I said. "I was there."

I was in a pleasant, clean room. There was no doubt that it was all over; I could see my feet under the bedspread.

"It's a girl," I said to my husband.

The door opened and the doctor came in. "Well," he said. "How do we feel?"

"Fine," I said. "It's a girl."

"I know," he said.

The door was still open and a face peered around it. My husband, the doctor, and I, all turned happily to look. It was the woman in the blue bathrobe.

"Had it yet?" I asked her.

"No," she said. "You?"

"Yep," I said. "You going home again?"

"Listen," she said. "I been thinking. Home, the kids all yelling and my mother looking sad like she's disappointed in me. Like I did something. My husband, every time he sees me jump he reaches for the car keys. My sister, she calls me every day and if I answer the phone she hangs up. Here, I get three meals a day I don't cook, I know all the nurses and I meet a lot of people going in and out. I figure I'd be a *fool* to go home. What was it, boy or girl?"

"Girl," I said.

"Girl," she said. "They say the third's the easiest."

RUSSELL LYNES

The
New
Snobbism

There was a time not long ago when a snob was a snob and as easy to recognize as a cock pheasant. In the days when Ward McAllister was the arbiter of Newport society and when there were precisely four hundred souls in New York worth knowing and only "nobodies" lived west of the Alleghenies, snobbishness was a nice clean-cut business that made careers for otherwise unoccupied women and gave purpose to otherwise barren lives. In those days the social order was stratified as tidily as the terracing of an Italian garden, and a man could take his snobs or leave them. But now the social snob, while not extinct, has gone underground (except for professionals such as head waiters and metropolitan-hotel room clerks), and snobbery has emerged in a whole new set of guises, for it is as indigenous to man's nature as ambition and a great deal easier to exercise.

Snobbery has assumed so many guises, in fact, that it is, I believe, time that someone attempt to impose order on what is at best a confused situation. There are a few basic categories of snobs that seem to include most of the more common species that one is likely to encounter, or, indeed, to be. None of these categories is new; there have always been, I presume, snobs of every sort,[1] but now that the pre-

[1] It is 102 years since William Makepeace Thackeray published his *Book of Snobs*, a series of facetious essays that originally appeared in *Punch*. Mr. Thackeray's snobs are largely of the social sort.

eminence of the social variety has been submerged in a wave of political and economic egalitarianism, and now that we find ourselves in an era in which the social scientists believe that it is somehow good for us to be ticketed and classified, let us sort out the most common practitioners of the sneer.

The Intellectual Snob is of such distinguished lineage and comes from such established precedent that he is dignified by a mention in Webster's ("one who repels the advances of those whom he regards as his inferiors; as, an intellectual snob"). The other categories are less well known and less well documented. For convenience, let us call them the Regional Snobs, the Moral Snobs, the Sensual Snobs, the Emotional Snobs, the Physical Snobs, the Occupational Snobs, and, finally, the Reverse Snobs or Anti-snob Snobs. Before we examine these, we should be aware that economic and social boundaries, while they may occasionally serve as guide ropes, are on the whole unimportant in considering the various forms of condescension and the various attitudes of superiority that distinguish the true snob from the merely vain man, woman, or child.

Snobbishness, as we will use the word, implies both an upward and downward movement—a scramble upward to emulate or outdo those whose position excel's one's own, and a look downward on (or sometimes straight through) those less happily endowed than one's self. The true snob never rests; there is always a higher goal to attain, and there are, by the same token, always more and more people to look down upon. The snob is almost by definition insecure in his social (in the larger sense) relationships, and he resorts to snobbishness as a means of massaging his ego. Since scarcely anyone is so secure that his ego does not sometimes need a certain amount of external manipulation, there is scarcely anyone who isn't a snob of some sort. As a matter of fact the gods of the Greeks and the Romans were frightful snobs, morally, physically, and emotionally, and it is not uncommon for civilized peoples to worship snobbery. It is the Christian religion that promoted the virtue of humility for us, and of all the virtues it is the most difficult to come by. Let us not, then, be snobbish about snobs—at least not yet.

It is not my intention to apply the scientific method to the definition of the categories which we shall examine, though each species will be seen to have its subspecies and each subspecies to have many variants. I mean this to be suggestive, merely a sketch that will enable the reader to glimpse the vast possibilities that a methodical study of snobs by a diligent social scientist might uncover.

Our first category is the Regional Snobs, commonly known in the South as Virginians, in the West as Californians, and in the East as Bostonians. This, however, should be recognized for what it is, a mere colloquialism. The Regional Snob can come from anywhere, and is readily distinguished by his patronizing attitude toward anywhere else. He lets it be known that there is no place to match the seat of his origin; indeed, he seems surprised or amused that people in other places are so much like people. The Asturians who live in the north of Spain, for example, look with special distaste on the citizens of the neighboring province, Galicia, and they have a saying that "a Galician is the animal that most closely resembles a human being." In Texas it is said that you should never ask a man where he comes from. "If he's a Texan," they say, "he'll tell you. If he's not don't embarrass him." These are not as extreme cases as they might seem. It was recorded a decade ago that a boy who lived on Martha's Vineyard, an island off the Massachusetts coast, was assigned the problem in school of writing a composition about the then Duce of Italy. His paper started with the sentence: "Mussolini is an off-islander."

But let us consider more common types of Regional Snobs. In Vermont, for example, the Regional Snob is generally called a "native" to distinguish him from the group known as "summer people." The aloofness of the Vermont native, a man proud of his thrift, of the bleakness of his winters, and especially of the fact that he has managed to squeeze a living out of rocky hillsides and out of "summer people,"[2] has a special laconic quality that is guaranteed to freeze the marrow of, say, a Texan. This kind of Regional snobbism is of the *We've had it tougher than anybody* variety, and is the opposite of the California type which is of the *We know how to live better than you do* kind, or of the Gracious Living types found in the South, notably in Virginia, in South Carolina, and in the New Orleans vicinity.

These types are, more or less, Area Snobs and should be distinguished from the local or home-town varieties which demonstrate certain cultural patterns quite different from those found in general geographical areas. The local snob does not even in many cases recognize his home town as anything very special; his vision may be myopic to the extent of permitting everything beyond the end of his particular street to go out of focus. "The other side of the tracks" is a phrase less frequently heard than it was a generation or so ago. We live in an age of "developments"—real estate developments, housing developments, community developments—of "projects" and of

[2] And more recently, with the advent of the Ski Snobs, out of "winter people" as well.

subdivisions, and the railroad tracks have lost some of their social significance in this age of buses and automobiles. So we have subdivision dwellers looking down upon development dwellers, and development dwellers turning their heads away from project dwellers, and project dwellers scornful of tenement dwellers. But the genuine home-town snob is rather more special than any of these.

Boston is too well known for its special brand of provincial hauteur to need discussion here, but the New York brand is less well documented and will serve to demonstrate one of the extreme forms of local snobbism. This is the Cultural Capital variety, or *Anything or anybody of any interest comes here* kind, that makes the New Yorker when visiting in any other city assume an air of condescension that has both an overhead spin and reverse twist. "You know," the New Yorker[3] will say when visiting a city in the Middle West, "I think it's really terribly interesting *out here.*" It is a wonder that so few New Yorkers get their throats cut in what they think of as (but do not call) "the provinces." In its most advanced forms Cultural Capital Snobbism will bend all the way over backward and touch its heels with its hair with some such observation as: "I think New Yorkers are the most provincial people in the world, don't you?" The born and bred New Yorker is rare (or at least thinks of himself as rare), and in general the New Yorker by adoption is the more virulent of the species.

At the other end of the scale we find Small Town Snobbism: the *I have lived here longer than anyone* type vies with the type who makes much of the fact that only people who rub elbows with the members of a small community really understand the meaning of life. This latter type, like the Cultural Capital Snob, is usually a member of the community by adoption, having fled from the city in order to discover what he calls "real values." Sometimes the members of this group are summer people gone native who retain certain characteristic attributes of their type such as station wagons, and dress themselves in more elaborately rural costumes (blue jeans, checked wool shirts, even straw hats) than any genuinely rural inhabitant would consider proper or necessary. Another variant of this species is the ex-urbanite who buys a farm in order to "get next to the soil." These might be called the Eternal Verities Snobs, Back to the Land Division, and are very likely to be authors.[4]

---

[3] Not to be confused with the magazine of the same name. It is not within the scope of this essay to discuss institutional snobbism.

[4] Indeed, Connecticut and Bucks County have been so overrun by authors that a real farmer can hardly afford to buy land there.

Before we proceed to our next category, there is one offshoot of the Regional Snobs which bears brief mention: The World Is My Home species,[5] made up of people who pride themselves on the fact that they are as much at home in Shepheard's Hotel in Cairo as in the Casino at Monte Carlo or in the Ritz Bar in Paris or in the Pump Room in Chicago or in less expensive saloons in any of these places. The members of this category like to think of themselves as "the international set" and are frequently remittance men, decayed nobility, career diplomats, overseas representatives (and their wives) of American industries, wealthy divorcees, or rich refugees. They regard every international problem or crisis chiefly as a personal inconvenience, and every visa in their passports as a mark of sophistication. The natives of any place they visit have no other function but to serve them, and their technique for insulting waiters is unsurpassed. Although the world is their home, they are in one sense the most provincial snobs of all, for their real world consists of a few thousand wanderers, and their horizons are limited to the chips on the table, the bottles on the bar, and the crystals in the chandeliers of hotel dining rooms, and when out of doors they darken their little world with sun glasses.[6] They have an unmitigated scorn for all tourists and are ashamed and embarrassed by their compatriots who travel abroad.

It is probable that as the world grows smaller, Regional Snobbism will increase. It is a logical antidote to political efforts to make man love his neighbor.

Like the Regional Snobs, the number of Moral Snobs is legion and they love their neighbors no more dearly. Oscar Wilde, a really accomplished snob, said that "Morality is simply the attitude we adopt toward people we personally dislike." But the Moral Snob carries it further than that; his snobbishness extends to people he doesn't even know. Morality is both a public and a private matter, to be sure, and it is characteristic of the Moral Snob to put a good deal of ornamental fretwork on his public façade and let the private places of his personality be slovenly. To call him a hypocrite would be to attribute vices to his virtues; he is not so positive a character as that. He does not necessarily want to get away with anything, but he is always quite sure that everyone else does, or would if he didn't keep a sharp eye on them.

---

[5] Not to be confused with the One World Snobs.

[6] There are two important variants of this species: (1) the Language Snob, who pretends to five or six languages and sprinkles his conversation with French, Spanish, and German phrases, and (2) the Reverse Language Snob, who prides himself on getting along everywhere with his native tongue on the assumption that anyone who doesn't know it is a fool or worse.

In our day there are two main categories of Moral Snobs—the Religious Snobs and the Tolerance Snobs. In mentioning the former, I am aware that I am on delicate ground, but the Religious Snobs are identified with no particular sect or creed, and the true believer is rarely, if ever, snobbish about it. The only thing that they seem to have in common is the conviction that those who disapprove of their faith or the methods by which they try to spread it are "bigots."[7]

Sometimes opposed to the Religious Snob and sometimes allied with him is the Tolerance Snob, a species of comparatively recent origin. It should be noted that he turns the tables on the Religious Snob for lack of tolerance toward disbelievers and backsliders, and in such cases he often calls the Religious Snob a "bigot." The bigot is a most useful foil to the Tolerance Snob. But whether he is at loggerheads with the Religious Snob or not, the *I am more tolerant than anybody* Snob has a special predilection for getting his name printed on the letterheads of societies for the prevention and furthering of things.

In contrast with the Moral Snobs are the Sensual Snobs who take special pride in being able to wrest more pleasure per cell from the flesh than anyone else. In this general category which is even more elastic than I mean to make it we find the Food and Drink, the Sex, the Indolence, and the Health and Hygiene Snobs.

The Food and Drink species is almost too common to require more than a passing word. In Food the Herb Snobs while somewhat old-fashioned still persist; but this species, I believe, is less in the ascendancy now than the Pot Luck Snobs, Casserole Division, or the *This is something I just threw together at the last minute* species. The mussels-snails-brains-and-garlic group continues to operate, especially in areas where mussels, snails, brains, and garlic are still considered somewhat outrageous, and the Plain American Food Group ("If you want a good cup of coffee and a decent hamburger, eat in a diner") flourishes in metropolitan areas where good foreign cooking is commonplace.

The Foreign Food Snob often can be identified by his attitude of frustration. The "little place" that he discovered and which used to be so good has always just recently gone to pot. "You know how it is," he says. "The frogs legs Provençal used to be superb, but now the place has got popular, and the food isn't fit to eat any more."

[7] The most extreme example of this type of snobbism I have heard of is credited to the family of the Duc de Levis-Mirepoix, one of the oldest important French titles that dates back to the ninth century. The family is purported to be descended from the sister of the Virgin Mary, and when the members of the Levis-Mirepoix family pray, they are said to say: "*Ave Maria, ma cousine. . . .*"

The Drink Snobs are, of all categories, the easiest to identify since the rules are so well established. They insist that their whiskey be bonded; they know what proof it is; and they drink it neat or "on the rocks"; their Scotch is "V.O." or "V.V.O."; their martinis are as dry as almost no vermouth can make them (in restaurants where they suspect the martinis may be somewhat amber in hue they order Gibsons and remove the onions); and they always nod at the waiter after looking at the date on a bottle of wine. Only the genuine connoisseur has the self-assurance to send back a bottle of wine. Some Drink Snobs take special pride in the amount they can consume and not show it; others take special pride in having a worse hangover than anybody ever had before.

The Sex Snobs have been adequately documented by the Physiology Department of Indiana University. It may, however, be interesting to note that the publication of Dr. Kinsey's first volume, *Sexual Behavior in the Human Male,* produced two new manifestations of the Sex Snob: first, those of the *I could tell Kinsey a thing or two* variety; and second, the species that insisted that the excitement about the book was all nonsense—"Why I've known that for years." The attitude of the British toward the Kinsey Report reveals an interesting provincialism. I was told by Dr. Kinsey that in general the reaction of the British professional and, if I may be permitted the phrase, the lay press, was: "No doubt this is all very true about Americans, but we are not interested. The British don't behave like that."

The Indolence Snobs, on the other hand, have been epitomized by an Englishman, Cyril Connolly, in his book, *The Unquiet Grave.* "Others merely live," he wrote; "I vegetate." An interesting counterpart to Mr. Connolly's form of snobbism is to be found in those who make a great show of doing nothing, of sleeping late, of lying in the sun, of always having time to amuse themselves and their friends, and who at the same time produce a great deal of work. These are the people who express their superiority by saying, "I just tossed off this novel in my spare time," or, "I just thought of this new international trade combine over a game of canasta in Miami one evening."

The Health and Hygiene Snobs may more properly belong with the Moral Snobs than with the Sensual Snobs. There is no denying, however, that there is sensual pleasure in the subjugation of the flesh, and that this is part of the routine behavior of the Health and Hygiene Snob. It is a far stronger motive than mere laziness that keeps a man or woman horizontal in the hot sun for a few hours in order to turn first red and then brown; it is certainly not morality that sends men and women to gymnasiums to reduce one portion of the anatomy and exaggerate another; nor is it laziness that makes them diet, abstain from (or at least be ostentatiously moderate about) liquor, and get to bed at what they call "a reasonable hour." It is the delight of being able to look down upon those who, to use their phrase, "don't take proper care of themselves." Sex, of course, enters strongly into this, but then so does a feeling of moral superiority. I have no doubt that the social scientists will in time be able to isolate the Health and Hygiene Snob from the Moral Snob.

While we are on the subject of the body, let us not overlook the Physical Prowess Snobs, more common among males than among females, but by no means limited to one sex. The Physical Prowess Snob is not necessarily an expert athlete; indeed he is likely not to be. It is the mediocre tennis player, for example, hitting everything hard if inaccurately, who is lofty about the player who may be able to beat him merely by getting the ball back.

No matter what you may think of the Sensual Snobs, it cannot be denied that, unlike the Moral Snobs, they are a great pleasure to themselves.

Since the emotions carry us rapidly in dangerous directions and soon lead us to the darkest corners of man's nature, we must proceed to the dissection of the Emotional Snobs with caution. This is the *I feel things more deeply than anybody* variety, and there is likely to be at least one in every family.

Probably the largest single subdivision of this category is the Love Snob, a type which finds its roots among adolescents, who since they are having their first encounter with sexual love, believe that no one has ever been so in love before. Their intolerance of their juniors is matched only by their scorn for their elders, and this can set a pattern for adult love that is difficult to break. The so-called "great lovers" do not, I believe, belong in the Love Snob category but rather in that of the Sex Snob. It was surely not about the intensity of his emotions that Don Giovanni, with his list of 1,100 ladies, was vain.

The Mother Love Snob, or *I give my all for my children* type, is not uncommon among women who are not Sex Snobs. The Filial Love Snob, or Mom Snob, is not in my experience nearly so common as English authors, such as Geoffrey Gorer, or Americans, such as Philip Wylie, contend that it is. That is not to say that the exploitation of Mom Snobbery by the florists once a year has not given it at least a seasonal boost.

The Marital and/or Soul Mate Snobs are not rare, though they are particularly tiresome because they are, by the very nature of their snobbery, raised to a higher power. Since it takes two to make Soul Mates, they are twice as tiresome as other snobs.

The Popularity Snobs also belong in the Emotional group; in a sense they are everybody's Soul Mate. To use their own vernacular, they have a "way with people" and can "get along with anybody." Theirs is the hauteur of affable condescension, and traditionally the species is common among traveling salesmen, Rotarians, public relations counselors, and politicians, though it would be a mistake not to recognize the far wider ramifications of this type wherever we meet them. Mass demonstrations of Popularity Snobbism are known as conventions.[8] The typical member of this species rarely uses the form "mister" in addressing anyone, no matter how brief or perfunctory the acquaintance. He is strictly a first-name man, and has little respect for anyone's dignity or privacy. He assumes that everybody loves him, and he reasons that there is no privacy in a public love affair.

By contrast the Unpopularity Snob, or *Nobody can get along with me* type, takes two principal forms.[9] The first is an imperious and often petulant species who by dint of the loftiness of his position or intellect makes much of the fact that he can't be bothered with boors and idiots. He works with his door closed; he throws all second-class mail into the wastebasket without opening it; and he never seems to be able to remember anyone's name, or if he does, he mispronounces it. When you meet him, he says "hello," but looks past you, as though you were obstructing his view. The second is the sensitive, or *I'm too special*, type who is "misunderstood" by crass and materialistic people. This species is likely to gravitate in the general direction of the arts and crafts and sooner or later to metropolitan areas.

Somewhere between the Emotional Snobs and the Intellectual Snobs[10] are the Sensitivity or Taste Snobs—those who are scornful of any whose aesthetic antennae they consider less receptive than their own. It is customary, I believe, to classify the Art Snobs, the Literary Snobs, and the Musical Snobs with the Intellectual Snobs, but it seems to me that they belong in a limbo between the Emotional

[8] College Reunions also figure in this category. They provide opportunities for the temporary renewal of Popularity Snobbism in those who were popular in college but have been slipping ever since.

[9] The persistence of one type of Unpopularity Snob is demonstrated by the number of adults who take special care to make the point that anybody who amounts to anything was "unhappy in school." It is likely to express itself in some such direct statement as "I was the most unpopular boy (girl) in my class."

[10] So commonly known and, as we have noted, so well established as to need no discussion in this brief survey.

and the Intellectual categories, with plenty of latitude to permit them to jump either way.[11] Furthermore the matter of taste comprehends more than just the arts (and, as we shall see, includes certain other vagaries of man's predilection for lording it over man). But let us take the arts first.

To categorize the Art Snobs into all of their many subdivisions would be an intricate and, I am afraid, tiresome business. We would, for example, have to consider the various shadings that range all the way from the Traditionalist or Permanent Value Snobs to the Modern or *I always keep an open mind* group. There are, however, a few basic behavior patterns that betray the Art Snob at any level. In a gallery he can be observed to stand back from a picture at some distance, his head cocked slightly to one side, and then after a rather long period of gazing (during which he may occasionally squint his eyes) he will approach to within a few inches of the picture and examine the brushwork; he will then return to his former distant position, give the picture another glance, and walk away. The Art Snob can be recognized in the home (*i.e.* your home) by the quick look he gives the pictures on your walls, quick but penetrating, as though he were undressing them. This is followed either by complete and obviously pained silence or by a comment such as, "That's really a very pleasant little water color you have there." In his own house his manner is also slightly deprecating. If you admire a print on his wall, he is likely to say, "I'm glad you like it. It's really not bad considering it is such a late impression." Or if he is in the uppermost reaches of Art Snobs and owns an "old master" which you admire, he will say, "Of course Berenson lists it as a Barna da Sienna, but I've never satisfied myself that it isn't from the hand of one of his pupils."

The Literary Snob has not only read the book you are reading, but takes pleasure in telling you the names of all the earlier and more obscure books by the same author, and why each one was superior to the better known one that has come to your attention.

Musical Snobs are in general of two sorts—Classical Snobs and Jazz Snobs. The former can sometimes be identified at concerts because they keep their eyes closed. This can for obvious reasons be misleading, but if closed eyes are accompanied by a regular movement

---

[11] It is interesting to note in connection with the publication of a new (1950) typographically eccentric magazine devoted to taste, that as an undergraduate Thackeray at Cambridge in 1829 contributed to a magazine called the *Snob*. An advertisement described it as follows: "Each number contained only six pages . . . printed on tinted paper of different colors, green, pink, and yellow." The *Snob* lasted for eleven numbers.

of the hands in time with the music, it is clear that the listener is
beating time to himself. This is characteristic of the lower orders
of Classical Snob. If he has a score of the music which he follows
while it is being played, he may be a professional musician looking
for subtleties of interpretation; he may, on the other hand, merely be
a higher order of Classical Snob. The surest way to identify the Classical Snob is to see whether he comes back after the intermission or not;
if he stays only for the more difficult or abstruse part of the program
and ignores the more popular portion, he is either a snob or a professional critic, or possibly both.

Musical Snobs, Jazz Division, beat time not with their hands but
with their feet. They do not talk about records or recordings but
about specific choruses, solo passages, or "breaks." They know the
dates and numbers of original pressings and occasionally they collect
never-played records much the way some book collectors prefer rare
copies with uncut pages. They are well grounded in the brand of jazz
they refer to as "authentic" (New Orleans, Memphis, Chicago) and
they are extremely partisan about what they consider to be "advanced" (Progressive Jazz, Bebop, or even Dixieland). There are
some overtones of social and racial snobbery in the way Jazz Snobs
identify themselves with jazz musicians.

Also among the Taste Snobs are to be found the Clothes Snobs,
both male and female. In this instance the female is a good deal more
interesting and varied than the male, for while the male "sharp
dressers" are snobs of a sort, there is only one male Dress Snob who
needs to arrest our attention: the Conservative Dress Snob. The buttons on the sleeves of his jacket actually unbutton. There is no padding on his shoulders. The collar of his shirt is a little too high for
him, so that it bulges and wrinkles slightly, and it buttons down. He
cares deeply about good leather and good tweed, but most of all he
cares about being conspicuously inconspicuous.

The female Dress Snobs offer a far more complicated range of types
and it requires some temerity on the part of a man to broach this subject at all. In general, however, women seem to fall into the following
categories of sartorial superiority:

(1) The Underdressed Snob, who wouldn't be caught
dead at a cocktail party in a cocktail dress, and a similar type,
the next on our list. . . .

(2) The Basic Dress Snob, who believes that she has so
much personality that she can get away anywhere in a simple

black ("basic") dress and one piece of "heirloom" jewelry.

(3) The Good Quality Snob, or wearer of muted tweeds, cut almost exactly the same from year to year, often with a hat of the same material. This type is native to the Boston North Shore, the Chicago North Shore, the North Shore of Long Island, to Westchester County, the Philadelphia Main Line, the Peninsula Area of San Francisco, etc. It rides horses and is rare in Southern California, except for Pasadena.

(4) The Band Box Snob—common among professional fashion models and among other young women trying to make their way in the big city. They look as though they had just stepped out of *Vogue* or *Mademoiselle*. They are never ahead of the fashion, but they are screamingly up-to-date.

(5) The Dowdy, or *Who the hell cares about fashion,* Snob.

(6) The Personal Style, or *I know more about my type than the experts,* Snob. This final type considers her taste to be above the whims of mere fashion. She is so chic that she believes that it is un-chic to be merely fashionable.[12]

Good taste is everyone's prerogative (no one willingly confesses to bad taste), and so nearly everyone is a Taste Snob of one sort or another, and often of many sorts at the same time.

Our next category, the Occupational or Job Snobs, are of two sorts; those who are snobbish about the kind of occupation by which they live, and those who are snobbish about how they perform in their occupation. Few women, for example, are snobbish about being housekeepers; many are snobbish about the way they keep house. Many men, on the other hand, are snobbish about the positions they hold and less snobbish about how they perform in them. But first let's take the women. The woman whose dearest ambition is an absolutely well-ordered and efficiently run house looks down upon the woman who firmly believes that it is nonsense to spend so much time over the household that there is not time for what she calls "life." She in turn looks down upon the whole-souled housekeeper. It boils down to a conflict between two aphorisms—"cleanliness is next to godliness" and "a little dirt never hurt anybody"—which, if we weren't careful, would lead us back to our discussion of Moral Snobs. Of

[12] The outstanding example of this in recent history was Queen Mary of England.

course both of these types are looked upon with scorn by the female Career Snob who manages with overbearing aplomb both a job and a household.

The hierarchy within which men work is quite different, and makes quite different demands. The professional man feels somewhat lordly toward the businessman or "money grubber" and considers him lacking in sensibility and intellectual curiosity and nearsighted to the point of seeing nothing beyond the sales chart but the golf course or the bridge table. He is likely to blame the world's ills on the businessman's greed and lack of cultural understanding. The businessman, on the other hand, thinks of many professional men as "dreamers" and "idealists" or even as "panty-waists." This applies especially to artists, writers, actors, musicians, scholars, and editors. The businessman is less likely to be snobbish about physicians, lawyers, and engineers because he considers them, like himself, to be "practical" men. His most unlimited scorn is for bureaucrats who "have never met a payroll."

Performance on the job is less likely to matter than position, as I have said, but there is the Efficiency Snob whose pose is primarily one of crispness. He answers the phone by barking just his last name; he is inclined to have rows of buttons on his telephone or desk and almost no papers. His memoranda are brief to the point of being curt, he considers the word "please" something that has no place among desks and typewriters, and he wants things done "soonest." He thinks of himself as a "trouble shooter" and makes lists of possible troubles to shoot. As each one is shot, it is crossed off the list with a firm black line. Accomplishment is measured by the number of black lines, and everyone who doesn't measure up to his particular standards of efficiency is "hopeless." The reverse of this type, also common, is the man who lives behind a mess of papers, pencils, and paper clips and "can never find anything" and yet manages to get out the work.

The results produced by the Efficiency Snob and the Inefficiency Snob are just about the same.

Performance off the job often reveals the Manual Dexterity Snob who can do complicated mechanical things with his hands and who considers all who can't to be fumbling idiots, and the opposite of this, the All-Thumbs Snob, commonly found among women. Men who are all thumbs are sometimes reticent about it; women rarely are.

We have noted as we went along that almost every kind of snobbism has its opposite; the Moral Snob contrasts with the Sensual Snob, the Manuel Dexterity Snob with the All-Thumbs Snob, the Efficiency Snob with the Inefficiency Snob, and so on. But these contrasting sources of the sneer should not be confused with our final category, the Reverse Snob or Anti-snob Snob. This is the snob who finds snobbery so distasteful that he (or she) is extremely snobbish about nearly everybody since nearly everybody is a snob about something. This is the man who tries so hard to be "natural," so hard to be "just folks," so hard to avoid having anyone else think he is a snob, that he plays a game which (if I may be forgiven for being a Language Snob for a moment) is *faux naïf*. He would not, for example, ever be caught using a foreign phrase, as I have, lest it be thought pretentious even when it serves better than any other he can think of to convey its meaning. Or if he is forced to use it (or even a foreign name, let's say) he Americanizes its pronunciation lest anyone think him up-stage.[13] He makes much of the fact that simple, uneducated people are wiser and nicer than sophisticated and educated people, even wise and nice educated people. He plays down his own education and accomplishments with an elaborate display of modesty and is likely to introduce a very erudite and perceptive observation with the phrase, "Of course I know so little about this I have no right to an opinion," or, "I know this is probably stupid of me, but . . ." Of all the snobs the Reverse Snob is probably the most snobbish; he is so sure of himself that he intentionally puts other people in a position where they have to play his game or feel like snobs themselves. The false simplicity of the Reverse Snob stands in direct and glaring contrast to the genuinely modest man.

By and large it is only the very great who are not snobbish at all. They are the ones who are modest about their accomplishments because they have devoted their lives to achieving some kind of understanding and so have developed a deep tolerance for ignorance. By the same token the serious professionals in any field are not likely to be snobbish about other serious professionals, whether they are doctors or actors or writers or mechanics or businessmen or masons or even, let it be said, housekeepers. As we noted at the outset, it is those who are unsure of themselves and are seeking security in their social relationships who have provided us with this incomplete list of Snobs.

It will not have escaped the reader (and so I might as well admit it) that this cursory attempt to classify and define snobs is an example not only of Intellectual Snobbism but of Moral, Sensual, Occupational, Physical, Emotional, and above all of Reverse or Anti-snob Snobbism. I am sure there is no greater snob than a snob who thinks he can define a snob.

---

[13] "They spell it Vinci and pronounce it Vinchy; foreigners always spell better than they pronounce."—Mark Twain, *The Innocents Abroad.*

PHYLLIS McGINLEY

A Quartet

 of

Elders

The Old Reformer
Few friends he has that please his mind.
  His marriage failed when it began,
Who worked unceasing for mankind
  But loathed his fellow-man.

The Old Actor
Too lined for Hamlet, on the whole;
  For tragic Lear, too coarsely built,
Himself becomes his favorite role,
  Played daily to the hilt.

The Old Philanthropist
His millions make museums bright.
  Harvard anticipates his will.
While his young typist weeps at night
  Over a druggist's bill.

The Old Beauty
Coquettes with doctors; hoards her breath
  For blandishments; fluffs out her hair;
And keeps the stubborn suitor, Death,
  Moping upon her stair.

SYLVIA WRIGHT

The Death
of

Lady
Mondegreen

When I was a child, my mother used to read aloud to me from Percy's *Reliques*, and one of my favorite poems began, as I remember:

> Ye Highlands and ye Lowlands,
> Oh, where hae ye been?
> They hae slain the Earl Amurray,
> And Lady Mondegreen.

I saw it all clearly. The Earl had yellow curly hair and a yellow beard and of course wore a kilt. He was lying in a forest clearing with an arrow in his heart. Lady Mondegreen lay at his side, her long, dark brown curls spread out over the moss. She wore a dark green dress embroidered with light green leaves outlined in gold. It had a low neck trimmed with white lace (Irish lace, I think). An arrow had pierced her throat: from it blood trickled down over the lace. Sunlight coming through the leaves made dappled shadows on her cheeks and her closed eyelids. She was holding the Earl's hand.

It made me cry.

The poem went on to tell about the Earl Amurray. He was a braw gallant who did various things, including playing at the bar, which,

I surmised, was something lawyers did in their unserious moments (I grew up during prohibition, though I was against prohibition and for Governor Smith). The poem also said that he was the queen's love, and that long would his lady look o'er the castle doun before she saw the Earl Amurray come sounding through the toun. Nothing more was said about Lady Mondegreen.

But I didn't feel it was necessary. Everything had been said about Lady Mondegreen. The other ladies may have pretended they loved the Earl, but where were they? The queen was probably sitting in Dunfermline toun drinking the blood red wine along with the king (he was in "Sir Patrick Spens"). As for the Earl's wife, hiding in the castle in perfect safety and pretending to worry about him, it was clear she only married him so she could be Lady Amurray. She was such a sissy she probably didn't even look doun very hard—she was scared she'd fall through the crenelations of the battlements. As a matter of fact, she looked like a thin wispy girl I once socked in the stomach while I was guarding her in basketball because she kept pushing me over the line when the gym teacher couldn't see her and who was such a sissy that she fainted dead away so that everybody said I should learn to be a lady when really she was cheating—but I won't go into that. Lady Mondegreen loved the Earl truly, and she was very brave. When she heard that Huntly (the villain) was coming after him, she ran right out of her castle and into the forest to be with him without even stopping to change from her best dress.

By now, several of you more alert readers are jumping up and down in your impatience to interrupt and point out that, according to the poem, after they killed the Earl of Murray, they *laid him on the green*. I know about this, but I won't give in to it. Leaving him to die all alone without even anyone to hold his hand—I won't have it.

The point about what I shall hereafter call mondegreens, since no one else has thought up a word for them, is that they are better than the original.

Take Hizeray. Hizeray is that huge hairy muscular Etruscan in the *Lays of Ancient Rome* who was such a demon with the broadsword and who committed one of the great betrayals of history. If Hizeray had been there, Horatius couldn't have held the bridge a minute. Horatius was very brave, but Hizeray was bigger. If not, why was he the first person Lars Porsena of Clusium thought of, when he swore by the Nine Gods that the great house of Tarquin should suffer wrong no more?

And named a trysting-day,
And bade his messengers ride forth,
East and west and south and north,
To summon Hizeray.

Hizeray was hard to find or the messengers wouldn't have been told
to go in so many directions, but he had no excuse. The messengers
blew so many trumpets that tower and town and cottage heard the
blast. I hoped Hizeray would rush in at the last moment and knock
Horatius into the Tiber. (I was on Lars Porsena of Clusium's side,
though you're not supposed to be, because his name was so much
better than anyone else's.) But he never did. When they say

Shame on the false Etruscan
Who lingers in his home,
When Porsena of Clusium
Is on the march for Rome—

they mean Hizeray.

Then there is Harold. You know Harold: "Our Father who art in
heaven, Harold be thy Name." It's not one I would have picked myself, but if He has to have a name, Harold will do.

Harold can do extraordinary things. There's a hymn which tells
about this. As it's printed in the book, it says that He "moves in a
mysterious way, His wonders to perform." Actually, of course, what
it really says is that Harold "moves in a mysterious way—He wanders
down a horn."

You must pray to Harold if you want something very specific. For
instance, if you have discovered how terribly hard it is to meet somebody there, you say to Harold, "Lead us not into Penn Station." At
the same time, Harold will protect you from those jittery, unreliable
New York, New Haven, and Hotfoot trains. They aren't so dangerous
when they're coming into nice motherly old Gran Central.

Even the mizz doesn't scare Harold. The mizz is a sort of elemental
protoplasm, which looks like a thick, pulpy, shifting fog. It is inhabited by all sorts of strangely shaped, white, squdgy animals, who moan
quietly to themselves from time to time. The mizz is in the Evening
Prayer Service: "Let the sea make a noise, and all that in the mizz."

If you decide that Harold is your shepherd, you can be sure of being
looked after. If He can't be there Himself, He will get in Good Mrs.
Murphy and "Surely Good Mrs. Murphy shall follow me all the days
of my life." I *knew* Mrs. Murphy, and I can't think of anyone I'd

rather have follow me, though, knowing her, I think she would more likely be several blocks ahead. She could do almost as many things as Harold. She told fortunes in tea leaves, baked delicious bread in a frying pan, and once when her little boy climbed onto the top of the roof and was too scared to get down, she shouted up to him, "You come right down, you little Irish basket," and like magic he got over being scared and came right down.

Mrs. Murphy lived in Massachusetts, where they have a holiday in April called Pay Treats Day. It always surprises and infuriates people who come from other states, because, just when they want to go out to buy shoes or bean pots, they find all the shops closed up tight, while the shopkeepers are out paying treats. This reminds me of Paul Revere, who rode to "spread the alarm through every middlesex, village, and farm." Middlesexes look a little like drumlins, if you know what they are, but they are made of hay, and so also look a little like haystacks. There is one middlesex exactly in between each village and farm, and people who are too poor to live in a village or farm live in a middlesex.

And where the middlesexes, villages, and farms slope down to the sea, beyond the dunes, beyond the rocky coast, stands the Donzerly Light on a rugged, lonely promontory. At twilight, the lighthouse keeper turns it on, and it begins to sprout rockets and bombs which light up the flag pole with the great big American flag which stands right next to it. This is where you go to pledge the legions to the flag.

There's a rude bridge around here somewhere, but I can't quite find it. It's so dilapidated that it touches the flood.

There are many mondegreens which give vivid new insights into tired old ideas. With all due respect to Rudy Vallee, "I'm just a vagabond lover" seems a pretty wet notion nowadays. A friend of mine sang it "I'm just a bag of unloving." If you've heard anything at all about psychiatry (who hasn't?) you'll realize that a bag of unloving is a significant and basic concept, and when you get a bag of unloving in search of a sweetheart, you've got the basis for a well-developed neurosis, because as long as you don't have adequate feelings of self-esteem and love yourself, you can't love someone else. See?

There's nothing very interesting about a vagabond lover, except that maybe he didn't like his mother.

The other day I found, on the back page of the New York *Post*, a headline: "Giants Struggle Under Weight of 'Dead' Bats." This is one of the most terrifying scenes I can think of, particularly since there is some doubt as to whether the bats are really dead. That would be bad enough, but if they were all stirring and squeaking—it would daunt even Hizeray. . . .

And some years ago, before World War II, there was a quiet Sunday morning when I discovered that on the front page of the *New York Times* it said: "World Blows Near." As I puzzled over this, I felt, in my room, the faint, fresh breath of the winds which were moving the turning world. Whose world was it? What was going to happen?

You see, if you lay yourself open to mondegreens, you must be valiant. The world, blowing near, will assail you with a thousand bright and strange images. Nothing like them has even been seen before, and who knows what lost and lovely things may not come streaming in with them? But there is always the possibility that they may engulf you and that you will go wandering down a horn into a mondegreen underworld from which you can never escape. If you want to be safe, guarded from the underworld and the creatures in the mizz, you have only to turn your back.

You have only to decide, as Humpty Dumpty put it (more or less), which is to be master, you or the word.

I am for the word, and against you.

Because there was a time, before she met the Earl Amurray, when Lady Mondegreen was a bag of unloving. Forlorn, in her embroidered dress, she looked out over her own crenelated battlement, wondering, all alone, about when the world would blow near so she could see what it was all about. Suddenly, beyond the moat, beyond the meadows, there is a stirring like dust far away on the horizon. A trumpet blasts, and she sees that it is the Earl Amurray, riding down the winding road, surrounded by men on prancing horses. Actually, these are Robin Hood's men, on a day off from Sherwood Forest, and the sun is glistening on their tunics of link and green. As the Earl Amurray spies Lady Mondegreen, he and his men spur their horses to a gallop and shout their wild, strange battle cry, "Haffely, Gaffely, Gaffely, Gonward." Lady Mondegreen rushes down the long winding stone stair. She reaches the portcullis and it rises as if by magic. The Earl Amurray seizes her, lifts her onto his horse and they ride over the drawbridge together and out into the world.

At noon, they come to a babbling brook and they stop and tie their horse to a tree. Upstream a little way (*Here* it is!) they see a rude bridge. The Earl Amurray pledges his legions to the flag to April's breeze unfurled and they go off, marching as to war, while the royal master leans against the phone, waiting for news of their victory.

Lady Mondegreen and the Earl Amurray are left alone by the brook. "Tell me," says Lady Mondegreen, as they sit down on the soft greensward in a crowd of gold and affodils, "Tell me [for she is beginning to get a little bit hungry] where is fancy bread?" And at this very moment, Good Mrs. Murphy, who has been riding a suitable distance behind on a sturdy mule, trots up and presents them with an Irish basket, which she has been carrying on her saddlebow. In it, wrapped in a damask napkin, is the fancy bread, a delicious small brown loaf, full of raisins and covered with white frosting.

After they have eaten, they wash their hands in the stream and they rest awhile. Lady Mondegreen lies back on the grass and listens to the soft sounds of the mumble-bees as they muzz among the affodils. The Earl Amurray entertains her by sounding through a tune in his fine baritone voice. Then they ride on. When night falls, they come at last to their own particular middlesex where they camp out under the stars, and Lady Mondegreen, because she loves him, does not say a word when he takes all the covers.

Tragedy lies ahead and there is no one who can save them. Hizeray is cowering in his home under a weight of dead bats. And alas, Harold, who has been watching them from above with a happy smile on His benign face, cannot help. His horn has vanished, and there is no way He can wander down.

But even though the worst will happen, Lady Mondegreen and the Earl Amurray have had their journey together. They have sniffed the delicate fragrance of the affodils, tasted the fancy bread, and slept together in the middlesex. Lady Mondegreen knows what the world is all about.

Lady Mondegreen is me.

The Seal
That
 # Couldn't
Swim

It is disproportionately distressing to me to hear people confusing ordinary seals with sea lions. Sea lions balance things and blow horns at circuses. They are slapstick clowns. Seals are sad-eyed creatures full of pathos and sentimentality. Clowns they may be, but of the school of Emmett Kelly. Their humor is often mixed with tears. If they had any musical talent it would be to sing "Sonny Boy." They don't grin like sea lions; they smile, and that rarely. Mostly they look helpless and forlorn. At least that is how Panayoti looked most of the time.

Devotion and a passionate need to be loved seemed to be the mainsprings of his character, but perhaps that was because he had lost his mother when he was still very young and I had saved him from a dreadful death at the hands of the fishermen who had found him in a cave. I say "him," although I never found out what his sex really was; probably because when I first saw him he looked and acted like a frightened little boy who is trying his best to be brave.

In those days I was abysmally ignorant about seals. I had no idea what I was letting myself in for when I ordered that the creature be brought aboard my raiding schooner. The last thing that crossed my mind when I determined to adopt Panayoti was that I would pass the

closing phases of the war in the Aegean playing nursemaid to an inexperienced seal and have to face something approaching mutiny among
my crew. All that I knew was that it was intolerable to watch a helpless little creature left to die of thirst under a pile of stones in a sun-
baked courtyard. My blood boiled at the thought that six brawny
fishermen were too superstitious to dare to kill the little animal outright, but had to immure it collectively so that the bad luck would
be spread among them.

Greek fishermen are poorer and more omen-ridden than most sea-
faring people, so it is not surprising that they both hate and fear seals.

The Mediterranean seal (Monachus Albiventer, the white-bellied
monk, the solitary one) is a clever animal. Long ago he discovered
that it is much easier for him to gather the fish that are caught in
nets than to go chasing after free ones. Monachus is neither very considerate nor very finicky, and he has extremely sharp teeth. When he
gets into a net and starts feeding, he doesn't trouble to disentangle
the fish. He simply swallows them, together with large pieces of the
net itself. Often the net is ruined beyond repair, and nets are a fisher-
man's livelihood. They are also expensive. Thus in a Greek fishing
village the cry "seal" is a cry of despair.

The superstitious dread in which the creatures are held is just as real
as the hate, although it is more complicated to explain and more
difficult to understand. Twice in his life the porter at my grand-
mother's house in Athens, who had once been a schooner captain,
had put back into harbor at great expense because when he set out
a seal had crossed his bow. The loss of his ship in a collision, he was
unshakably convinced, was due to his having ignored a third such
warning.

It was from him that I first heard the old, old story of the Gorgon,
that monstrous mermaid who frequents the blue Aegean Sea. She rises
out of the water and stops ships with her hand. She looks into the
eyes of the captain and asks him whether Alexander the Great is alive.
If he says, "Yes. He is alive and reigning," she lets the ship go on its
way. If he has not heard of the legend and says, "No," then he and
his ship are dragged down to the depths.

The legend is that Alexander acquired a tiny phial of water from
the spring of immortality. His sister found it in a cupboard and drank
it out of curiosity. When Alexander was on his deathbed, he called for
the water and was told that his sister had drunk it. With his dying
breath he cursed her. In desperation she tried to kill herself by jumping off a cliff into the sea. Since she had drunk the water, it did no

good, and she has lived ever since with her intolerable guilt. From time to time she rises to the surface, hoping to find some seaman who will tell her that Alexander did not die.

How it has happened that a seal should be identified with a mermaid, the mermaid with a snake-haired monster of antiquity, and that monster with the great Alexander's sister, I don't know. I don't suppose anybody knows just how beliefs are changed and molded and transferred. But to the old schooner captain there was no incongruity in believing simultaneously that the little round head which showed for a moment among the waves was both an animal of no great strength and a female demon who could root his ship to the spot. And he was no exception among Greek seamen.

But I myself did not learn all these things until later, and as far as seals went I lived in a fool's paradise. First of all, I was under the illusion that they knew how to swim and that they lived on fish. It never occurred to me that these things did not come naturally. All I had wanted to do was to rescue Panayoti, provide him with a good meal of fish to restore his strength, and then give him his freedom. I was quickly disabused.

From the very first moment everything went wrong. To begin with I antagonized the whole village by curtly ordering the fishermen to deliver the seal to me. They may have been too frightened to kill the seal outright, but they were damned if a young whippersnapper of a reserve lieutenant would boss them around, even if he did control the hungry island's supply of food and had enough fire power at his command to blast the village to hell. What is more, my own crew was not at all enthusiastic.

Since I could not very well open hostilities with my countrymen over a seal, I found myself in the position of having to swallow my anger and negotiate. The villagers for their part did not wish to press matters too far. After a decent interval the fishermen offered to sell me the seal. I paid for him with food which they would have received anyway, together with some discarded clothing, and everybody's pride was saved. Panayoti was brought aboard, looking filthy and miserable after his ordeal.

Then and there I found out that I had made a second and more serious mistake. Panayoti simply refused to have anything to do with the fish which I bought for his dinner. Every time I offered him one he would turn his head away and start crying. The noise he made was heart-breaking—something between the wail of a baby and the bleat of a lamb. I tried everything. I rubbed his nose with the fish, but he

only cried louder. I pushed the fish into his mouth. He spat it out.
Thinking that perhaps the fish was too big for him to swallow, I cut
it up into small pieces and tried to force them down his throat. He
spat them out too. I decided that the only thing to do was to let
Panayoti go on his way without a meal, since probably he preferred
to catch his own fish.

I dropped Panayoti overboard, expecting to see him streak off. The
next thing I knew he was drowning: his head went down and his tail
flippers came up out of the water. They beat wildly for a time, then
more and more feebly. A stream of bubbles rose from his mouth.
There could be no doubt that Panayoti did not know how to swim.
I dove overboard and fished him out, which took some doing, since he
was very slippery and I didn't know then that the best way to pick up
a seal is from under the flippers, the way one picks up a baby. Besides,
I was still not at all sure he wouldn't bite.

I needn't have worried. The poor creature was more dead than alive
when I got him aboard again. I was afraid he might die and gave him
artificial respiration as best I could. After a while he revived and
started crying again weakly, moving his head from side to side in the
most dejected manner. In a few minutes he seemed completely recovered and went crawling about the deck in that hopelessly inept,
broken-boned way seals have out of the water. But at least he was
clean now and his fur was fluffing up in the sunshine, turning from
black to a soft dove gray on top and ivory underneath.

By then it had belatedly occurred to me that Panayoti was only a
baby. I know it sounds stupid that I had not thought of it earlier, but
I had never seen a seal before and I had no basis for comparison. A
length of nearly three feet did not seem to me conclusive one way or
the other. I began suspecting it when I found out, on trying to feed
him more fish, that he had no teeth. So I tried milk. First I gave him
some in a saucer, but he only turned away and spilled it with his flippers. Then I made a feeding bottle out of an empty gin bottle with a
nipple made from the little finger of a rubber glove which we used for
handling the smoke-screen apparatus. It was a complete flop. Panayoti
didn't even want to look at it. The mere sight sent him into tantrums.
He became hysterical when I tried to force the nipple into his mouth
and went dragging himself round and round in circles across the deck
screaming his head off.

More in self-defense than from compassion I opened a can of New
Zealand butter, of which we had a lot, and stuffed his mouth full of
it. He spat most of it out, but a good deal stuck and for a time he was
too busy choking and spitting to make much noise. He was so quiet

that I almost forgot about him, and when I looked for him later I discovered to my delight that he was engaged in licking the butter off his nose. I spent the rest of the day carrying the can of butter around with me and smearing Panayoti's nose every time I passed him.

Since this method could not be used in the darkness and Panayoti was still very hungry, nobody got much sleep that night. The following day I decided that a new system had to be devised. It was, after all, unseemly for a raiding captain to spend his time buttering the nose of a seal, nor could I very well ask any of my sailors to take over the duty. Watching Panayoti crawling over the deck in his endless rounds, it occurred to me that a self-smearing technique could be devised. If a part of the deck were enclosed with cases to limit him in his movements, and pats of butter were scattered at random all over it, he was bound to run into some of them and butter his nose automatically. It worked like a dream.

Then there was an alarm. The lookout reported an unidentified vessel on the horizon. I ordered action stations and the men streamed aft to man the machine guns. Those on the starboard side forgot about the butter in their excitement and ended up in a cursing, tangled heap in the scuppers. The boatswain, a very irascible man, was among them. When he managed to pick himself up, dripping butter, he scowled at me and delivered himself of a dire prophecy: "It was an evil day when you brought that animal aboard. It will go ill with us, Captain, but with you worst of all. Mark my words," and he stalked off.

By good fortune the ship which had caused all the commotion turned out to be one of ours, and the incident fizzled out. But the obvious drawback of slippery decks gave me a brilliant idea. I drilled a hole in the deckhouse wall near the level of the deck and stuffed it full of butter, leaving a big, tempting pat on the outside. When Panayoti eventually found it and began to suck, I dashed down into my cabin and very gently inserted the nipple of the milk bottle into the hole. Finally all the butter was gone, but Panayoti kept on sucking, and, triumph of triumphs, the milk in the bottle started going, at first slowly and then, as he got a taste for it, so fast that I thought for a minute the nipple had come off.

When I saw the last drops disappear I was exultant. I filled the bottle again and scrambled up on deck thinking that all I had to do now was offer Panayoti the bottle and he would feed. Not at all. The moment he saw it he set up an ungodly racket and crawled away. I tried all sorts of ruses. Nothing worked. It was mortifying and also extremely undignified. The original curiosity of the men was rapidly giving way to surreptitious snickers.

So I decided to go to extreme lengths. I had the carpenter make a sort of wooden shield with a hole in the middle, which I stuffed with butter. For a couple of days I left it standing in the same place until Panayoti got used to it. Then I let him go for twenty-four hours without any butter until he was good and hungry. His complaints were heart-rending, but I was adamant. On the following day I passed the nipple through the hole, covering the projecting end with butter and advanced upon Panayoti, hidden behind the shield. It was absurd but effective. Panayoti made a beeline for the butter and began to suck. No sooner had he taken one swallow than I pulled the bottle away and slid the shield aside. Panayoti gave a cry of anger and frustration, but before he could do anything else I stuck the nipple into his open mouth. For a moment he looked surprised. Then he settled down to sucking steadily, eyes closed and a beatific expression on his face. That was the first time I saw Panayoti smile.

From that day on the feeding problem ceased to exist and he started gaining rapidly in size and strength. Our relationship also became much more intimate, not to say exclusive. Panayoti had at last become convinced that he had a friend in the world, and Panayoti was not a seal to do things by halves. His gratitude and affection were embarrassing. He would not let me out of his sight. When I was standing on deck, day or night, he would come and rest his head on my bare feet. If I moved he gave forth pathetic little moans. To avoid hurting his feelings I often found myself rooted to the same spot for what seemed like hours. To stumble into him, as I often did on dark nights, was a major calamity. It upset him terribly, and he would go on whimpering until he was picked up and comforted.

As his strength and devotion grew, he would not even let me go down into my cabin unescorted. When I was below for only a few minutes, laying a course or checking a bearing, he would get so restless and unhappy that he even overcame his dislike of heights. He would come to the open hatchway and cry. If I paid no attention he would wriggle forward over the combing until he overbalanced and slid forward down the ladder to land at my feet with a bump. I often watched him at it from between parted fingers. He obviously did not like doing it. He always looked miserable and reproachful as he prepared to take the plunge, and at the last moment just as he was about to tip forward, he always closed his eyes tight. But apparently being picked up and stroked was compensation enough.

The matter of getting out of the cabin up the almost perpendicular ladder was something else again. That he never mastered. He always had to be lifted out.

Sliding down into the cabin and setting up a to-do until he was taken out was nuisance enough, particularly if it happened at night when we were sailing and had to keep our ears open for the first, faint sound of enemy engines. But when he took to falling overboard every time I rowed away in the dinghy or went swimming over the side, it became really insufferable; for in spite of several unpleasant experiences, Panayoti had learned neither how to swim nor the obvious truth that he couldn't. He had to be rescued from drowning every time.

In desperation I decided to teach him how to swim. Every morning after the schooner was moored against the rocks and camouflaged under nets, after the machine guns were emplaced and the lookouts posted, I took Panayoti in the dinghy to some secluded cove. First we began in the shallows with Panayoti barely awash. I would walk away on the beach following the edge of the sea, and Panayoti would try to wriggle after me, splashing and thrashing about in the foot-deep water. As often as not he would give up his allegedly native element and crawl out onto the sand. If he didn't, the lesson usually ended up with his swallowing a mouthful of water and choking.

If I set him out on the sand and went and squatted in the water a few feet away, he would try to come to me. All went well until he got beyond the depth of his flippers. Then his head went down and he had to be pulled out by the tail. It never fazed him. After I had picked him up and he had spluttered for a few seconds, he would put his head on my shoulder and nuzzle my neck contentedly.

In spite of the disappointing results, I persevered with the lessons, using every method that I had ever heard of. I took him out beyond his depth and held him under the chin while swimming away backward. In the beginning this seemed promising. He began to move his flippers in a reasonable imitation of a swimming stroke, and his tail assembly, that absurd appendage which on dry land looked more like the wet hem of a skirt than anything else, became an admirably contrived instrument of propulsion. The trouble was his head. Whenever I let go of him it sank like a piece of lead and his tail beat uselessly in the air. I even strapped a Mae West on him, but he was so slippery in the water that after a few minutes it worked loose, and he slid out of it head-first to assume his usual perpendicular position.

Then one night we had an unpleasant experience. We were making a long crossing to one of the more distant islands, in company with another schooner, and we were caught in the open by a German Ems Craft. Being shelled at night on the sea by a more powerful enemy vessel against which you have no means of retaliating is very unnerving. We spent a desperate half-hour dodging right and left until the Germans lost us in the darkness. In the morning when we had made port the atmosphere on the schooner was distinctly ominous. Much as I tried to laugh it off it was clear that the crew attributed the previous night's alarms to the presence of a seal aboard. This was a serious matter, for a discontented crew could mean disaster. I was a worried man when my fellow captain hailed me and invited me to go swimming. I put Panayoti in the dinghy and rowed across.

My friend and I discussed our narrow escape and my crew's disaffection as we swam slowly round and round, with Panayoti propped up in the dinghy's stern, watching our every movement. We got so engrossed in our conversation we did not realize the boat was drifting further and further away, until with a splash Panayoti, unable to stand the separation any longer, slipped overboard. We dashed to rescue him, but he had disappeared. We dived and dived. There wasn't a trace of him. Then my friend pointed with his hand and shouted, "There he is!" A hundred yards away a little black head was bobbing up and down among the waves at the mouth of the cove. I was torn between a terrible sense of loss and the joy of knowing that Panayoti had come into his own at last. After all, I thought, this was the best, the only way, for it to end. I waved to him, and he disappeared.

My friend and I stood treading water, both of us wondering, I suppose, whether Panayoti was well enough equipped to face the challenge of the open sea, when, with a flurry of churning waves, his glossy head bobbed up between us. His face wore the broadest, most triumphant smile I have ever seen. He kept on looking from one of us to the other, his whiskers twitching with excitement, his round eyes opened wide as if to say, "You see, I've done it." Then, as though he needed to prove the point, he dived, nipped me playfully in the calf and was off at such speed that I had hardly time to turn around before he had served my friend in the same way.

We tried to catch him but he always slipped between our fingers. He darted through our legs and brushed across our backs; he dived, he leaped out of the water, and every now and then he surfaced to look at us and make sure that we were enjoying it too. Then he'd be off again like a cockeyed torpedo. We spent a wildly exciting quarter of an hour until he got tired and came to me and put his flippers on my shoulders, wanting to be lifted back into the dinghy. From that time on the days became one long delight. We were in the water whenever we had a chance. From early morning Panayoti would start worrying me to take him swimming, and by nightfall we were both exhausted.

Fortunately the war in the Aegean was drawing to its close and all we had to do was follow the retreating Germans. Even so, fate had some further blows in store for us. A fierce gale sprang up one night and separated us from the rest of the flotilla. A man was injured falling from the mast. Another was killed in an encounter with a German patrol vessel. And the temper of the crew grew uglier and uglier. One night while I was below they picked up Panayoti and dropped him overboard. I missed him half an hour later and much to their disgust put back and found him in the darkness by his cries. He had been desperately trying to keep up with us and was utterly exhausted. The following day they sent a deputation to me to say the seal must go or else. I told them to be their age and sent them packing. But I don't know what would have happened if the war had lasted longer.

Even so, I had a very hard time of it for the few remaining days. To make things worse Panayoti was growing teeth and he began to bite. It was all in fun, but it could be very painful. It was this new development which put an end to his career aboard one of His Hellenic Majesty's men o' war.

Our commanding officer was a brave and charming man, but somewhat pompous and with a passion for showing off. As we approached Athens he put his miserable little flotilla of raiding schooners through fleet maneuvers. Now that the danger of enemy aircraft was passed he made us practice blue turns and white turns and lines ahead and lines abreast until our heads were spinning. Then, on the day of liberation when we anchored off Piraeus harbor, he went ashore and returned to carry out an inspection, accompanied by several dignitaries and some pretty lady friends. We had to pipe him aboard with our men in summer whites drawn up at the rail as if we were real warships and not filthy little wooden death traps.

The men were understandably angry. After so many years we were returning home as liberators, but instead of being allowed to go ashore we had to be stared at like strange animals and listen to a silly speech about the gratitude of our country. It was at this stage that Panayoti intervened. The captain was delivering his oration when Panayoti crept up behind him and bit him smartly in the calf. There was a most undignified yowl of pain and the speech came to an abrupt end. The men had a hard time of it trying to hide their grins. Afterward they came one by one, the boatswain first, and patted Panayoti on the head. The commanding officer said nothing at the time of the incident, but a few hours later I received a curt, formal signal ordering Panayoti ashore forthwith.

For one last time I tried to coax Panayoti into starting a new life on his own, but he would have none of it. So having no choice I decided to take him to Athens with me. Taxis were scarce and when we finally got one, seven of us piled into it. I sat in front with three others and with Panayoti on my lap. He was very curious and kept sticking his head out of the window the way dogs do.

When we arrived at my aunt's apartment the maid who opened the door nearly fainted at the sight of the seal. My aunt too only managed to overcome her revulsion for a rather grimy Panayoti because of her great pleasure at seeing me return from the wars. But she put her foot down when I suggested that Panayoti should be bathed in the bathtub. We struck a compromise eventually, and a tin hip bath was brought out to the balcony overlooking the street. Panayoti hated getting soap in his eyes and started an awful ruckus. The strange bleatings attracted the attention of the people sitting on their balconies in the flats above my aunt's, and they leaned over to see what it was all about. The sight of so many people staring at something that was going on above the street intrigued the passers-by and soon a large enough crowd had formed in the street below to block the traffic. Drivers, after honking their horns futilely for a while, got out and joined the others. The people in the street started calling up to those in the balconies above, "What is it?" The people in the balconies answered, "We're not sure. We think it's a seal," and presently the whole crowd started shouting in unison, "Show us the seal!"

When I had rinsed Panayoti, I picked him up from behind and he bowed to the people of Athens right and left as if he were a young prince. He was roundly applauded. Perhaps for many of those people he was as good a symbol as any for the end of the occupation. A seal being bathed on a balcony may not be what one ordinarily conceives of as a return to normalcy, but it was certainly a departure from the grim mood of the previous years.

A few days later I was ordered to go on a patrol to the north, where the Germans were still fighting a rear-guard action. I took Panayoti to my mother and left him with her in our home in the country. We put him in a kennel next to the pool so he could take a swim.

When I returned a few weeks later, after the last German had been driven out of Greece, my mother told me that Panayoti was dead. The weather had suddenly turned bitter, and she thought that he had died of a cold. She had had him buried in the garden at the foot of a young cypress tree. I went to say good-by and standing next to the little grave with the icy wind moaning mournfully in the branches, I couldn't help thinking that Panayoti had died of loneliness.

The
Young Man
 # Who Came
to Visit

June 11—Friday

Letter arrives which proves agitating. Linda writes from college she is appearing a week later than originally planned. Friend is motoring her on last lap, and will remain for a few days. He is absolutely terrific. I will understand him but Daddy won't.

Charles reads this at least three times with an inflamed face. Asks me to point out a single creep who has pursued Linda in past whose character he has not grasped far more swiftly than I. Try to calm him down but am secretly flattered that Linda is aware of my quality of comprehension.

Linda's sisters Rachel and Cissie view visit from different angles. Rachel, aged thirteen, peeks into looking glass and runs small pocket comb through her new wave. Cissie, aged seven, says she is using the bathtub to exercise her goldfish and is unwilling to relinquish it again for a guest.

June 18—Friday

Long distance call from Linda who in a blissful voice tells me that she and Bowie—Bowie NORMAN, Mummie—will arrive in late afternoon.

Repeat to Charles who, though skeptical of name Bowie, on the whole takes it calmly. Concludes on what seems to me rather thin evidence that Bowie sounds like Varsity hero, part of a cheer, and in spite of Linda's comment he knows the type like the palm of his hand. All he will desire is exercise so Charles will arrange some men's doubles for tennis.

Point out that Bowie Norman is visiting Linda and that she may have other plans for his amusement but Charles replies that Linda has no net and he has yet to meet a man who does not prefer men's doubles.

June 20—Sunday

Rapture of all when at twilight Linda at wheel in black slacks and pink shirt drives in, with young man at her side. Dogs bark with excitement and I, filled with an emotion I cannot explain, hug and kiss her and tell her that she is too thin.

Linda in voice that is surprisingly low for her usual protest, answers that it would not be like coming home if I had failed to say that.

Under Charles' supervision Bowie Norman backs car behind tree and introductions are made. Bowie is small and ashen colored and speaks in so hushed a voice that first impression is of one coming out of ether and having difficulty in articulating the words. Linda with manner of protective dove keeps large eyes fastened on Bowie's face and tunes own speech on same remote wave length so that at times tones of both appear to fade out "due to circumstances beyond our control."

Conclude, as have often before with young men from the age of thirteen on, that Bowie is shy and must be made to feel At Home. This is not helped when Cissie asks if the cat has got his tongue, Bowie says, Pardon? and Linda with vocal cords suddenly restored, cries, Cis, how dare you! Charles opportunely brings in tray of juleps and welcoming atmosphere again re-established.

Charles now raises his glass to Linda and says the Old Man has missed her. A lot of surprises for her here including re-surfaced tennis court. Big match tomorrow and your friend Bowie is to make a fourth.

The Dove with a whir of feathers as though distracting a serpent from a rabbit exclaims that Bowie is writing Thesis for his Ph.D., therefore no time for anything but work "while we are here." Last phrase highly disturbing and am only thankful that no one picks it up.

We sit down to supper and immediately plunge into account of recent events but give way to Rachel the most vociferous as she tells Linda of Aunt Julie's arrival, Toona's departure, Louise's home life, new kitchen, permanent wave, and what does Linda Honestly think about it?

Sense that Rachel's news broadcast has not been particularly favorably received, for Linda's response is to gaze at Bowie with rather curious look at which he ejaculates single word "Maintenance" and gives her a compassionate smile.

Not unnaturally Charles asks what that means.

Maintenance, repeats Bowie—a generic term . . . a symbol . . . (voice fades).

Linda flies in, all feathers raised, crying, Bowie you are too modest —yes you are—it was sheer genius. You invented it—explain it to Dad.

Charles asks what the Hell they are talking about.

Bowie studies Charles for a few moments as though weighing his powers of comprehension and then begins in faint voice:

Maintenance, sir, is a Protest aimed at what one might call the civilized world of today. The Protest concerns itself with the delusion of this world that they know how to converse. (Can see that in spite of himself attention of Charles is arrested.) Many of the allegedly intelligent believe they are having a conversation when they are actually talking Maintenance. Maintenance as defined in this so-called Protest is the discussion of all material plans. The term includes talk of money, domestic problems, hospitality, alterations, plans for holidays, state of health, automobile, or wardrobe—the list is infinite. It may be necessary to discuss these practicalities but it is false to believe it is conversation.

There is complete paralysis at the table and Cissie looks as if she were about to cry.

The Sponsor of the Protest now gazes rather intently at Charles, and continues: According to our theory (It's *yours*, Bowie, you invented it) it is permissible to discuss the mundane provided, provided, sir, one labels it audibly as Maintenance and is not deluded into believing one is having a meeting of the minds.

Linda now clarifies it further. Let me give you some examples, Dad, so that you will really grasp it. . . . By by-passing the parkways in the traffic hour I can make better time driving to the city. . . . I believe in trading in a car every year for in that way in effect you rent a brand-new car for $294.00. . . . I have found an automatic coal feeding furnace is better than gas—ten minutes of details supplied. (Charles winces.)

Bowie contributes *sotto voce:* . . . I do not agree that the 17-inch television screen is as satisfactory as the larger model but I am going to wait for color anyhow.

There is again a stunned silence and creator of the Protest gives us a thread-like smile.

And what, asks Charles, is Conversation?

It is I would say, sir, the interchange of facts and ideas by the informed, given in disciplined style.

Linda gives a triumphant there I told you so glance at table as Bowie adds: But of course there has been no conversation in the Western World for two hundred years.

Do not like expression on face of Charles and try to give him grueling look of warning as he responds in controlled and noncommittal voice: It is obvious, Bowie, that in your researches you have not read the memoirs of the nineteenth century.

Bowie however also appears to possess the art of hewing to the line and is undeflected by that which does not appear pertinent. He inquires of Linda: Would you not agree that the last renaissance of the art of conversation of which there is testimony occurred among the Encyclopædists—Voltaire, Madame du Deffand, etc., he adds in an exclamatory aside.

That's absolutely true, Bowie, is Linda's response.

Well, if it is so lost, like how to make old mosaics, why bother? suggests Rachel in a helpful voice.

Charles rises heavily and looking at Bowie says I have some work to finish, if you and Glaucon will excuse me, This subtle shaft however is spoiled by his signaling to me in rather obvious fashion from door to join him. Cissie asks Linda a little timidly if she and Bowie would like to play parcheesi. Leave the Encyclopædists with Rachel and Cissie and take dogs on stroll in order to avoid Charles and then find him in hammock. Beg him to lower his voice.

In tones of stinging moderation Charles asks for how many days he is going to have to put up with this gas-bag? Explain that gas-bag is visiting Linda and I found his ideas enlivening. (Do not know why but am instinctively on opposite side of Charles when he attacks.)

Charles with an *et tu Brute* look inquires how I could conceivably be enlivened by this Demosthenes exhorting the Western World in a whisper to step up its mental intercourse to meet the criteria of said authority.

Repeat that I was enlivened and found it salutory to be made aware of how much I talk Maintenance in twenty-four hours.

We swing for a moment in hammock when Charles bursts out demanding how Linda—so level-headed, so astute—could have been taken in by such sophistry. Make error of telling him Rachel has already learned from Linda that Bowie is genius of University, and five publishers are struggling for Book called Philosophy of History, as yet unwritten.

Charles springs from hammock and says he is going to find Rachel. Beg him not to, as unfair to pump sister about sister.

Charles returns in three minutes leading Rachel.

Rachel obviously flattered at being confidante and adviser to her parents sinks into hammock and informs us that (A) Linda in frightful state of nerves over what Bowie will think of family, especially— I am sorry—you, Dad; (B) Linda passionately in love; (C) Rachel not sure to what extent Bowie responds; (D) Linda learning typing to help Bowie with Thesis and Rachel must not repeat it but she believes he will ultimately become President of U. of C. or Harvard. Rachel adds that she has been in Bowie's room. He has four shirts, no top to his pajamas, picture of Linda on skis, and half a bottle of bourbon.

Charles listens in deepest concentration and asks what They are doing now. They, Rachel replies, are sitting in hall and Cissie is sitting with them.

Charles wakes me twice during night, once by lighting cigarette with three matches, the second time to ask if I am asleep and if I am not do I think I heard a car drive away?

Suggest he go downstairs and look which he does not do. Asks me what I think is happening to Education in our country? Does not wait for my views but exclaims two four-letter words which I completely understand. Finally inquires of me if I do not think it is rather late to get into an argument and he must get some rest. Immediately falls asleep and I toss and turn until dawn.

Almost
Strictly

for the
Birds

The island of Lundy is a big, grizzled, windswept hunk of granite in the Atlantic Ocean, not very far from Land's End, England, which is inhabited for the most part by untold thousands of rabbits and birds, notably puffins, and by a dozen or so grizzled, windswept human beings who stoutly maintain that Lundy is an independent nation, with an hereditary king, Mr. Harman. Great Britain, a neighboring and more heavily populated island twelve miles to the east, maintains antithetically that Lundy is nothing but Lundy, with an hereditary queen, Elizabeth. I myself would have hoped that a matter so vital as this would have been settled ages ago, but the awkward fact is that Lundy's status has been uncertain since 1135 A.D., and, after eight hundred years, a clarification of it isn't in sight.

Consequently, there has been no end of confusion. Not the least of it was in 1929, when Mr. Harman, the king, or non-king, depending on whose side you're on, having already issued his own postage stamps, began to issue his own coins, and shortly thereafter was hauled into court on the neighboring island, Great Britain, for allegedly violating its Coinage Act of 1870. (Mr. Harman's specie, portraying the face of Mr. Harman, was in two denominations, a one-puffin coin and a

half-puffin coin, neatly convertible to a penny and a ha'penny at the
legal rate of exchange. The postage stamps were in several denominations, the twelve-puffin stamp portraying twelve puffins, the nine-
puffin stamp nine puffins, etc., and the half-puffin stamp half a puffin
—the upper half.) The trial, in Great Britain, was held at the King's
Bench Division of the High Court, and, it was hoped at the time,
would resolve the status of Lundy once and for all. It didn't do anything of the sort, for, as anyone studying a transcript soon realizes,
Mr. Harman, the defendant, was the only person at the trial who took
it seriously. The following excerpt is typical:

> *Mr. Harman:* The mainland has never interfered when
> Lundy was reasonably well governed. And it
> repudiated all responsibility when anything
> really called for investigation, like the murder
> of the whole population.
> *The Lord Chief Justice:* Does that often happen?
> [Laughter.]
> *Mr. Harman:* It happened two or three times in the past.
> *Mr. Justice Avory:* The population of what? Rabbits?
> [Laughter.]
> *Mr. Harman:* There are about one thousand rabbits to every
> human being, but the residents number forty-
> five, apart from visitors.

Such arguments as these having been heard, the justices deliberated,
and subsequently opined it had been a very entertaining case—it was
to *them*—which had been lost by Mr. Harman. That was in 1931.
Today, notwithstanding, the residents of Lundy *still* aren't paying
taxes and when they visit Great Britain are liable to customs. There
aren't any policemen on Lundy and the laws of Britain are unen-
forced. Lundy publishes its own postage stamps, portraying, in addition to puffins, such eminent non-puffins as Eric Bloodaxe, Mrs. Graham in her aerial balloon, and a horse named Betty Brown, and a
letter cannot be gotten off the island without one; and Mr. Harman's
coins, which he priced at a penny and a ha'penny when they were
legal tender, are considered nowadays to be historical relics, and are
sold on Lundy to tourists and numismatists for forty-eight times as
much. Mr. Harman is dead, but his son, Mr. Albion Harman, is reigning in his stead, and stoutly maintains that Lundy is "a vest-pocket
size, self-governing dominion," out of the realm for every practical
purpose.

Unfortunately, I wasn't able to attend the trial in 1931, being ten months old at the time, but in 1955 I happened to be in London, and I made it a point there to visit the king, Mr. Albion Harman, to learn how Lundy finds itself in such a curious position. Mr. Harman is a healthy, middle-aged man with a quiet smile and a spray of un-kempt white hair, and, when I found him, was himself in a curious position—sitting amidst a pile of junk in his old, weather-beaten auto. He told me he was employed, in London, as a mining engineer for the Balakhany Black Sea Oil Company, and often used the car on geological field trips, accounting for its condition.

Presently, we decided to continue our conversation at a nearby pub, and drove to one of Mr. Harman's favorites, the Horse and Groom, ordering a Worthington apiece. Worthington, Mr. Harman commented, is the only beer or ale continuously aging in the bottle, and he started to explain how this singular chemical process occurs when I steered the conversation to Lundy; thereupon, he revealed that he visits the place once or twice a month, that he enjoys it hugely, and that its sovereign status arises, principally, from the English penchant for keeping things just as they always were.

In 1135, Mr. Harman said, Lundy apparently was the domain of the king of England, but in that year he gave it to the Marisco family, one of England's foremost. Since then, it has belonged, essentially, to whoever was there at the time, a heterogeneous group that includes not only the Messrs. Harman, father and son, but also a Reverend Mr. Heaven and *his* son; Mr. Thomas Benson, a smuggler, who fired on any ship that didn't dip its colors; a pirate named Salkeld; a pirate named Nutt, who still haunts the place; and other pirates of Turkey, Spain, France, and Holland, the last of whom murdered the whole population in the 1700s, to the immense amusement of the Lord Chief Justice in 1931. In all these years, Mr. Harman said, Parliament never interfered in Lundy's affairs or tried to tax it, apparently feeling it was too far away to bother with, and thereby setting a precedent that still obtains.

Next, Mr. Harman recalled that the pirates on Lundy had enacted a total of two laws, and observed that nowadays, in the twentieth century, its body of legislation still is admirably brief. The pirates' laws were these:

The man who shall snap his arms or smoke tobacco in the hold or carry a lighted candle without lanthorn shall receive Moses' law [forty lashes]. If any man meet with a prudent woman that offers to meddle with her, without her consent, he shall suffer death.

The laws of contemporary Lundy, Mr. Harman explained, are contained in half-a-dozen letters and scribbled notes, which he and his father left about. The first time they were codified was today, by me, as follows:

THE LAWS OF LUNDY

ARTICLE I. Nobody can come here if Mr. Harman doesn't want him to.

ARTICLE II. Anybody with a gun must give it to Mr. Gade at night before it gets dark.

ARTICLE III. Nobody can shoot any birds, especially puffins.

ARTICLE IV. Every dog must be the same sex, and visitors can't have dogs at all.

ARTICLE V. Anybody who wants to do something very odd, like bring a kangaroo here, has to ask Mr. Harman.

A few explanatory notes and judicial interpretations on this body of laws seems to be called for, at this point. Article I, Mr. Harman told me, has resulted in a blacklist, a dozen or so persons forever banned from Lundy—for example, a trawlerman who used naughty language there, an alcoholic, a homosexual. Article IV, the anti-canine statute, is to prevent their proliferation about the island, and the sex that Lundy's dogs currently must be is female. Article II, relative to the use of firearms, was enacted in 1927, when two residents were feuding over a woman; now, Mr. Gade doesn't enforce it.

Mr. Gade, I learned, is Mr. Harman's viceroy and the King of Lundy *pro tem*, as well as the postmaster, innkeeper, grocer, bartender, Lloyd's of London agent, Volunteer-in-Charge of the Rocket Life Saving Apparatus, and official representative of the Shipwrecked Fishermen and Mariners Society or the Shipwrecked Mariners and Fishermen Society—no one can remember which, including Mr. Gade. Also, Mr. Gade is judge and jury at Lundy's trials, of which historically there have been two, one civil and one criminal. In the civil action, he handed down a writ of mandamus, so to speak, constraining the longshoremen to divvy up their tips; in the criminal one, he fined a visitor five dollars for accompanying a dog to Lundy, in contravention of Article IV. The corpus delicti, incidentally, a chow-chow, got lost on Lundy shortly afterwards. It was discovered in a cleft of rock, dead, thereby demonstrating to the satisfaction of everyone resident on Lundy the simple, laconic wisdom of their country's legislation.

Having familiarized myself with the laws of the realm, and having thanked Mr. Harman for the interview, and for the Worthington, I went to Lundy itself. Formerly, a three-seater plane had gone there —at various times, it was called the Lundy and Atlantic Airlines, the North Devon Flying Club, and Devon Air Ltd.—but several weeks earlier, it fell into the Atlantic, so I traveled to Lundy on a boat, a big white paddle-wheeler that makes the trip every two or three days from Ilfracombe, Great Britain's equivalent of Atlantic City.

Besides myself, there were seven hundred passengers—all of them excursionists. I am utterly unable to account for such an extravagant number of them, and, after observing their behavior at close range, on Lundy itself—they looked at one or two pigs there, had a beer, and returned to the paddle-wheeler—I find it even the more mysterious. The tourist's lot is a difficult one almost anywhere, but on Lundy his adversities are of epic proportions. Many of the seven hundred were seasick; as we got off, drizzle fell upon them, and the ocean slapped over the flimsy wooden pier, soaking their skirts and trousers. A man fell into the water, and a middle-aged lady, after enduring some unknown misfortune at shore, was carried back to the paddle-wheeler all bloody, while the rest of us were getting off it.

The tourists bore their crosses stoically. Huffing and hawing, they climbed the palisades of Lundy by a steep, switchback trail, and hurried to the only gay spot, the Marisco Tavern; like subway riders, they pressed inside, and were given beer furiously by an old, gaunt, eminently harried man, whom I took to be Mr. Gade. He, Mr. Gade, was afforded no quarter by the tourists; in his capacity as postmaster, he was called upon for postage stamps; in that as grocer, for fig newtons and crumpets; meanwhile, his assistant, Audrey, equipped the tourists with puffin book ends, puffin ash trays, and plaster puffins of no apparent utilitarian value. The tiny tavern was full of smoke, darkness, and noise: of men calling for beer, of plaster puffins falling to the floor, of a boy crying,

"Buy a pennant, Mommy, so they'll know we've been to Lundy."

"Hush, dear, we already have a puffin."

I surveyed this Doré-like scene for a minute or two; then, I pushed outside for a breath of air. The drizzle had stopped, and the sunlight fell in ribbons; the island of Lundy dried beneath it, a desolate plain of scrub, stones, and faraway, gray sheep. The color of everything was gray—the stones, the abandoned lighthouse, the Marisco Tavern and the ashen huts nearby—an island that was built of rain-clouds. I strolled to the edge of the cliff, watching the sunlight's glare on the water, four hundred feet below. When I returned to the Marisco Tavern, the tourists had gone, and Mr. Gade, Audrey, and two or three islanders were sitting quietly in the darkness, desperately trying to get their bearings.

Now, the Marisco Tavern was a friendly, easygoing place. Mr. Gade, with all the slow deliberation of a bartender making a pousse-café, had filled his pipe, and leaned against the gray stone wall, cheerily smoking it; the others, with beer mugs in their laps, talked idly of the unimportant, important things of life. Charlie and the Captain, who worked at the waterfront, came from there in black turtleneck sweaters, nodded for a beer apiece, and started throwing darts at a raggedy bull's-eye, inaugurating each of their games with an esoteric cry, "Middle for diddle!" or "Muggs away!" A few others drifted in, and every now and then the assemblage raised its glasses, toasting itself with enthusiasm: "*All* the very *best!*"

"All the *very* best," cried Charlie, at the dart board, "and muggs away!"

These were the "islanders," the dozen or so persons who live on Lundy, as distinguished from the seven hundred "trippers," or "bluebottles," who just had left. (A bluebottle, my dictionary explains, is *Calliphora erythrocephala*, a pesky insect that flies about in circles, going buzz.) They were a friendly crowd, and, later in the evening, as every evening, we made it a point to get together again. Audrey, the girl who sold puffinware, sat herself at a piano, and we all sang "Home on the Range" and "The Whiffenpoof Song"; then, "What d'ya say you jive it, Audrey, up a bit?" cried Charlie, and we all sang "Tavern in the Town," "Landlord, Fill the Flowing Bowl," and two choruses of "The Halls of Montezuma." At ten o'clock, we were given a solo by a retired sea dog with a vivid, animated face:

> When I catch Alfonso Spugoni, the toreador,
> With one mighty swipe I will dislocate his bally jaw,
> I'll fight the bullfighter, I will,
> When I catch the bounder, the blighter I'll kill,
> He shall die. . . .

Whenever the old sailor came to this particular point, he swiped himself on the jaw. Presently, Mr. Gade was called upon, and maintained the toreador theme by singing "Flow Gently, Sweet Afton" in a voice that is occasionally heard in Spain, emanating from mortally wounded bulls, and I, being an American, was asked to obtain a fiddle somewhere and call a square dance. A good time was had by all, and there were cries until early in the morning of "*All* the very *best!*"

Lundy seemed like such a delightful place to live that I wondered, naturally, how the Harman family had managed to come by it. I asked about this the next day and discovered that the late Mr. Harman—Mr. Harman I, or "M.C.H.," as his subjects knew him— had set his heart on Lundy when only a bluekettle, aged eighteen, and finally bought it in 1925 for $80,000, a thousand times what it went for in the Mariscos' days. Theretofore, Lundy had been owned and operated by the Reverend Mr. Heaven, and was known as the Kingdom of Heaven, of course, while the voyage to Lundy was known as Purgatory.

Lundy, I also learned, has gone by many other names, historically, but all of them sound decidedly like Lundy—*viz.*, Landy, Londi, Londey, Londay, Lounday, Lunday, Lundeia, Londia, and Londai— and scholars have just as many explanations for the word, one of the more extravagant being that of Westcote, who suggested in 1646 that it was "island" backwards. In fact, Lundy is from the Icelandic *lundi*, meaning puffin, and *ey*, meaning island, and so means Puffin Island. Etymologically, then, we must note that "Lundy Island" is a tautology, and that a resident is properly a Lundyskeggi, two or more of them being Lundyskeggjar. The late Mr. Harman was in the forefront of the battle to prevent the ungrammatical use of "Lundy Island," and, a few years before his death, he wrote an impassioned letter about it, saying, "I hope [the residents] will help me to combat this practice. As the British Post Office insist on perpetuating the error we shall never quite succeed, but we can at least do our best." It is not recorded, however, that Mr. Harman ever called himself a Lundyskeggi.

So much has been said, on these pages, of puffin islands, puffinware, half-puffins, and non-puffins that a word or two about the puffin itself seems to be called for. Puffins, on Lundy, are residents in the spring and early summer, and as I was there in the fall, we missed one another; however, the Lundyskeggjar told me they're a small, black-and-white sea bird, with an outrageous beak of every color, a singing voice that somewhat resembles Mr. Gade's, and a gait like a rolling ship. Further research turned up the news that puffins were eaten in the Middle Ages; that they themselves eat animals 98.22 per cent of the time and algae 1.78 per cent of the time: that they are popularly known as sea parrots, Lundy parrots, tommie noddies, tammy nories, and bottlenoses, and ornithologically as *Fratercula arctica*—"little arctic brother."

In addition to puffins, I learned, one hundred and forty-five species of birds inhabit Lundy, and many others visit it from time to time, including such transoceanic rarities as the Sardinian warbler and the American robin. Personally, I'm not a practicing bird-watcher, and none of this stuff especially fascinates me, but, I realize, there are readers of mine whom it *does*, who are anxious to hear even more, and for their benefit I have studied some of the voluminous, ornithological logs that were kept, on Lundy, for not only years but centuries, and I have recorded, in the next three paragraphs, and in no particular order, a few of the sightings that seem of more than routine interest. They are paragraphs that persons like myself, who aren't markedly fond of birds, might very profitably ignore.

Lundy, anyhow, I learned from my readings, has been visited by such exotic feathered creatures as the great auk, the great tit, the twite, knot, teal, stint, snipe, shag, rook, widgeon, and wood pigeon, as well as by two apparently distinct species, the chaffinch and the chiffchaff. The chaffinches were seen in great profusion at lunchtime, September 9, 1880, and, in the following year, one was caught by a fellow named Ward, who gave it to Annie. The chiffchaff, for its part, was duly noted but escaped captivity from March 12 to October 23, 1954, and a fate worse than a chaffinch's was meted to a gray phalarope on December 9, 1881, when it was shot by W.B.; Cecilia Harriet Heaven called it "an evil deed," and so do I.

Mr. Norman H. Joy saw an arctic skua on August 22, 1905. A peregrine falcon was recorded in 1274 A.D., and an albatross on June 13, 1874, and, on an unspecified date in April 1906, Mr. Norman H. Joy saw a cirl bunting. Crespi saw a goshawk, but Loyd says he is "obviously in error," and Hendy saw a tree pipit, but Davenport says, "As may be imagined, we saw no tree pipits"; the consensus on yellow wagtails, is three to four, with Perry, Davenport, and an unnamed bluebottle maintaining the affirmative, Crespi, Rousham, Ross, and Cummings upholding the negative, and Loyd keeping his own counsel on the matter.

On September 23, 1954, a spotted flycatcher caught a butterfly, hitting its head against a tree, and in October 1874, a yellow-billed cuckoo hit *its* head against a tree and dropped dead, after flying uninterruptedly from America. Jack snipes, by way of contrast, have been hitting their heads against a lighthouse, while the foghorn there has frightened away the choughs, which were "as common as crows" in 1860, and the gannets, which were as common as choughs since 1321 A.D. A nightjar was churring at 10:30 in the evening, May 30, 1922. Bluebottles on Lundy have reported nightingales, white-tailed eagles, and lesser gray shrikes, but nobody ever believed them, and, in 1953, a cook at the Lundy Field Society reported a pelican, becoming the laughingstock for days. Well, it *was* a pelican; it just escaped from the Bristol Zoo.

While W.B., the lighthouse, and the foghorn have, of course, played an unparalleled role in the lives, respectively, of the gray phalarope, the jack snipe, and the gannet, there surely hasn't been anything of such profound consequence to the average bird, on Lundy, as the founding of the Lundy Field Society there, in 1946. Since then, the birds have scarcely known a moment to call their own. Not only are they kept under a constant surveillance which, anywhere else, would be reserved for suspected criminals, but a full blotter is being maintained on their comings and goings, their associations with other birds, their sexual indiscretions, and such intimate details of personal hygiene as the name, number, and whereabouts of their body lice.

Many of these birds, on Lundy, after a dozen years of such scant privacy, are beginning to betray the same signs of nervous collapse that might be expected in a human being. A case in point is the manx shearwater, a shy, rather introverted bird, whose mental state became so desperate that, in 1948, the elder Mr. Harman was forced to memorialize the Lundy Field Society on its behalf.

"This particular colony," he wrote, "has suffered from rats, but has also suffered a bit from being over-birdwatched. I don't take any exception to this, for it is all in the cause of science, but I understand that not a single bird was hatched."

Mr. Harman's charitable attitude toward the Lundy Field Society was manifested as early as 1946, when, welcoming the Lundy Field Society to Lundy, he gave it $250, its first subscription, and the abandoned lighthouse to live in. Today, the lighthouse is still the society's roost, being inhabited in the migrating season by a half-dozen earnest bird-watchers and in *every* season by Miss Barbara K. Whittaker, its warden, a young, personable, studious woman whose tireless devotion to the birds is almost a byword there. One afternoon, I visited the lighthouse and introduced myself to Miss Whittaker, and she, in turn, introduced me to several other bird-watchers and to Mr. Oliver Hook, an old, lively Englishman who watches seals but hasn't anything in particular against birds. The lighthouse itself was a perfect chaos: of tables and rickety orange crates, of dirty dishes, of unwrapped butter, marmalade tins, Spam cans, and dismembered bits of liverwurst and boloney, of shaggy, gray-green books in topless heaps, of bulletin boards, broadsides, and ornithological pin-ups, and, in the interstices of all this, moving guardedly, of Miss Whittaker and the bird-watchers, all of them wearing baggy woolen sweaters and looking absolutely in the pink of health.

For the most part, the bird-watchers were eating liverwurst, and Miss Whittaker was writing assiduously in the daily log. I saw that her entry was a curious one, this:

> *Wednesday*, Sept. 7. Oliver Hook arrived. O.H. entered straight way into L.F.S. activities and visited Seal Hole with B.K.W., where a calf about 24 hours old was found. The spirited young lady left her imprint on O.H.

Puzzled by this, I asked O.H. for a fuller explanation, and hastily was told that the spirited young lady wasn't Miss Whittaker but the seal, and that the imprint was of its teeth—now, a purple, terrifying welt on his forearm. Mr. Hook assured me it wasn't malignant and, when I inquired about the seal, observed it had been shooed away by splashing water in its face, apparently, in England, the accepted procedure for shooing away seals. Later, Mr. Hook said, he managed to weigh the seal, measure it, and tag it for future reference with a small aluminum band. Both parties to the operation set a record for Lundy, the seal being the first of its species to be tagged by a human being, and Mr. Hook being the first of *his* to be bitten by a seal.

Mr. Hook now remarked that, for the time being, he proposed leaving the seals to their own devices and investigating the birds, and, if possible, even catching some for more particularized study. The idea of catching a bird rather fascinated me, and, although I confessed I wouldn't know how to begin, he invited me along, and Miss Whittaker came, too. When we left the lighthouse, it was late afternoon, and the fading sunlight swept across the island like a wind. Below us, the beach already was in twilight; sea gulls circled in the warmth above it, and black cormorants stood on the rocks, spreading their wings like Prussian eagles. Miss Whittaker, Mr. Hook, and I walked silently for ten minutes and came, presently, to a sizable thicket of bramble and rock, rising out of which, like a dinosaur, was an extraordinary contrivance of wire fences, wood, and rope, of doors and pulleys moaning in the breeze. This, Miss Whittaker said cheerfully, is a Heligoland Bird Trap, the most serviceable kind there is. Flabbergasted, I stared at the Heligoland Bird Trap, estimating it one hundred feet long, thirty feet wide, and eight feet high—roughly, one million times as large as the average bird.

Presently, Miss Whittaker saw my dismay, and observed that a Heligoland Bird Trap—although, on Lundy, such elemental devices as dead herrings, balls of wool, and W.B.'s rifle had been used instead —is superior to any of these because of its vast, intricate mechanism, which only the most scholarly of birds could hope to grasp. Its proper utilization begins, she continued, when she, Miss Whittaker, thrashes about in the bramble, and, after frightening a bird into the trap, closes a screen door behind it. Thereupon, the bird flies about in consternation; more and more doors are closed, all of them being actuated by Miss Whittaker, who, it ought to be pointed out, is also inside the Heligoland Bird Trap; progressively, the woebegone bird finds itself in smaller and smaller quarters and, finally, when the last door closes, in a small, accessible, wooden box. As she explained this, Miss Whittaker scurried about the trap, thrashing her arms, yanking ropes, and closing doors by way of demonstration, and when she had finished, she put her hand demonstratively into the wooden box, discovering, to her astonishment, there *was* a bird inside. It was a female redstart, which apparently had been there all along, and Miss Whittaker drew it forth in triumph.

Until now, I hadn't considered what Miss Whittaker would do with a bird in the hand once she had it there; so she explained that the customary procedure is to weigh it, measure its wing, bill, and leg bone, observe the color of its eye, put all this in a notebook, appropriate its body lice, put all *that* in a bottle, assign the bird a serial number, put this serial number—a tiny aluminum band—on its leg, and, finally, let the bird, band, and serial number fly blithely away. So saying, Miss Whittaker carried the redstart to a little shack and began to perform these operations, and, as she did so, commented "The Lundy Field Society ringed more than a thousand birds last year—one thousand and ninety-eight, I believe, of forty-six different species. Birds that were ringed on Lundy have turned up, later, in such places as Chaves, Portugal; Alicante, Spain; and Izmozen, Spanish Morocco; and, of course, that helps us to understand how they migrate, as do the ectoparasites. On Lundy, the birds are lousy—they have a lot of lice, that is—and as you can see, this redstart has two or three, in the scruff of her neck. I don't care for ectoparasites myself, but Mr. Gordon B. Thompson *does*, and asked us to save them. Mr. Thompson has discovered that the most common ectoparasite here, on Lundy, is a tick, *Ixodes reduvius*."

Mr. Hook and I listened to this attentively, but the redstart, apparently, had heard it all before. It didn't look frightened, it looked bored, and, after its release, it flew to the bramble and sat on a juniper twig, as if nothing out-of-the-way had happened. It didn't even make its experiences known to the other redstarts, to whom, I gathered, the whole bird-ringing business was old hat.

Presently, Mr. Hook observed something to the effect that two birds in the hand are worth one in the bush, and proposed that the three of us attempt to capture, measure, and ring another one, having had such notable success with the redstart. This struck Miss Whittaker as an excellent idea, so she, Mr. Hook, and I equipped ourselves with branches and began thrashing about in the bramble, in front of the Heligoland Bird Trap. We managed to rouse a single bird— another redstart, which popped from the underbrush like a champagne cork, flying over my shoulder to distant, unknown parts. Miss Whittaker and Mr. Hook watched it go, and turned to me with disappointment.

"I'm awfully sorry," I said.

"That's all right," Miss Whittaker said, but I knew that her heart wasn't in it.

A few days later, before departing from Lundy and returning on the paddle-wheeler to England, I visited the old lighthouse again, to see what sort of mention had been made of our activities in the Lundy Field Society's daily log. I knew, of course, that these logs had been preserved for centuries and would be kept, inevitably, for centuries more, so I was delighted to see the following:

> *Thursday*, Sept. 8. B.K.W. swallow-watched all day, but in the evening she, an American author (or journalist) Mr. Fach (?) and O.H. worked the Heligoland Trap on the terrace and caught and ringed a ♀ redstart.

The hesitant nature of this entry doesn't trouble me at all. The bird was the first and only ♀ redstart in whose capture and subsequent enringment I've been to any degree responsible, and I'm proud as a peacock, happy as a ♀ lark, to have been granted this unsolicited measure of immortality.

FREDERICK LEWIS ALLEN

These

 Intelligence

Tests

Last October I had to take a literacy test. I had recently moved to
New York State, and it appeared that I could not vote in the election
unless I either produced a school or college diploma or certificate, or
passed a literacy test; and though I searched the house from top to
bottom, not a single certificate could I find. I found documents which
to my simple mind seemed to bear on the case, such as college class
reports with my name in them, and letters which mentioned my
being in the publishing business (a fact which ought to establish at
least a fair presumption in my favor); yet when I took them to the
local schoolhouse and showed them to the State of New York as
embodied in the person of its authorized agent, the schoolmistress,
I was told they wouldn't do. The law said certificates, and these were
not certificates. So I laughed a little nervously and sat down in the
schoolroom to take the test, in a tiny chair before a tiny desk designed
for a child of eight, and a little deficient in knee-room for a child of
thirty-four.

It was a formidable paper which the schoolmistress set before me.
First I had to write my name and address, which I did with great
care. Then came a series of detailed directions to the effect that I
was to read the paragraph of text which followed and write out the

answers to some questions bearing on it. The paragraph began somewhat as follows:

> Theodore Roosevelt was a great American. His letters to his children have been collected in a book since his death. He was interested in animals and birds. He read many books and magazines. . . .

It ran on in this sprightly and coherent style for some distance. Then came the questions:

1. Who was a great American?
2. What has been done to his letters to his children since his death?
3. What was he interested in?
4. What did he read?

And so forth.

I started to answer the first question when suddenly (as sometimes happens) a thought struck me.

One of the candidates for Governor of New York State in the coming election was named Theodore Roosevelt—and here were humble citizens like myself, of doubtful literacy, being subtly subjected to propaganda on his behalf. Was I to submit to any such nefarious scheme? I was not. I resolved to write:

1. Alfred E. Smith; and still is.

They would throw me out of the schoolhouse for an illiterate fellow, but I would appeal the case. If necessary I would carry it to the Supreme Court, where able counsel would argue brilliantly that *Alfred E. Smith; and still is* was a demonstrably literate reply. There would be a triumphant vindication, and—

But suddenly I cooled. By that time Election Day would be past, and I should have lost my vote. No, there was a better way. So very firmly I seized my pencil and wrote *Theodore Roosevelt*. I received a certificate of literacy, and a few weeks later I went to the polls— and you all know the result.

I had almost forgotten the incident when the other day I picked up a set of the intelligence tests prepared by the learned ones of Columbia University for the selection of young Columbians. As I looked at them I marveled again—as I had marveled that day in the schoolroom —at the abject docility of mind which so many examiners seem to expect of their victims. To them there is only one right answer to any question—the one they had in mind when they framed it—and all others are wrong. If they want you to write *Theodore Roosevelt,* write it you must or flunk.

With most of the Columbia tests I had no quarrel. There were printed alphabets in which you were told to cross out the letter just after A and draw a line under the second letter after K; there were nice little problems in arithmetic, and pictures of rabbits with one ear missing in which you had to point out what was the matter with the rabbit. But soon appeared a lot of questions of a different sort. Each of these questions had several answers appended to it. The miserable examinee was instructed to mark a cross before the "best answer" to each question. No chance for argument; he would be given credit if he picked the right answer and lose credit if he picked the wrong one. For example:

> When you are out of funds, should you—
>> get to work and earn
>> borrow from your friends
>> write home to your people
>> steal

Now what on earth is the "best answer" to that question? I am willing to concede that the worst is *steal.* But as between the other three, it seems to me a toss-up, with the wise selection depending on the circumstances. Presumably *get to work and earn* is the answer favored on Morningside Heights; but to the average sub-freshman I should certainly recommend writing home to his people, and to myself I should recommend borrowing, and then evening things up by striking the editor for more cash for my next contribution. Yet apparently there is no chance for the examinee to rise in his wrath and say, "That depends." He must pick the "right answer."

Here is another:

> If you are lost in the forest in the daytime, what is the thing to do?
>> go straight ahead to a big tree
>> hurry to the nearest house you know of
>> sit down and cry
>> use the sun or compass for a guide

Now here is a very pretty problem, on which whole chapters could be written (and have been). The orthodox Boy Scout would say, *Use the sun or a compass for a guide;* but the only time I ever got lost in a forest the sun was well hidden by clouds and I had no compass—which shows that the kind of answer which will get you into Columbia won't always get you out of the woods. The fellow who would get lost in plain sunshine with a compass in his pocket would be such a nut that he ought to be admitted to a good safe campus and kept there.

There is something to be said for the answer *Hurry to the nearest house you know of.* I happen to live in a thoroughly wooded suburb, a section so wooded that the real-estate agents sometimes pleasantly refer to it as a forest; and often visitors have told me that they got thoroughly mixed up driving around in the network of roads and succeeded in finding where I lived only by inquiring for me at the nearest house. Ought I to say to them, "Tut, tut, you should have used the sun or a compass for a guide"?

There are occasions when I should recommend going straight ahead to a big tree, climbing it, and getting a good long look at the surrounding country, being very careful—and here is a real test of intelligence—not to climb out on the end of a dead branch. But after all the most delightfully satisfactory answer is *sit down and cry.* There are few enough opportunities for a good long cry in this busy modern life of ours; so if you are all alone and there is nobody to tell you to move on, why not settle right down on a stump and enjoy yourself? Besides, after you have cried for a little while you may have a good idea about what to do next (such as not climbing out on the dead branch), or the sun may come out, or somebody may hear you and come along with a compass, or even point out the moss growing on the north side of a Doctor of Philosophy, thus enabling you to make your triumphal exit according to the best Boy Scout traditions.

In these tests there are also a number of sentences which the victim is to mark T if they could possibly be true and F if they could not; and several of these sentences seem to me equally debatable. For instance, take this one: *Coming down the hill on his bicycle the chain broke, but he rode back again to get it fixed.* I can see the examiners shaking their heads and saying, "Impossible." But who said it was a bicycle chain which broke? In my version of the incident our friend was carrying something heavy by means of a chain (very likely a dangling participle such as the examiner perpetrated in the sentence above) when the chain broke. No damage was done to his bicycle or any part thereof. Will Nicholas Murray Butler raise his right hand and swear to me that our friend could not ride back again (to the English department, let us say) to get the damage repaired?

Here is another: *Fearing that he might waken her patient by his impudent talk, the nurse gave the detested dummy what he wished.* "Impossible!" goes up the cry at Morningside Heights. But what if we were to tell them the whole sordid story? As I recall it, there were four men in the convalescent ward of a hospital, playing bridge. As the game progressed, one of them (who was not taking part in it at the moment) wandered off to the private corridor and, hateful creature that he was, demanded a kiss of a pretty nurse. Whereupon, fearing that he might awaken her patient by his impudent talk, the nurse gave the detested dummy what he wished. I am not quite sure what happened next, though it is my impression that the patient—a former Yale football star—had one eye open all the time and, despite his enfeebled condition, got up and spoiled the dummy for any more bridge that night, subsequently marrying the nurse, much to the regret of several eligible interns. Is it impossible? It is not. Yet if you, ardent bridge-player that you are, were taking the examination and marked that sentence as possible, the scoring clerks would set you down as unintelligent.

I have nothing against intelligence tests or literacy tests or any other sort of tests as such. Personally I find them as diverting and twice as ingenious as crossword puzzles. When I see a question like *A man whose salary is $16 a week spends $10 a week: in how many weeks can he save $300?* I like to see how soon I can get the answer, which is, of course, 50 weeks or more, depending on (a) his private income, and (b) the size of the doctor's bills resulting from his attempt to live on an insufficient diet. But I do wish examiners would try not to be so arbitrary. Young John Keats was a pretty intelligent boy and as Keats, '14, might have been spoken of as one of the more successful members of the Alumni Club of London; but what chance would he have had of picking the "best answer" if he had been up against something like this (which isn't from a Columbia test but might be)?

> Mark a cross before the best answer to this question: What can ail thee, knight at arms, alone and palely loitering?
> I have mislaid my compass
> I have indigestion and my companions have deserted me
> I voted for the Republican candidate for Governor of New York
> I met a lady in the meads.

DAVID McCORD

New Twilight
on
Old Gods

I

Sisyphus, rolling up the hill his stone,
Found that he could not make the grade
   alone : alone
Today the best of us say this of us,
We are no better rollers than was Sisyphus.

II

Atlas at last unable to sustain
The heavens' weight sank down to earth
   again : again
We cry for someone huge and hatless.
You'll have to bear the world though, this time, Atlas!

III

Pandora never has received our praise
For singling out the lid that she did
   raise : raise
Every lid, the eyelid first. Sand or a
Speck of dust can hide like Hope, Pandora.

IV

Calypso *ipso facto* played it cool;
Penelope employed the golden
                rule : rule
Out old Zeus, for whom the gods eclipse so
Easily is always a Calypso.

V

Poseidon, Greek for Neptune, has in hand
The trident as he rides from sea to
                land : land
Sakes, old fellow, look which way you're ridin'!
Much better off at sea these days, Poseidon.

VI

Calliope, concerned with eloquence,
How graciously you lived one present
                tense : tents
Of another kind your recent tie-up, he
Is younger now who loves you so, Calliope.

ROBERT NATHAN

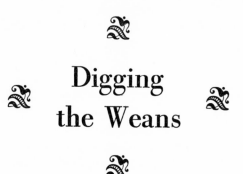

Digging
the Weans

The inscription on the north wall of the temple at Pound-Laundry
on the east coast of the Great West Continent has finally been
deciphered by the team led by Sr. B'Han Bollek. This work brings
us certain assurance of the theory expressed by Bes Nef, Hanh Shui,
and Nat Obelgerst-Levy that a people of considerable numbers and
power formerly inhabited this salt and desolate land. It is a triumph
for those archaeologists who have been working ever since the fortunate discovery of an ivory cross and string of beads at the northeast,
or "Bosstin" tumulus, along with a rusted iron wheel which seems
to have been designed to run along some kind of track or trolley.
These artifacts, as everyone knows, are now in the museum at Kenya.
What we have been unable to discover is the fate of these ancient
people. That they perished in some sort of upheaval many thousands
of years ago is clear from the inscription itself, which Sr. B'Han
translates as follows: "nor [for north?] rain nor hail nor snow . . ."
there are some hieroglyphics missing, and the inscription ends with
the phrase . . . "their appointed rounds."

However, it must be remembered that the *r* and the *w* are readily
interchangeable, both in Hittite and in ancient Hivite, and Bes Nef
prefers the reading: "their pointed wounds." This naturally suggests
a catastrophe, possibly an invasion from the east, a belief, I may add,
greatly encouraged by the findings in the Valley of the Sun, which
will be discussed later. On the other hand, if, as some believe, includ-

ing B'Han Bollek, that the phrase should be read: "their appointed rounds," the meaning of the full inscription might well be as follows: "The north rain, the hail and the snow [also from the north] have accomplished their appointed 'rounds' [or tasks]" . . . namely, have annihilated the inhabitants.

So much, then, we do know; but very little else is known of these ancient people. Professor Shui believes that they may have been Brythons, and related to the still older, Druidic culture whose stones are still to be seen in the East Island. Professor Shui bases this theory upon a certain similarity in the two glyphs, the Brythonic "bathe" and the Wean "bath"; but his theory necessarily comes to grief when one examines the glyph for "that which rises"—the Brythonic "lift" and the Wean "elevator" having obviously no common root.

I have called these people the Weans, because certain archaeological findings incline us to the belief that they called their land the We, or the Us; actually, in the southern part of the continent, the word Weuns (or Weans) does appear, as well as the glyph for Wealls, and the word Theyuns.

To return for a moment to the theory of catastrophe, and the "pointed wounds" of Bes Nef. In the Valley of the Sun there have been unearthed many bronze, and tin, and even stone figures of what would seem to be a kind of huge praying mantis. There are many groups of such figures, usually including male and female, and sometimes with young; it is curious that in every case the male figure is larger and more powerful than the female, which we know to be untrue in the case of the actual praying mantis. These figures nevertheless have the small, cruel head, the long savage arms, the spindly legs, and the attenuated bodies of the mantis. Is it possible that a civilization of men and women, more or less like ourselves, might have been overwhelmed by an invasion of mantis-like insects? Where could they have come from? and where did they go? The conjecture is, of course, fascinating; but no mantis skeletons or remains of any kind have been found, except the above-mentioned statues.

Pound-Laundry is in itself the richest of the diggings. It is believed that at one time this city (for recent excavations indicate "the laundry," as we call it, to have been a city of considerable culture) may at one time have been, in fact, the capital of We, or at least to have had some political or historic importance. Obelgerst-Levy translates the first word of the name as "washing"; the second is obviously the sign for "weight." It is not known what—if anything—was washed there.

In the middle mound, or Cha'ago, near the Lakes, there have been unearthed several paintings; badly discolored, they yet show enough to prove that the inhabitants of Cha'ago were not entirely without visual art. However, they show almost nothing else. They portray squares, lines, lozenges, and mathematical figures; perhaps they were used in some way by the astrologers of the period. One finds no recognizable human face or figure. We cannot be sure what the Weans of Cha'ago looked like.

(In this relation, it is interesting to note that among the artifacts unearthed at Cha'ago were some unbroken jars and other ceramic objects; also statues of what appear to be eggs, and certain nightmare shapes in stone, iron, and bronze. One is allowed to wonder if there was not some correspondence between these art objects and the praying mantises who may have taken over the country. It is also believed that the Weans had music, but so far at least only a few brass instruments and some drums and cymbals have been found; no sounds have come down to us from those faraway people except a high rasping cry from a slender horn-like object found in Oleens.)

To return again to the matter of what the Weans may have looked like; no human bones have been found. Although we have turned up many artifacts of the period, we have nothing for the anthropologists to work on. It is probable that the bones of these people were brittle, and turned to chalk soon after interment.

The greatest difficulty in reconstructing the life of the Weans has not been the deciphering of the inscriptions and the scrolls—due to the brilliant work of Professors Bollek and Shui—but the fact that the Weans, unlike the true ancients, used little gold, preferring to build everything of steel or other metal, and of some curious substance which Bes Nef translates as "gastric," or "plastric." As a result, little is left for the archaeologist. Stone was used mainly for monuments, as was bronze, but those which have been uncovered are too heavily encrusted with bird-droppings to be easily recognizable. One theory is that the Weans collected guano; but it is not known what they did with it.

It is here, for the first time, that I must take issue with my esteemed colleague, Professor Kowly of the Institute for Ancient Arts and Letters, who has discovered in one of the scrolls at Pound-Laundry a glyph of what he believes to be a bird-man. Professor Kowly sees in this some correspondence to the djinn of the even more ancient civilizations of Akad and Sumer. While agreeing in the translation of the glyph, I must dispute its meaning: I believe it to have a purely domestic significance, and not religious at all. For one thing, it is often found along with the glyph of a woman, and the sign of a host, or hosts; there seems to be another letter between the final *t* and the *s*, possibly an *a* or an *e*, which would make it hostas or hostes. I cannot help but see this as a picture of an ordinary family, the man in winged splendor, as befits a husband, the woman merely one of a number, or host (or hostes).

In this relation, it is interesting to note that the Hittite plural, in the feminine gender, often adds the *e*. I am not one of those who hold that these unknown Weans were actually Hittites, although I admit to some strange correspondences. In any case, a Sumerian djinn would never be found accompanied by a woman, unless she were a sorceress. There is no suggestion that the woman-hostes was in fact a witch or sorceress, which I believe effectively disposes of Kowly's untenable hypothesis.

Apropos of the mounds or tumuli of the Weans, each one of which appears to contain and cover the ruins of a city or congregation of habitations, an expedition under Hulay-Beneker has been for several seasons in the field in search of a mound thought to cover the most extensive congregation of all. The name of this lost city, or congregation, which is believed to have been more influential in Wean affairs than Pound-Laundry itself, was—as deciphered by both Eretebbe and Bes Nef—Mil Town. So far no trace of it has been found.

All that we have been able to learn of Wean manners and customs we have been obliged to decipher from the copper and silver tablets found in the mounds, and in the Valley of the Sun in the southwestern part of the country. As a matter of fact, it would appear that a considerable civilization flourished in the southwest, not in any way inferior to the middle mound at Cha'ago, or to the eastern tumuli such as n.yok. Here, in transcription, is Bes Nef's account of a religious occasion, translated from scrolls found in the Valley:

"[for that] he did cause them . . . [by] rock and roll . . . to [give out] cries and screams . . . loudly . . . and . . . in the corridors[1] . . . in syncope[2] . . ."

The word "roll" or "rolls" suggests a feast, possibly a feast of communion on a grand scale. So far no one has been able to explain the presence of the word "rock."

However, it is apparent that the people came together, and were seized by an ecstasy of some sort in which they lost reason and

---

[1] "Columns"—Bollek. "Aisles"—Obelgerst-Levy.
[2] "Syncopation"—Obelgerst-Levy. But this makes no sense, apparently.

decorum. This belief is further strengthened by another scroll found in the same tumulus, in which the scribe reports: "and the spirit came down."

So the evidence points to the fact that the Weans were a religious people. There is additional witness in a silver coin dug up in one of the smaller mounds, which carries the inscription "In God We Trust" —or "Trusted." The translation is by the Bantu scholar, Eretebbe; the tense of the verb "to trust" is obscure.

Neither Eretebbe nor any other member of the Academy has as yet been able to discover what god was meant. It is extremely unlikely that these ancient people had only one; inscriptions found among the ruins of Pound-Laundry suggest, in fact, a number of religious differences among them. There are definite traces of Hebrew culture in the ruins of n.yok; and although nothing has so far been found at Pound-Laundry to suggest Babylonian or early Egyptian influences, there are hints here and there of the Cyprian cult of Antinous, particularly among the arts.

It is probable, too, that the Weans worshiped, among others, a sort of horse-god or centaur. Professor Rass points out that the fragment unearthed at s.nita, and known as the Rass fragment, contains the unmistakable glyph for "horse," and the simple statement: "Schwaps [schnaps?] was first." Yet another glyph, found not far from s.nita, is that of a bearded god; it, too, states that "Schwepps [schwaps?] was first."

In this regard, it is interesting to note that in a fragment unearthed at Oleens, and known as the Oleens fragment, the word "schnaps" is written: "cocacola," which was the name of an Aztec root-deity.

In politics, we are on surer ground. It is possible to say with absolute certainty, from scrolls unearthed at Pound-Laundry, and also from the ancient city of Boxton, or Bosstin, known to archaeologists as mound x-5, that the Weans were divided into hegemonies or states, each ruled by a theocrat or autocrat, and all loosely joined in a confederacy under one ruler (who, however, was not a theocrat) whose duty it was to retire after an interval varying in length from four to twelve years, and to issue warnings and oracles. These groups, or states, were in turn divided into counties, which were in turn divided into wards. As for the system of government itself, it appears to have been conducted by means of barter, each county or state getting what it could for itself in exchange for helping its neighbor to do the same.

Public servants, we know, were paid little; they were expected to enrich themselves as best they could in private. When this enrichment, which was illegal, was discovered, they were beheaded. This curious fact did not keep the majority of Weans from seeking public office; but one is forced to conclude, from inscriptions found at Nassaw, that the most admired citizens lived in actual poverty, and rarely spoke at all, except in musical sounds or mathematical formulae. As we have already seen, no musical sounds have come down to us, which is unfortunate.

It is true that two scrolls, bound each in oblong form, were found by the team of Haph-Bukong and Sumer, digging one winter among the ruins of what may once have been some sort of library. That it may have been a repository of many such scrolls—or as we should say "books"—is suggested by the remains of metal shelves which may have held the scrolls (or else jellies, but informed opinion veers toward the scrolls).

Unfortunately, both scrolls, though easily legible, due to the brilliant work of the scholars Bes Nef and Obelgerst-Levy, are unintelligible; that is to say, the words, although translatable, make no sense when put together. One of these scrolls appears to be an account of a god or hero named Finigan, or Finnegan; the size of the scroll and its rare state of preservation attest to its importance as a religious or historical document, but it is impossible to make out what happens to him. The second scroll is in what appears to be a metrical, or verse form; nothing can be gathered from it at all.

A tablet unearthed at n.yok gives us a welcome glimpse into business transactions in We. "[Having] borrowed a million," it reads in the transcription of B'Han Bollek, "[I acquired] thereby credit to twice that amount." This suggests an economy not unlike our own: one thinks of the motto of our Treasury Department: "To the Borrower, All." Throughout history there has never been anything more useful than credit, to establish credit. Without a debt, there is nothing.

As for the history of these interesting and almost unknown ancestors[3] of ours, no more is known than is known of the Romans, and later the Brythons: they established themselves in the land by killing off the native tribes already there, and built their empire by the sword; when the sword rusted, they perished, along with Egypt, Babylon, and Greece, leaving behind them only these curious mounds, some scrolls, monuments, and glyphs, a few statues of eggs and mantises, and no music.

[3] Nat Obelgerst-Levy denies that the Weans were ancestors of ours.

Stranded in Kansas City, or a Fate Worse Than Vaudeville

My sister, June, was thirteen years old when she eloped with one of the boys in our vaudeville act. I was fifteen and a half. There was no act left, without June, until Mother decided, one day, to pick up the tangled threads of her life, as she put it, and organize another company. The new act was all girls. (Mother wasn't taking any more chances.) It was named "Madam Rose's Dancing Daughters." Mother had called herself Madam Rose for many years—ever since we headlined on the Orpheum Circuit. There were six girls in the new act besides me. Mother found them in dancing schools and amateur contests in Seattle, our home town. None of them received a salary; Mother convinced their parents the experience the girls would receive would be worth more than money.

The oldest girl, little Mary, was sixteen, but so tiny everyone thought she couldn't be over ten. Two of the girls, Nancy and Millie, were sisters. They were comediennes in the act so they didn't have to be pretty. Nancy's blond head sat on her long, thin neck like a jonquil.

Millie sang June's comedy number and did a bustle dance with me. The braces on her teeth added to the comic effect. None of the girls could do my sister's ballad about her little dog, but Ruby did a contortion dance in place of it. Contortionists didn't have to be pretty, either. Ruby's neck was even longer than Nancy's. Her legs were long too and thin, with red chapped knees that looked like candied apples on sticks. The brassiere part of her costume was ruffled to hide the two tiny swellings that embarrassed her when she did the back bends.

Then there was Dorothy with her big brown eyes and sweet little singing voice and Hazel, the only one of the girls with any stage experience. Hazel, who was thirteen, had appeared in six dancing-school recitals. She learned June's Russian toe tap dance, minus the more difficult steps, and appeared in the walking doll number and the Military Finale, where we all did a drill complete with gilded guns and costumes that lighted up in the dark spelling out the name of the act in radium letters on our backs. I sang "I'm a Hard-boiled Rose" in a striped skirt and comedy jacket. I had been doing the same number since I was four years old—mainly because I couldn't learn a new one.

Mother had been told, before we left Seattle, that talking pictures were killing vaudeville, but she wouldn't believe it. "They said the same thing about radio," Mother replied. "We weathered that storm and we'll weather the talkies, too. Nothing will ever take the place of flesh."

In Yuma, Arizona, I bleached all the girls' heads until they were albino-like and we changed the name of the act to "Rose Louise and Her Hollywood Blondes," but with all of that, and Mother's confidence and salesmanship, she still couldn't find bookings. The few places we did play only confirmed the fact that our new act was a dismal failure.

Mother sat on the foot of the bed in our hotel room in Kansas City and counted the money again. There was eleven dollars and eighty cents left. She put it back in the shabby gray suede money belt and fastened the strap around her waist. "It's always darkest before dawn," she said cheerfully to the girls who watched her with wide frightened eyes. "You'll see," she added, "God won't let a little act like ours lay off."

The phone rang and Mother ran to it. "What did I tell you?" she said triumphantly as she took down the receiver.

"Now here's the deal, Rose," the agent was saying on the phone in a loud shrill voice. "They bought some act out of Chicago but because of the snowstorm the act can't make it. It's for a full week, right here in the city, two shows a day—"

"What is the salary?" Mother asked.

"Well," he replied, "I might as well be frank with ya, it's short money, but you gotta look at it like this, two shows a day, right here in town—"

"What," Mother repeated, "is the money?"

"Three hundred," the agent said.

We had been asking for five and taking two fifty. Mother tried to keep the elation out of her voice. "As a personal favor to you, Sam, we'll take it."

"Fine. Now write this down, it's the Missouri Theatre, Tenth and Missouri Avenue. Rehearsal at twelve noon, sharp. I'll meet you there with the contracts."

Little Mary grabbed up her long underwear and began pulling it on. "I'm glad it isn't another night club," she said, wrapping the leg of the underwear neatly around her ankle and holding it in place while she unrolled the brown stocking over the fold. "I don't think my parents would like me working in a night club."

At a quarter of twelve we were on our way to the theater, all except Hazel, who had been sent on ahead in a taxi with the scenery and costumes. We all wore scarves tied twice around our necks and fastened with safety pins. Under them, pinned to our underwear we each wore a small bag filled with camphor cubes, which was Mother's precaution against pneumonia. The dogs wore two sweaters each. It was very cold and my hand, carrying the bag with Porky, our performing pig, was almost frozen in its mitten. I shifted the bag to my other hand and Porky made an angry oinking noise. His pink snout pressed close to the air hole looked like a rosebud.

Dorothy, carrying two of the dolls and the gilded guns, ran up beside me. "Wait for me, Louise. I don't want to walk alone on this awful looking street."

I hadn't noticed anything unusual until she mentioned it, but then I saw what she meant. There was something sinister about it. The all-night movie theatre we were passing, for instance, with the lurid pictures out front advertising "Pitfalls of Passion."

We passed a barbershop with a sign in the window reading: "Tattooing Artfully Done." Samples of the artist's work decorated the sign. One was of a woman clinging to a rock with MOTHER written under it, the other, a dagger being thrust through the skin of an arm.

Nancy let out a whoop. "There it is, there's the theatre!" she yelled.

Next door to a hotel advertising beds for fifty cents was the Missouri Theatre. In electric lights was the word BURLESQUE. Mother closed her eyes, then opened them, as though in that time the sight ahead might have been altered. A canvas banner hanging from the marquee read:

40 girls 40
Burlesque As You Like It
40 Girls 40

"*Burlesque,*" Mother gasped. "Sam wouldn't dare do a thing like this to us."

She advanced on the theatre, a steely glint in her eyes. Stopping at the stage-entrance alley she gave Millie the dogs' leashes. "Wait here," she said, "and stay close together. I'm going in to get Hazel." She made it sound as though she was about to rescue Hazel from a burning building, but I knew exactly how she felt. Vaudeville performers looked down on Burlesque. For an act to play such a theatre was professional suicide. Mother took a deep breath before she opened the stage door and strode purposefully through it.

While we waited, the girls and I watched a man on a ladder adjust an electric fan under the marquee of the theatre. He was aiming the breeze from it down on a larger-than-life-sized photograph of a blond woman who wore nothing but a triangle patch where she should have worn panties and two smaller patches for a brassiere. Another man was nailing black silk tassels to the brassiere part of the photograph. As he stepped aside the breeze from the fan picked up the tassels and made them spin like windmills.

The girls and I inched closer to the lobby so we could see more. The animated picture of the blonde had silver-flittered letters nailed around the head, and above it in flittered letters that sparkled like rhinestones, was her billing: *Tessie, the Tassel Twirler.*

Inside the lobby there were other life-sized photographs. The women in them were all half-naked; each of them peeked out from behind something such as a parasol, a fur muff, or a balloon. Millie, her eyes like saucers, nudged me.

"Look at that!" she said pointing to an easel that read "*Wine, Women and Song. Beauty! Form! Shimmy!*" At the bottom of a long list of names was "Rose Louise and her Hollywood Blondes."

"We're not even headlining," Millie whispered. "Wait'll Madam Rose sees that."

We scooted back to where Mother had told us to wait, and just in time, too. Mother, holding Hazel by the arm, was marching up the stage alley. At the same moment a taxi stopped at the curb and Sam, the agent, got out.

"Did ya bring the pictures for the lobby?" he asked.

"Pictures?" Mother said, glaring at him. "Do you think for one minute I'd let these innocent little girls play this filthy dive?"

"Dive?" Sam repeated. "This happens to be one a the cream de la cream houses on the whole Burlesque wheel. Plenty of acts'ed give their eye teeth to play this theatre."

"Not our little act!" Mother said. "Come along girls, we're going back to the hotel!"

"Now wait a minute," the agent said. "I okayed this deal. You walk out on me and I'll blacklist you in every theatre in Kansas City—"

Little Mary began to cry. "What are we going to do, Madam Rose?" she wailed. "Where can we go? We're stranded!"

The word stranded was all the other girls needed. They weren't sure what it meant, neither was little Mary, but it had a terrifying ring to it. Nancy's face screwed up, then she began to blubber and they all started. The agent, his polo coat flying behind him, ran from one girl to another pleading with them to be quiet. "Not in front a the theatre," he begged. "If you gotta bawl, for crissake bawl inside, we got trouble enough with the cops. Let's go inside, Rose, and talk it over."

Mother pulled her arm away from his hand. "I'd rather starve first!"

"Well, I wouldn't," I said, and the sound of my own voice startled me. For the first time in my life I had contradicted Mother. "I mean it," I said. "I'm tired of starving to death. That's all we've been doing for years—even before June left us—"

Mother caught her breath in a tight gasp, and I was afraid for a moment she was going to have an asthma attack.

"You don't know what you're saying," she cried. "Something will turn up. It always has and it always will."

"Nothing better is ever going to turn up for us, Mother. There's no place left for us to work any more." I picked up Porky's bag and walked toward the stage entrance. "We'll play the date," I told the agent. "We need the money."

As I walked down the alley I knew Mother and the girls were following me because I heard Mother sobbing.

There was a star on the door, but even so it was the dirtiest dressing-room I had ever seen. Mother wrinkled up her nose at the stale, sour odor. I hesitated in the doorway, "The doorman told us to take one of the empty rooms," I said.

For an answer Mother moved a few of the sweat-stained, sleazy costumes to make room on the hooks for ours. I took Porky out of his bag and tied him to a pipe under the sink, along with the dogs. Ruby, surveying the littered make-up shelf, picked up a glittering patch of rhinestones and held it to her thin neck.

"It's kind a big for a necklace," she murmured.

"Put that down!" Mother commanded. "Don't touch anything in this room that doesn't belong to you. You don't know *what* you might catch!"

A blond woman wearing a black satin dress stood framed in the doorway, her hands on her big soft-looking hips. "Of all the gawddamn nerve," she said. "The only thing you'll catch around here is a swift kick in the butt if you don't leave my stuff alone!"

She was fatter and older looking than in her picture, but I knew this was Tessie, the tassel twirler.

"Hey, you with the neck," she said to Ruby. "I just paid six bucks for that G string. It's no play toy. Put it down."

Ruby was too frightened to move. The woman strode into the room and snatched the glittering thing from Ruby's hands. "Who told you to come busting in here like it was a public bathhouse?"

"The door was open," I said. "We've always had the star dressing room and I assumed we'd have—"

"Oh, you did, huh? Well, you can just assume yourselves to hell out."

"We'll see who gets out," Mother said. "Girls, unpack the make-up!"

The blonde's anger left her like the air sputtering out of a busted balloon. She flopped onto a chair and let her head hang down between her legs. "Ohmigawd," she moaned, "what a hang-over I got. I love my drinks, but they sure don't love me. . . . Why I slop up all that gawddamn beer when I know I got a rehearsal the next day I dunno."

Mother picked up the music case. "Stand by for rehearsal," she said; then with a slight curl to her lips, she added, "and no talking to strangers."

The blonde gazed up at her sadly and belched. "I wanta apologize," she said when the belch was over. "I didn't mean to chew your heads off like I did—it's just that I got this lousy hang-over—then to find a troupe a acrobats sprawled all over my room—"

"We aren't acrobats," Mother said witheringly. "We happen to be a vaudeville act. We were booked into this theatre by mistake."

"Weren't we all!" the blonde exclaimed; then she belched again.

A voice called out in the hallway, "Everybody on stage for the opening number. Step on it. We're late gettin' started."

The hallway began filling up with chorus girls wearing red satin brassieres and abbreviated pants to match. The pants were open at the sides and held together with pink elastic straps that cut into the flesh, making their hips look corrugated. Long red satin tails were attached to the backs of the pants. The girls' hair was tucked up under red satin skullcaps with tiny horns at the ears. Each girl carried a spear and, as they ran chattering and complaining toward the stage, they poked one another playfully with the pointed ends.

In a moment the orchestra played the introduction to "Lucky Little Devil" and the chorus girls pranced lackadaisically on stage singing the lyrics of the song in several different keys. The stage hands yelled even louder than the chorus girls as they gave instructions to one another: "Let that tab in a few inches—okay, now tie it off and bring in the front traveler—not so fast—give the broads a chance to finish the number—"

"Is it always this exciting on opening days?" Nancy bubbled. "I love all the noise and the people running around—"

Tessie didn't answer her. She had spotted Porky who woke up from his nap in a bad humor. He pulled on his leash and squealed in fury, kicking out with his hooves at Nancy, who tried to quiet him. "He's hungry," Nancy explained. The dogs began barking, and she raised her voice above the din, "We use him in the act."

"Gawd help us," the blonde said, "and they wonder what happened to vaudeville."

Then we heard our music and Mother's voice as she gave the orchestra leader our cues. I tugged at my long brown stockings and walked down the hallway to the stage. The girls, staying close together, followed me. The stage hands watched us as we took our places for the rehearsal of our opening number.

"*This* is supposed to keep the cops out?" one of them remarked.

"Yeah," another one said. "Next week 'East Lynne.'"

The agent sat in the front row of the gloomy theater with another man who looked just like him. "You won't recognize 'em when they get their make-up on," he was saying. "The costumes and lights help a lot, too, ya know."

"I hope so," the other man said grimly.

The orchestra leader pounded out our music on the piano and the girls and I tried to pretend we couldn't hear the men as we went through our act.

"That big one," the man said, "can she talk?"

"Sure, talks great," Sam replied. "Why? You wanna use her?"

"Maybe. I dunno yet. Think she could handle the 'Illusion' scene?"

"Sure," Sam said expansively. "They don't look like much but they all got a load a talent."

"Hey you," the man yelled suddenly and loudly. "You, the big one on the end." The music stopped and the girls and I looked at one another. Little Mary was on one end of the line. I was on the other.

"Do you mean me?" I asked, my voice going funny on the last word.

"Yeah. Lift up your skirts and lemme see your legs."

"Her *what?*" Mother screamed from the wings.

"It's nothing, Rose," Sam yelled reassuringly. "This is Herbie Michaels, the boss. He just wants to see if she's bowlegged or something—"

"Rose Louise is not showing her legs and that's final!" Mother said firmly, striding on stage.

"All right, all right," Sam muttered, waving her off into the wings. He turned to Herbie Michaels. "You can take my personal word for it. The legs are okay."

The stage hands were moving a big pink satin-lined sea shell on stage behind us.

"Speed it up, will ya?" Sam yelled up to me. Mother ran out on stage with the guns and hurriedly shoved them at us, then called out the directions from the wings as we went through the gun drill and into our Finale dance.

Before we could get off stage the chorus girls were dancing on, dressed as sea sprites. "Where's Gladys?" someone yelled, and a girl with brassy red hair, wearing a flowered print robe, scurried across the stage, sat herself in the sea shell, took her knitting out of a bag and began to count off the stitches. "Knit two, purl two, knit two—"

"Isn't it exciting?" Nancy whispered. "This is what I always dreamed show business would be like."

It wasn't like any show business I'd ever known, but I had to admit it was exciting. I glanced back at the undersea ballet number and turned my head away quickly. Gladys had dropped her knitting and was standing up in the sea shell with nothing on but a string of big fake pearls.

The girls and I walked, close together, back to the dressing room.

"I'm not going to write home about this," Millie said thoughtfully. "Mom isn't professional enough to understand."

In our dressing room we took off our street clothes and hung them on the hooks we had cleared for ourselves. We were busily passing the community powder puff when there was a knock on the door.

"Don't come in," we screamed in a chorus, "we're not dressed."

The door flew open and Herbie Michaels stood there with a man in a funny sailor suit. The girls and I grabbed for make-up towels, kimonos, anything at all to cover our long underwear, but the men didn't appear to be looking at us.

"We want ya to be happy here, Joe," Herbie was saying to the man in the sailor suit. "We just done the 'Dirty Restaurant' or you could do that, but if you wanna do the 'Illusion' scene, okay, we got a fine talking woman to play it with ya. She's that big one over there."

They both looked at me and I tried to shrink so the make-up towel would cover me.

"Will she do?" Herbie Michaels asked.

"Who's got a choice?" the man in the sailor suit replied.

"Get hold a hula skirt," Herbie Michaels threw over his shoulder at me as he left. The man he called Joe sat down in Tessie's chair and bent his rubber cigar back and forth.

"Ever done the 'Illusion' scene before?" he asked.

I shook my head.

"Well, it don't matter," he replied. "I do a rehash on it, anyway. I don't use none of that Tondelayo dialogue, I go right inta the switch on the Joe the bartender bit only I use a ukulele instead of a bull fiddle. And after the yok yok with Stinky, the second banana, the lights come up and you're lying stage left in front of a grass hut. I give you a skull, then a slow triple, and you get up and start giving me the business. You do about four bars a bumps and grinds while I chew a hunk outta the grass hut, then you throw me your lines, 'I'm no illusion,' you say. 'I'm real—here, take my hand—touch me, feel me.' "

"I'm no illusion," I repeated slowly. "I'm real, here, take my hand, touch me, feel me."

"Great," the comic said, "you got it already. You scram on the blackout and I finish the scene with Stinky."

"What finish?" I asked faintly.

"Him and me clinching—the old tried and true. Is it clear?" Then without waiting for my answer, he walked out of the room and left me standing there behind the make-up towel, confused and be-wildered.

Mother was delighted when I told her about the scene but Tessie wasn't. "It detracts from your prestige," she said. "Look at me, for instance. I do only two numbers. One in the first half a the show, the other in the second. In Burlesque, you gotta leave 'em hungry for more. You don't dump the whole roast on the platter."

She didn't approve of the hula skirt, either. I had it hooked on around my waist, and she pulled it down low on my hips. I tugged it back up again. "I couldn't wear it down there," I said. "My navel shows."

"I'll fix that," Tessie said. Rummaging through the mess on the cluttered make-up shelf, she found a red pear-shaped jewel and putting a bit of glue on the back, she stuck the bauble on my stomach. "There," she said, "how's that?"

It looked silly, but I didn't want to hurt her feelings, and I had to admit the skirt was better around my hips; it didn't make me look so fat that way.

"I like a covered navel," Tessie said. "It's more classy." Then she looked down at my patent leather dancing shoes. "You can't wear those. They make you look like a rube comic. Here—put these on." She fished a pair of gold high-heeled sandals out of the litter under the make-up shelf and tossed them to me.

I'd had on high heels only once before. I had the same feeling now as I had then, as though I were going to fall flat on my face.

"You oughtta see how much better ya look," Tessie said approvingly. "For a kid, you got a lot of sex in your walk."

Mother came hurrying into the room. "Hurry, dear," she said. "The Illusion scene is next. My, how nice you look."

Then she looked at me more closely. "Pull up that skirt!" she commanded. I ran out of the room and down the hallway. "Louise! You come back here and take off those ridiculous shoes and pull up that hula skirt!"

I ran as fast as I could toward the stage. Then I heard Tessie calling Mother, and they were both behind me. I stood in the wings, nervously waiting for my cue. Mother was right and I knew it. The shabby gold shoes were silly. The red stone glittering in my navel was vulgar and ugly. The lights suddenly blacked out. That was my cue but I couldn't move.

"I can't do it," I cried. "I can't go on!"

"The hell you can't," Tessie said, giving me a shove. "There ain't anything you can't do. You got the world on a string, kid, and don't you forget it."

Peeking around the side of the grass hut I could see Joe and Stinky lying on the mat. "Six long months on this God-forsaken island," Joe was saying. "Six months and not a human being in sight!"

"What am I," Stinky mumbled, "chopped liver?"

"There you are, my beautiful darling," Joe cried throwing his arms around Stinky. "I wanna go home!" Stinky yelled, trying to pull away from him.

"Come to my arms," Joe said. "I've always loved you. I adore you. I dream of you by night and think of you by day—I can't get you out of my mind. Your eyes are like burning pools, your lips are like rubies, your teeth like pearls—are you following me?"

"Following you Hell," Stinky chortled, "I'm way ahead of you."

"Kiss me, my darling—"

The lights blacked out and Stinky passed me in the darkness. "You're on," he whispered, and I found my way to the front of the hut before the lights came up.

"You *are* real!" Joe cried as he saw me. "You're not an illusion—"

"Louise!" Mother whispered from the wings. "Hold in your stomach!"

I took a deep breath, "I'm real," I said. "I'm no illusion—here, take my hand, touch me—feel me—"

Tessie greeted me as I stumbled into the wings on the blackout. "There, that wasn't so tough, was it?"

I looked back at the comics who were doing what I presumed was the tried and true. "He said he was going to give me a skull," I murmured. "I guess he forgot."

Tessie roared with laughter. "A skull's a take," she said. Then seeing the question in my eyes, she added, "He gives you a slow look, then he looks away, and looks back again—that's a take, a skull, see?"

Back in the dressing room, the girls were already dressed in their opening number costumes.

"Take that thing out of your navel," Mother said, "before you get an infection."

I picked out the red bauble and laid it on Tessie's place on the make-up shelf, then I put on the cretonne pinafore and my hair bow and snatched up my walking doll.

Mother, leading the way, escorted us on stage.

Flossie the ingenue was finishing her song, "I'm Looking at the World Through Rose-Colored Glasses," and at the end of each phrase, she crinkled her newspaper costume provocatively. There didn't seem to be any connection between the song and the costume but from the occasional hoots of approval from the audience, I knew they liked her. I squeezed closer to the wings so I could see better.

I had seen the runway at rehearsal and wondered what it was used for. Now, as Flossie stepped daintily onto it, I knew. It was a narrow strip, with a frosted glass floor, extending out into the audience over the heads of the men who sat alongside it. As Flossie wiggled the newspaper costume at a baldheaded man, lights came on under the glass floor and made her bluish legs take on a rosy glow. She tore off a strip of the newspaper and tickled the man with it, then with a little cry of girlish abandon she darted toward the wings. Just before she exited, she tore off a larger piece of the newspaper and her whole backside was bare—all but the pink net pants which hardly showed at all. There was a bit of scattered applause and a lot of hooting and hollering from the audience.

The orchestra played "Whispering" and Flossie came out again, tearing at the newspaper, this time in a slower tempo. As she tore off the strips, she rolled them into balls and threw them into the audience. She danced out onto the runway and asked a man in the audience to help her. "Would ya, Daddy?" she asked in a baby voice. The man struggled to his feet holding his overcoat with one arm. He winked at the men sitting beside him and hauled off and slapped Flossie on her net-covered bottom. He appeared to be quite pleased with himself as he sat down. Flossie, squealing like Porky the time he got his tail stuck in the door, limped off the runway. Just as she reached the wings, she tore off the last bit of newspaper covering her front, and rolling it into a ball held up her arms to cover herself. The audience yelled, "Take it off!" and Flossie obligingly revealed her breasts that were cupped in soiled flesh-colored net like two used tea bags.

Someone tapped me on the shoulder and I jumped a foot. "You're on after the next scene," the man said. It was Herbie Michaels and he was smiling at me. "You looked great in the scene," he said.

The orchestra played the introduction of the "Doll Dance." There was a surprised silence from the audience as the girls and I walked our dolls on stage in time to the music.

Mother, in the wings, whispered, "Count four, Louise; then start." I counted to myself, then made the doll kick out a chubby leg.

The piano player had a container of beer beside him. He raised it to his lips and took a swig as he played our music with one hand. The girls and I walked the dolls through the routine. "Forte on the last eight bars," Mother hissed and the music swelled as we walked the dolls off the stage.

Then I was on in my "tough" number. "I will now sing a little number entitled 'When your hand itches you're going to get something—when your head itches you got it'—I'm a Hard-boiled Rose—"

Matches flared up here and there in the darkness and I realized the men were lighting cigarettes. The smoke threw a glow around the spotlight. My eyes became accustomed to the haze and I could make out the figures of the men in the front row. They sat slouched way down in their seats, their feet up on the orchestra railing. Their faces were expressionless as they looked up at me. But there were a few laughs from the balcony. At the end of my number there was a bit of applause. Not the kind of applause Flossie received, but enough anyway.

When the Finale was over Mother helped us hang up our costumes. "The orchestra just about butchered our music," she said, "but all in all, I think it was a pretty good opening show."

Sam and Herbie Michaels agreed with Mother. Before the night performance, we had signed to stay on for another week. I was to have a new hula skirt with a higher waist band on it, and the following week, if the scenes were ladylike and met with Mother's approval, I was to appear in several of them.

As Mother said, it all came under the heading of experience.

"A lot of big stars played Burlesque," she said. "There isn't a reason in the world why we can't—at least until vaudeville comes back."

AGNES ROGERS

 ## Conversation
 ### Piece

Come live with me and be my love
And we will our devotion prove
By sweet adjustments, compromises,
Embracing what the other prizes.

"I'll tolerate your sulky cat,
Attend you while you choose a hat,
I'll risk a weekend on a yacht,
Although, God knows, I'd rather not."

"I'll go to every Indoor Meet,
Applaud Bob Richards' fifteen feet;
I'll stumble after beagle hounds;
And trail you to the Polo Grounds."

"I'll do my best to tell apart
Abstractionists in modern art—
If you will cultivate, my sweet,
A taste for Lower Basin Street."

"And I will learn such manly matters
As batting averages of batters

And horse's pedigrees—and, yes,
I swear I'll even master chess."

"For me, already I've begun
To memorize the works of Donne,
And though they're not what I am used to
I'll tackle Eliot and Proust, too."

So may these bonds 'twixt you and me
Augment our similarity
Till presently none can discover
Where I leave off, and you take over!

MARCEL AYMÉ

The Man
 Who Walked
Through Walls

In Montmartre, on the third floor of 75A Rue d'Orchampt, there lived a good man by the name of Dutilleul who was gifted with the singular ability to walk through walls, without being inconvenienced in any way. He wore a pince-nez and a small black goatee, and worked as a clerk at the Ministry of Registration. In winter he went to the office by bus, and when the weather was kinder, he walked the distance under his derby.

Dutilleul had just turned forty-three when this power was revealed to him. Caught one evening, by a brief electrical breakdown, in the foyer of his small bachelor apartment, he groped about for a moment in the darkness. When the current was restored, he found himself on the third-floor landing. The fact that his front door was locked on the inside made him pause and reflect. Reason notwithstanding, he decided to return the way he had come; going straight through the wall. This strange faculty, apparently gratifying none of his aspirations, was a source of annoyance, and, as the next day was Saturday, he took advantage of the five-day week to visit a neighborhood doctor and explain his troubles. The doctor ascertained for himself the truth of Dutilleul's story, and after a thorough examination, discovered the cause of the affliction in a hardening of the helix of the strangulary

Translated by E. and M. Teichner

278

wall of the thyroid. He prescribed a very active life and pills compounded of pirete powder (tetravalent), rice flour, and centaur hormones, taken twice a year.

Dutilleul swallowed the first pill, put the medicine away in a drawer, and thought no more of the matter. As for living a very active life, his bureaucratic existence, bound by routine, precluded excesses of any kind. Nor did his leisure-time occupations oblige him to any unreasonable expenditure of energy, taken up, as it was, with the reading of the daily paper, and his stamp collection. So, at the end of a year he had kept intact his faculty to pass through walls, without putting it to any use. This was not by way of inadvertence, but, rather, because of a lack of curiosity and a mulish resistance to the force of his imagination. It never even occurred to him that he might enter his rooms by any means other than the front door, after duly turning the lock. He might have aged in the peace of his daily routine, without being tempted to put his gifts to the test, had not this existence been suddenly turned upside-down by a disconcerting event.

His immediate superior at the Ministry of Registration, M. Mouron, was called to other duties, and was replaced by a certain M. Lécuyer, a man of few words and a clipped mustache. From the first day his new boss looked askance at Dutilleul's pince-nez hanging on a chain, and his black goatee. Lécuyer treated him like an old and slightly unclean nuisance. But what was most serious was that the newcomer aspired to introduce certain reforms calculated to disturb the complacency of his subordinate. For twenty years Dutilleul had begun his letters with the following formula:

"Referring to your esteemed letter of such and such date, and for your knowledge, to our previous correspondence, I have the honor to inform you . . ."

For this, M. Lécuyer wished to substitute another introduction with a more American turn of phrase:

"In response to your letter of such and such date, I wish to inform you . . ."

Dutilleul was incapable of adapting himself to these epistolary fashions. Despite himself, he returned to the traditional mode of address, and the mechanical obstinacy with which he accomplished this gained him the growing enmity of his superior. The atmosphere of the Ministry of Registration seemed almost oppressive. In the mornings he set off to work with apprehension, and in the evenings, in his bed, he often meditated for a whole quarter-hour before falling off to sleep. Disgusted by this negative attitude which compromised the success of his reforms, M. Lécuyer had relegated Dutilleul to a dark hole next to his office. Entrance was by a low, narrow door, opening on the corridor. It still bore in capital letters the inscription: STOREROOM. Dutilleul resigned himself to this unprecedented humiliation, but once at home, while reading in his paper the story of some bloody incident, he caught himself dreaming of M. Lécuyer as the victim.

One day his superior burst into the cell brandishing a letter, and began to bellow: "Do this damn thing over! This stupid nonsense which dishonors my department!"

Dutilleul tried to object, but M. Lécuyer treated him like a low order of cockroach, and before leaving, crushed the letter and threw it in his face. For all his diffidence, Dutilleul was a man of spirit. Left alone in his little office, his temperature rose, and suddenly he felt himself inspired. He got up from his chair and entered the wall that separated the two offices. But he entered prudently, so that only his head emerged on the other side. M. Lécuyer was seated at his desk, still upset, relocating a comma in the text of some underling, when he heard a cough in the office. Raising his eyes, he discovered, with indescribable panic, Dutilleul's head, stuck on the wall like a hunting trophy. And this head was alive. Through the pince-nez, it pierced him with a look of hatred. Better still, the head spoke. "Sir," it said, "you are a cad, a scoundrel, and a knave."

Agape with horror, M. Lécuyer was incapable of taking his eyes off this apparition. Finally, he tore himself from his armchair, rushed into the corridor, and ran into the storeroom. Dutilleul, pen in hand, was seated at his usual place in a peaceful and hard-working pose. His superior scrutinized him carefully and at length, mumbled a few words, and returned to his office. Hardly had he seated himself, when the head reappeared on the wall. "Sir, you are a cad, a scoundrel, and a knave."

In the course of that one day, the dreaded head appeared on the wall twenty-three times, and it reappeared as often in the days that followed. Dutilleul had acquired a certain ease at this game, and no longer restricted himself to invective directed at his superior. He uttered vague threats; for instance, he declaimed, in a sepulchral voice, punctuated with truly demoniacal laughs, a nursery rhyme which began with the words, "Garou! Garou!" and conveyed a sense of overpowering menace.

Hearing this, poor M. Lécuyer paled still further, gasped a little more than usual; his hair stood straight up on end, and a horrible sweat of agony flowed down his back. The first day he lost a pound.

In the week following, aside from melting away almost to the point of transparency, he took to drinking his soup with a fork and saluting policemen. At the beginning of the second week, an ambulance came to his door and took him away to an asylum.

Rid of M. Lécuyer's tyranny, Dutilleul was able to return to his cherished introductory sentence:

"Referring to your esteemed letter of such and such date . . ."

Nonetheless, he was dissatisfied. Something inside clamored, a new and imperious need, which was nothing less than the urge to go through walls. Undoubtedly, he did not lack of facilities. At home, for instance, he indulged himself. But the man who possesses such brilliant gifts is not long content to exercise them on such mediocre objects. Besides, going through walls cannot be considered an end in itself. It is the beginning of an adventure that provokes a sequence, a development, and, inexorably, a retribution. This Dutilleul understood well. He felt a need for expansion, a growing desire to fulfill and outdo himself, and a kind of nostalgia, which appeared to be something like the call from beyond the wall. Unfortunately, he lacked a goal. He sought inspiration in the newspaper, particularly in the political and sports sections. These seemed like honorable pursuits, but he finally decided that they offered no outlet to people who could go through walls, and he fell back on the one field that showed promise.

Dutilleul's first burglary took place in a large banking establishment in the financial district. Having gone through a dozen or so walls and partitions, he entered several vaults, and filled his pockets with banknotes. Before leaving, he autographed his crime, under the pseudonym Garou-Garou, with an extremely elaborate flourish that was reproduced in all the newspapers the next day. By the end of a week, the name Garou-Garou had attained an extraordinary fame. The public gave its sympathy without reservation to this wonder-working thief who so mystified the police. Every night he made his presence known by some new exploit, at the expense of a bank, a jewelry store, or some wealthy person. There was no dreamy-eyed woman, whether in Paris or in the provinces, who did not desire ardently to belong body and soul to the terrible Garou-Garou. After the lifting of the Burdigala diamond, and the looting of the Municipal Bank, both in the space of a week, popular enthusiasm reached delirious heights. The Minister of the Interior was forced to resign, and in his fall pulled along the Minister of Registration. While all this was transpiring, Dutilleul, now one of the wealthiest men in Paris, was always punctually at his office. He was even spoken of for academic palms. His pleasure, in the mornings, was to listen to his colleagues' comments on his exploits of the previous night.

"A genius, this Garou-Garou," they said, "a remarkable man, a superman."

Hearing such praise, Dutilleul blushed with confusion, and under his pince-nez, his eyes shone with friendship and gratitude. One day this sympathetic atmosphere put him in such an expansive mood that he felt no longer capable of keeping the secret to himself. The remnants of a shy personality made him first apprise his colleagues, clustered about a newspaper telling about the robbery of the Bank of France. He said in a modest voice: "You know, this Garou-Garou, that's me."

An enormous and interminable laugh assailed his ears, and Dutilleul, by way of scorn, was nicknamed Garou-Garou. At quitting time, in the evening, he was the butt of endless scoffing from his comrades. Life seemed less beautiful.

Some days later, Garou-Garou had himself nabbed by a night patrolman in a jewelry store on the Rue de la Paix. He had inscribed his signature on the cash register and was singing a drinking song, while shattering show-cases with a massive gold goblet. It would have been simple to bury himself in a wall, and thus to escape the patrolman, but everything leads one to believe that he wanted to be arrested, probably with the sole aim of confounding his colleagues, whose skepticism had been so mortifying. And indeed, Dutilleul's photograph on the front pages of the papers the following day caused great surprise amongst them. They regretted bitterly having so misjudged their genial comrade, and rendered homage to him by growing goatees. Led on by a combination of remorse and admiration, some of them even tried to snatch the billfolds and watches of friends and acquaintances. Undoubtedly, the fact that he allowed himself to be captured by the police in order to astound a few colleagues will be taken as evidence of a frivolous turn of mind, unworthy of so exceptional a man. But such temptation overwhelms the will. In renouncing his liberty, Dutilleul thought he was merely yielding to an arrogant desire for revenge, while, in fact, he was really accomplishing his destiny. For a man who can go through walls, no audacious career is complete if he has not, at least once, been imprisoned.

Dutilleul felt that he was being spoiled by fortune as soon as he entered the premises of the Santé. The thickness of the walls was a real treat. On the second day of his imprisonment, the guards were stupefied to discover that the prisoner had hammered a nail into his wall, and had hung thereupon a gold watch belonging to the warden. The prisoner was either unwilling or unable to tell how the object had come into his possession. The watch was returned to its owner, and was found on the morrow at the head of Garou-Garou's cot, alongside a copy of the first volume of *The Three Musketeers*, borrowed from the warden's bookshelves. The staff of the Santé was on edge. Besides, the guards complained of being kicked in the rear by an unknown agency. The walls seemed to have sprouted feet, as well as ears. Garou-Garou had been imprisoned at the Santé for a week when the warden, one morning, was greeted by a letter on his desk:

> My dear Warden:
> Referring to our talk of the 17th inst., and for your reminder, to your over-all instructions of the 15th of May of last year, I have the honor to inform you that I have just finished the second volume of *The Three Musketeers*, and that I plan to escape tonight, between 11:25 and 11:35.
> I beg of you, my dear sir, to accept the expression of my profound respect.
>
> Garou-Garou

Despite the strict surveillance under which he was placed, Dutilleul escaped at eleven-thirty. This news, published the next morning, aroused enormous enthusiasm everywhere. In the meanwhile, having brought off a new robbery, which capped his popularity, Dutilleul appeared unconcerned about hiding, and circulated freely in Montmartre. He was arrested three days after his escape at the Café du Rêve, Rue Caulaincourt, a little after midday, while drinking a glass of white wine and lemon with some friends.

Returned to the Santé, and imprisoned under triple lock in solitary confinement, he escaped that very night, and went to sleep in the guest room of the warden's apartment. The next morning, just before nine, he rang for the maid to bring his breakfast, and allowed himself to be plucked, without resistance, from the bed by the alerted guards. Incensed, the warden established a guard post at the door of his cell, and put him on a diet of dry bread and water. At noon, the prisoner went to eat in a nearby restaurant, and, after drinking his coffee, phoned the warden:

"Hello, Warden? I am terribly embarrassed, but just a little while ago, when leaving, I forgot to take your wallet, and now I'm stuck at a restaurant. Would you be so kind as to send someone to pay the bill?"

The warden rushed over in person, and lost his temper to the point of threatening and cursing. His pride touched, Dutilleul escaped the following night, never to return. This time, he took the precaution of shaving off his black goatee, and replaced his pince-nez glasses with a pair of horn-rimmed spectacles. A sports cap and a loud checked suit, with plus-fours, completed the transformation. He set himself up in a small apartment on the Avenue Junot, where, before his first arrest, he had sent part of his furniture and his most treasured possessions. The tumult and fame surrounding his name had become tedious, and since staying at the Santé, his enthusiasm for going through walls had become jaded. The most massive and pretentious now seemed mere screens, and he dreamed of penetrating to the heart of some great pyramid. While this project of a trip to Egypt was taking form, he led a most uneventful existence, dividing his time between motion pictures, his stamp collection, and long strolls about Montmartre. So complete was the metamorphosis that, with shaven face and horn-rimmed glasses, he brushed against his best friends on the street without being recognized. Only the painter Gen Paul, observant of the slightest changes in the physiognomy of old Montmartre residents, penetrated his disguise. One morning, finding himself face to face with Dutilleul, at the corner of the Rue de l'Abreuvoir, he could not refrain from saying in his vulgar way: "I see you got yourself rigged up like a plush duck to dodge the cops."

"Ah!" murmured Dutilleul, "you recognize me."

He was worried and decided to hasten his departure for Egypt. But on the afternoon of that very day, he fell in love with a blonde beauty whom he saw twice in the space of a quarter hour on the Rue Lepic. All thoughts of stamps, Egypt, and the Pyramids vanished from his mind.

For her part, the blonde looked him over with considerable interest. Nothing strikes the fancy of modern young ladies like a loud checked suit and horn-rimmed spectacles. They see stardom, and dream of cocktails and California nights. Unfortunately, so Gen Paul informed Dutilleul, the beauty was married to a brutal and jealous husband. Besides, this suspicious spouse led a life of pleasure and license. Regularly, he deserted his wife between ten in the evening and four in the morning, but, before leaving, he took the precaution of locking her in her room and barring the windows. In the daytime, too, he maintained this strict supervision, even following her through the streets of Montmartre.

"The old rascal's always on the watch," said Gen Paul. "He won't stand for any muscling in on his territory."

But Gen Paul's warning served only to inflame Dutilleul. The next day, running across the young woman in the Rue Tholozé, he ventured to follow her into a dairy. While waiting his turn to be served, Dutilleul declared his respectful passion, adding that he knew everything—the wicked husband, the locked and barred room—but that he would visit her that very night. The blonde blushed, the milk pitcher trembled in her hand, and her eyes became dewy with tenderness. She sighed weakly and said: "Alas, Monsieur, that is impossible."

At ten o'clock in the evening of that joyful day Dutilleul was on duty at the Rue Norvins, inspecting a robust garden wall. Behind it stood a small house, of which only the chimney and weather vane were visible. A door opened in the wall, and a man after carefully locking it behind him, set out down the hill toward the Avenue Junot.

Dutilleul waited until he had disappeared from view, turning a corner at some distance, and counted to ten. Then he jumped like a gymnast into the wall, and going through all subsequent obstacles, finally entered the room of the beautiful recluse. She greeted him rapturously, and they made love until a late hour.

The following day, Dutilleul had the misfortune to suffer severe headaches. He judged the matter to be of little importance, and did not intend, because of it, to miss his rendezvous. Nevertheless, by chance discovering a few scattered pills at the bottom of a drawer, he swallowed one in the morning, and another in the afternoon. By evening, the pains were tolerable, and they were forgotten in his exaltation. The young woman awaited him with an impatience rekindled by the memory of the previous night, and they made love until three in the morning.

After leaving, while going through the partitions and walls of the house, Dutilleul had the impression of an unaccustomed friction about the hips and shoulders. However, he did not at first give it much attention. Besides, it was only in penetrating the garden wall that he had the clear sensation of resistance. He felt that he was moving in a still fluid medium, but one that was coagulating rapidly with each of his movements. Having succeeded in lodging his whole body in the thickness of the wall, he noticed that he could not advance further, and remembered with horror the two pills he had taken during the day. He had thought them aspirins, but, in reality, they were the tetravalent pirete powders the doctor had prescribed the previous year. The effect of this medication, on top of a very active existence, manifested itself suddenly.

Dutilleul was, as it were, congealed in the interior of the wall. He is still there, solidly ensconced. The evening strollers who walk down the Rue Norvins when the rumble of Paris has abated, hear a muffled voice that appears to come from beyond the grave. They take it to be the wind whistling through the square at the Butte Montmartre. It is Garou-Garou, who laments the end of his glorious career, and regrets his love cut short. Some winter evenings, the painter Gen Paul takes his guitar down from the wall, and in the sonorous solitude, wanders down the Rue Norvins in order to console the poor prisoner with a song. The notes, winging from his numbed fingers, penetrate to the heart of the stone like drops of moonlight.

KINGSLEY AMIS

Who Needs
 No
Introduction

Public lecturing in America is the perfect vehicle for that rich compound of vanity and greed which makes up the literary character. I
say "in America" not because Americans are particularly devoted to
the two qualities mentioned, but because in Britain, at least, neither
of them will get much of an outing at this form of sport: "I'm sorry
so few people have turned up," one is likely to be told, "but our Mr.
Snodgrass is also lecturing tonight—on French cathedrals—with lantern slides," and again, "I'm sorry the fee is so tiny, but we find
if we charge admission nobody turns up at all."

In America, under I know not what system of inducement or threat,
enough people will turn up to tickle even a writer's vanity, and greed
is abundantly satisfied. Instead of having to wait a couple of months
for five pounds, the common fate in England, one will probably be
given the check before the audience has finished assembling, and if by
any chance payment should be deferred until afterward a good reason
will be forthcoming: in Washington, I seemed to gather, a compatriot
of mine got his little envelope after the preludial dinner and was
never seen again.

Conscious of having had either one martini too few or one too many (a finer literary judgment is needed here than most of us possess) the lecturer makes his way to the podium and does his stuff, imperturbable and trying to sound improvisatory with his dog-eared script, uneasily alert for any face in the audience that even slightly recalls anybody who may have heard him deliver the identical talk last week in a different part of the town. This phobia is perhaps an integral part of the academic neurosis, likely to afflict all who have had to go through the motions, year after year, of sounding sprightly about *The Mill on the Floss* or *Martin Chuzzlewit* in front of undergraduate audiences; this year's lot look and behave so much like last year's lot that you can never quite convince yourself they are not the same lot. You need all your reasoning power for the reflection that nobody who has had to take two runs at the Freshman Novel Program (as it might be called in this country) is in danger of recognizing a supposed epigram however often it might be repeated.

But to abandon thoughts of home: our literary lecturer in America will meet, if he has been at all conscientious in preparing his remarks, a polite and attentive reception. The only man who ever made faces at me while I was holding forth turned out to be an official of Her Majesty's Government, which I was mildly denouncing at the time; they were mild faces too. Even that potentially dreadful aftermath, the question period, will generally slip harmlessly by without intervention from the aggressively well-informed or even the plain madman. Those well-tested life belts—asking for a 250-word question to be repeated, answering it with a monosyllable, breaking into uncontrollable laughter, etc.—can be left unused.

My one major error (the only one I know of, anyway) was committed when I gave an address at a well-known university in Philadelphia. Exhausted by the ceaseless search for wit, I had decided to abandon trying to tell jokes and deliver instead what was conceived as a hideously sophisticated joke in action: a long, humorless, pseudo-academic diatribe on the comic spirit recited absolutely deadpan by a supposed comic writer. As I recall—and one does not recall these things well, being concerned only to maintain continuity and aplomb, for all the world like somebody who has had too much to drink—as I recall it went down rather badly, except for a reference to vomiting which laid a single undergraduate in the aisle. But retribution was swift: during the postludial party at the fraternity house somebody stole my script, which naturally, having a living to earn, I had been intending to run off elsewhere a few weeks later. I see now, of course, that the right way to interpret the felony was as (a) a blow against authority, to be welcomed as such, and (b) a second joke in action, a good deal more pointed and economical than my own. But I thought differently then.

It must have been vanity rather than greed which induced me to appear on a kind of public panel in a playhouse in New York: the topic, *Is There a Beat Generation?* My colleagues were Mr. James Wechsler, the editor of the New York *Post*, Mr. Ashley Montagu, the anthropologist, and Mr. Jack Kerouac, who as they say needs no introduction. At the preludial dinner it was explained that Mr. Kerouac was very nice, perfectly charming in fact, provided he was convinced that those present were on his side, felt sympathetic to him, in short *liked him*. I said I saw what was meant. Over in the theatre we encountered Mr. Kerouac, conservatively attired in giant's-chessboard shirt, black jeans, and pigskin ankle boots. With hand on hip he piped to me, "Hallo, my dear" (I did need a haircut at the time, admittedly) and said to Mr. Montagu, "I saw you on the Jack Paar show. You didn't have anything new to say."

Having thus variously put the pair of us at our ease, he crossed to the backstage piano without giving us the chance to tell him how much we liked him. Then, seating himself at the instrument, he began a version of the dear old "Warsaw Concerto," but broke off every now and then to appear before the photographers. When he did this he weaved and bobbed rather as if about to start what we squares used to call jitterbugging. The "Warsaw Concerto" gave place at one stage to a boogie-woogie left hand, but was resumed after an interval when no boogie-woogie right hand was forthcoming.

Though Mr. Wechsler had still not arrived, some sort of gesture toward getting started was obviously called for. We trooped onto the stage and huge high-pitched enthusiasm arose from certain sections of the audience, a salute intended not for Mr. Montagu or me, I recognized sadly, but for Mr. Kerouac, who responded with more weaves, bobs, and a chimpanzee-shuffle or two. After some determinedly sedate remarks from the chair, Mr. Kerouac arose for what we all thought was understood to be a ten-minute stint. During it, a stocky figure with overcoat thrown open entered at the back of the hall and made its way on to the stage; no beatnik anarch, as I had begun to fear, but Mr. Wechsler, in pretty good shape after a three-day editorial crisis and soon disabused of the idea that I was Mr. Montagu. Mr. Kerouac was talking about a swinging group of new American boys intent on life, forecasting the appointment of a beat Secretary of

State, and saluting Humphrey Bogart, Laurel and Hardy, and Popeye as ancestral beats. Half an hour or so later he said he would read his poem on Harpo Marx. The texture of his discourse did not change. Throughout it seemed to illustrate the theme of the symposium rather than actually expound it.

Next there was me. Then there was Mr. Wechsler, who performed the considerable feat of advocating political commitment in terms that were both rational and free of cliché. Right at the start of it Mr. Kerouac muttered, "I can't stand this activist crap," and, wearing Mr. Wechsler's hat, began a somnambulistic pacing of the stage, occasionally breaking off to wave balletically at the photographers in the wings. He went on doing this while Mr. Montagu's ironies flew above the beat sections of the audience.

Finally there was "discussion." Mr. Kerouac accused Mr. Wechsler, very inaccurately, of having said a lot about what he didn't believe in and nothing about what he did believe in. Mr. Wechsler gamely responded with a capsule version of positive views. Mr. Kerouac leaned on the podium and said, "Admit it, Wechsler, you came here tonight determined to hate me." It was clear that none of us had managed to convince him that we liked him.

Disengaging myself from a 250-pound brunette who had leaped onto the stage to assure me that, contrary to my apparent belief, there was a beat generation, I followed the others out, reflecting that Mr. Kerouac's performance had acted as a useful supplement to his novels in demonstrating how little spontaneity has to do with talking off the top of the head. I also wondered, and still do, just what it is that people anywhere in the world get out of attending discussions or lectures by literary persons. For the majority, I imagine, one might as well speak in Choctaw; the visual appeal is what counts. For all his evident casualness, Mr. Kerouac was shrewd enough to have grasped that.

Protection

 ## for a

Tough Racket

When I started working in a New York night club, my mother asked me to forget that fact in writing home to the neighbors.

"I know teaching pays very little," she wrote from Texas, "and your father thinks you're clever to find an extra job after school. But we are horrified at your choice. Teaching may be dull, as you say, but at least it's respected and safe."

I left her with her dreams.

I taught in a school for problem boys in Manhattan, and no regular teacher would stay there. As a young substitute just out of college, I didn't know how to quit. Any likeness the school had to my mother's halls of learning was purely coincidental.

It was at Tony and Nick's night club, The Tonic, that education was truly esteemed. My college degree, though not as expensive, was rarer than sables. I was only a sort of errand girl—part-time secretary was the official title—yet the Kohinoor diamond was never handled more reverently than I.

Added to my intellectual prowess was Tony's touching tribute. "She's a virgin," he said simply, but proudly to anyone who entered the club. "I can always tell."

This made my stock soar so high I was sorry I couldn't sell it on the

exchange. I was as sheltered as though I were in purdah. Before
The Tonic got really interesting each evening, Tony and Nick would
send me home. It was flattering to be a vestal virgin, but it didn't
seem to have a big future.

Because of my varied accomplishments, Nick and Tony asked my
advice about everything. My pupils might not want an education,
but my bosses did.

I taught them good manners in letter writing. My students would
have said, "We don't wanna loin none a dat junk." I showed Tony
a graceful way to hold his knife and fork. At school, knives were
weapons and not to be handled lightly. I subdued, somewhat, Nick's
choice of ties. My boys didn't wear any.

Every day at school brought some new defeat. Each night at the
club, the torch of learning burned a little brighter.

Tony was my star pupil. He was dark and handsome, I believed,
although The Tonic's lights were so subdued I took a lot on faith.
Over six feet tall and massively built, he never had to hire a bouncer.
To get what he called the glass-door clientele, for the club was in a
fashionable Manhattan district, he longed to become a more elegant
greeter.

Nick was the financial brains of the partnership. He was crazy
about great big hundred-dollar bills and rather fond of the small
change, too. He'd been through the first grade in PS 11 and he'd
learned to add. Luckily, he never got to the second grade and
subtractions. When the club had a slow night, he'd kick and yell
at the cash register. The next evening, business always picked
up.

When Tony had his office redecorated, he asked me to get some
books for it.

"What kind of books, Tony?" I asked.

"Big ones," he said.

He had an American flag hanging above his desk.

"You don't need that flag, do you?" I asked, thinking of the new
color scheme.

"We're legitimate," he protested, "we're legal. Buy me some books
for under the flag."

At school, the book for my class was about King Arthur and the
Round Table. The Board must have hoped the chivalry would rub
off. But the boys never complained. They thought it was a story of
Robin Hood. They used copies to bang each other on the head or
chuck them out the windows at innocent pedestrians.

Just that day I'd picked up a book in the school gutter on my way to the club. Tony opened it.

"Jeez," he exclaimed, "this is English?"

I nodded.

"Translate it," he said.

I gave him a little background.

"I don't want no foreign language round here," he explained. "Jus' buy me some American ones."

Tony had come to America when he was twelve and he was fiercely patriotic. Before I knew him well, I'd made some casual remark that showed him I thought he'd been born here. The Congressional Medal couldn't have pleased him more.

He'd gone back to Italy just once. But walking past the Colosseum or sitting near the Pantheon, he'd wept for Brooklyn. He cut his visit short and flew back home.

At school, a few weeks after choosing Tony's library, two of my boys began a fight. It happened without warning. Not a word spoken nor a signal given. Suddenly they were slugging it out and blood was flowing freely. Fifty boys jumped up on desks and yelled advice and approval.

I tried to push my way through to stop the slaughter. A sharp pencil in one of the boys' hands was accidentally, but painfully stabbed into my cheek.

That night at The Tonic I appeared with a bandage over my wound. Tony and Nick were shocked.

"Those hoods!" exclaimed Tony.

"She needs protection," said Nick.

"She's in a dangerous racket," Tony agreed. "She needs a body-guard."

When they suggested sending me right home in a taxi, I accepted the offer gratefully.

The following morning I had to force myself to go to school. I'd been so angry the day before I hadn't been frightened. Now I was suffering from delayed shock. I felt sick at my stomach.

The bell rang and the boys came stumbling and pushing into the room. Elephants were infinitely more graceful. One of the boys in the fight grinned amiably at me. Two front teeth were missing. The other boy was absent.

It always took twenty minutes of hard work to get them quieted down. They shoved. They crashed to the floor. They shouted with laughter. Suddenly, they were appallingly still. Every eye was focused on the door in back of me. I turned around—usually a fatal move in that class—and there stood Tony, glaring down at the boys in front of him.

I had never seen him in daylight before and it was a shock. Years of working at night had yellowed his naturally olive complexion. Running along one cheek was a scar I hadn't noticed under the dim club lights. But there was fire in his eyes and his huge figure was remarkably lithe and catlike as he walked up to my desk.

"Are these the hoods that hurt a innocent—" I flinched, waiting for him to say "virgin" but he said "girl" instead.

"How'd you get here?" I asked stupidly.

The boys stared speechlessly at him. They didn't know who he was or what he was doing in the room, but he had an authority and power they recognized and which I had never had.

"Get outcha books," he ordered. "I wanna see can you read English."

For the first time in their lives without a protest, the boys flipped out their books from pockets, sweaters, pants' legs and from even more personal hiding places. The books peppered onto the desks like shelling peas in a pan.

Tony walked slowly around the room until every book was opened, every face turned to me. He nodded and I began the lesson.

The deathlike silence was frightening. My Hooper rating was fabulous.

We read of fair Elaine and Guinevere. And Lancelot, "seam'd with an ancient sword-cut," which I hoped Tony wouldn't take personally. But he was absorbed in the story as I translated it, and the boys were fascinated by him.

When I had finished, he walked up to my desk. King Arthur ascending the throne could not have been more regal. He glanced at me, a gentle maiden in distress. Then he turned and looked imperially at the boys.

"A fine buncha knights!" he said. "A great buncha jerks. Ya couldn't even make cub scout!"

They squirmed under his wrath.

"Let's begin the turniment," he continued. "I challenge all comers."

No one moved.

"Brave knights!" said Tony. "Ya jus' hit women and children here?"

The class winced.

"Too yellow to touch someone your size?"

"It was a accident," said one boy.

"We din' mean to do it," explained another.

"But her face is cut up jus' the same," Tony replied.

"That's all right, Tony," I said.

"Ya gotta real doll here," Tony went on and pointed to me. "A pure hunert per cent American Beauty doll. Smart, too. Knows everything. Ya gotta show her respect. Ya hear me?"

The boys nodded.

"I don' wanna see no more marks on her frame! Ya understan' English?"

He glared at the boys. They looked admiringly at him.

"If I haf' to come back," he warned, "I'll take ya row by row. Want I should draw a picture?"

The boys' eyes were shining. They almost burst into applause.

As Tony paused at the door, he hurled his last and most humiliating insult. "Don' ever forget what I toldja, ya buncha FOREIGNERS!" he said.

C. NORTHCOTE PARKINSON

How to Tell
 When You
Are Obsolete

Every student of human institutions is familiar with the standard test
for assessing the importance of any given individual. The number
of doors to be passed, the number of his personal assistants, the
number of telephones on his desk—these three figures, combined with
the depth of his carpet in centimeters, have given us a simple formula
which is reliable for most parts of the world.

It is less widely known that the same sort of measurement is ap-
plicable—*but in reverse*—to the institution itself.

Take, for example, a publishing organization. The most successful
publishers have a strong tendency, as we know, to live in a state of
chaotic squalor. The visitor who applies at the obvious entrance is
led outside and round the block, down an alley, and up three flights
of stairs. A young and vigorous research establishment is similarly
housed, as a rule, on the ground floor of what was once a private house,
from which a crazy wooden corridor leads to a corrugated iron hut in
what was once the garden.

Are we not all familiar, moreover, with the layout of an international airport? As we emerge from the aircraft, we see (over to our
right or left) a lofty structure wrapped in scaffolding. Then the air
hostess leads us into a hut with an asbestos roof. Nor do we suppose

for a moment that it will ever be otherwise. By the time the building is complete the airfield will have been moved to another site.

The institutions already mentioned—lively and productive as they may be—flourish in such shabby and makeshift surroundings that we might turn with relief to an institution clothed from the outset with convenience and dignity. The outer door, in bronze and glass, is placed centrally in a symmetrical façade. Polished shoes glide quietly over shining rubber to the glittering silent elevator. The overpoweringly cultured receptionist will murmur with carmine lips into an ice-blue receiver. She will wave you into a chromium armchair, consoling you with a dazzling smile for any slight but inevitable delay. Looking up from a glossy magazine you will observe how the wide corridors radiate toward Departments A, B, and C. From behind closed doors will come the subdued noise of an ordered activity. A minute later and you are ankle-deep in the director's carpet, plodding sturdily toward his distant, tidy desk. Hypnotized by the chief's unwavering stare, cowed by his Matisse, you feel you have found real efficiency at last.

In point of fact you will have discovered nothing of the kind. It is now known that a perfection of planned layout is achieved only by institutions on the point of collapse.

This apparently paradoxical conclusion is based upon a wealth of archaeological and historical research, with the more esoteric details of which we need not concern ourselves. In general, however, the method pursued has been to select and date the buildings which appear to have been perfectly designed for their purpose. A study and comparison of these proves that perfection of planning is a symptom of decay. During a period of exciting discovery or progress there is no time to plan the perfect headquarters. The time for that comes later, when all the important work has been done. Perfection, we know, is finality; and finality is death.

Thus, to the casual tourist, awestruck in front of St. Peter's in Rome, the Basilica and the Vatican must seem the ideal setting for the Papal Monarchy at the very height of its prestige and power. Here, he reflects, must Innocent III have thundered his anathema. Here must Gregory VII have laid down the law. But a glance at the guidebook will show that the really powerful Popes reigned long before the present dome was raised, and frequently somewhere else. More than that, the later Popes lost half their authority while the work was still in progress. Julius II, whose decision it was to build, and Leo X, who approved Raphael's design, were dead long before the buildings assumed their present shape. Bramante's palace was still building until 1565, the great church not consecrated until 1626, nor the piazza colonnades finished until 1667. The great days of the Papacy were over before the perfect setting was even planned.

This sequence of events is in no way exceptional. Just such a sequence can be found in the history of the League of Nations. Great hopes centered on the League from its inception in 1920 until about 1930. By 1933, at the latest, the experiment was seen to have failed. However, its physical embodiment—the Palace of the Nations—was not opened until 1937. It was a structure no doubt justly admired. Deep thought had gone into the design of secretariat and council chambers, committee rooms and cafeteria. Everything was there which ingenuity could devise—except the League itself. By the year when its Palace was formally opened the League had practically ceased to exist.

It might be urged that the Palace of Versailles is an instance of something quite opposite; the architectural embodiment of Louis XIV's monarchy at its height. But here again the facts refuse to fit the theory. For granted that Versailles may typify the triumphant spirit of the age, it was mostly completed very late in the reign, and some of it indeed during the reign which followed. The building of Versailles mostly took place between 1669 and 1685. The King did not move there until 1682 and even then the work was still in progress. The famous royal bedroom was not occupied until 1701, nor the chapel finished until nine years later. As against that, Louis XIV's real triumphs were mostly before 1679; the apex of his career was reached in 1682; and his power declined from about 1685.

In other words the visitor who thinks Versailles is the place from which Turenne rode forth to victory is mistaken. It would be more correct to picture the embarrassment, in that setting, of those who came with the news of defeat at Blenheim. In a palace resplendent with emblems of victory, they can hardly have known which way to look.

Mention of Blenheim calls to mind the palace of that name built for the victorious Duke of Marlborough. Here again we have a building ideally planned, this time as the place of retirement for a national hero. Its heroic proportions are more dramatic perhaps than convenient, but the general effect is just what the architects intended. No scene could more fittingly enshrine a legend. No setting could have been more appropriate for the meeting of old comrades on the anniversary of a battle. Our pleasure, however, in picturing the scene is spoiled by our realization that the Duke never even saw it finished. His actual residence was at Holywell, near St. Albans, and (when in town) at Marlborough House. He died at Windsor Lodge and his old comrades, when they held a reunion, are known to have dined in a tent.

What of the monarchy which the Duke of Marlborough served? Just as tourists now wander, guidebook in hand, through the Orangerie or the Galerie des Glaces, so the future archaeologists may peer around what once was London. And he may well incline to see in the ruins of Buckingham Palace a true expression of British monarchy. He will trace the great avenue from Admiralty Arch to the palace gate. He will reconstruct the forecourt and the central balcony, thinking all the time how suitable it must have been for a powerful ruler whose sway extended to the remote parts of the world. Even a present-day American might be tempted to shake his head over the arrogance of a George III, enthroned in such impressive state as this.

But again we find that the really powerful monarchs all lived somewhere else, in buildings long since vanished—at Greenwich or Nonesuch, Kenilworth or Whitehall. The builder of Buckingham Palace was George IV, whose court architect, John Nash, was responsible for what was described at the time as its "general feebleness and triviality of taste." But George IV himself, who lived at Carlton House or Brighton, never saw the finished work; nor did William IV, who ordered its completion. It was Queen Victoria who first took up residence there in 1837, being married from the new palace in 1840. But her first enthusiasm for Buckingham Palace was relatively short-lived. Her husband infinitely preferred Windsor and her own later preference was for Balmoral or Osborne. The splendors of Buckingham Palace must therefore be associated with a later, and strictly constitutional, monarchy. It dates from a period when power was vested in Parliament.

It is natural, therefore, to ask whether the Palace of Westminster, where the House of Commons meets, is itself a true expression of parliamentary rule. It represents beyond question a magnificent piece of planning, aptly designed for debate and yet provided with ample space for everything else—for committee meetings, for quiet study, for refreshment, and (on its terrace) for tea. It has everything a legislator could possibly desire, all incorporated in a building of immense dignity and comfort. It should date—but this we now hardly dare assume—from a period when parliamentary rule was at its height.

But once again the dates refuse to fit into this pattern. The original

House, where Pitt and Fox were matched in oratory, was accidentally destroyed by fire in 1834. It would appear to have been as famed for its inconvenience as for its lofty standard of debate. The present structure was begun in 1840, partly occupied in 1852 but incomplete when its architect died in 1860. It finally assumed its present appearance in about 1868. Now, by what we can no longer regard as coincidence, the decline of Parliament can be traced, without much dispute, to the Reform Act of 1867. It was in the following year that all initiative in legislation passed from Parliament to the Cabinet. The great days were over.

The same could not be said of the various Ministries, which were to gain importance in proportion to Parliament's decline. Investigation may yet serve to reveal that the India Office reached its peak of efficiency when accommodated in the Westminster Palace Hotel. What is more significant, however, is the recent development of the Colonial Office. For while the British Empire was mostly acquired at a period when the Colonial Office (in so far as there was one) occupied haphazard premises in Downing Street, a new phase of colonial policy began when the department moved into buildings actually designed for the purpose. This was in 1875 and the structure was well designed as a background for the disasters of the Boer War.

But the Colonial Office gained a new lease of life during World War II. With its move to temporary and highly inconvenient premises in Great South Street—premises leased from the Church of England and intended for an entirely different purpose—British Colonial policy entered that phase of enlightened activity which will end no doubt with the completion of the new building planned on the site of the old Westmister Hospital. It is reassuring to know that work on this site has not even begun.

But no other British example can now match in significance the story of New Delhi. Nowhere else have British architects been given the task of planning so great a capital city for so vast a population. The intention to found New Delhi was announced at the Imperial Durbar of 1911, King George V being at that time the Mogul's successor on what had been the Peacock Throne. Sir Edwin Lutyens then proceeded to draw up plans for a British Versailles, splendid in conception, comprehensive in detail, masterly in design, and overpowering in scale.

But the stages of its progress correspond with equivalent steps in political collapse. The Government of India Act of 1909 had been the prelude to all that followed—the attempt on the Viceroy's life in

1912, the Declaration of 1917, the Montagu-Chelmsford Report of 1918, and its implementation in 1920. Lord Irwin actually moved into his new palace in 1929, the year in which the Indian Congress demanded independence, the year in which the Round Table Conference opened, the year before the Civil Disobedience campaign began. It would be possible, though tedious, to trace the whole story down to the day when the British finally withdrew—showing how each phase of the retreat was exactly paralleled with the completion of another triumph in civic design. What was finally achieved was a mausoleum.

The decline of British imperialism actually began with the general election of 1906 and the victory on that occasion of liberal and semi-socialist ideas. It need surprise no one, therefore, to observe that 1906 is the date of completion carved in imperishable granite over the British War Office doors.

The elaborate layout of the Pentagon at Arlington, Virginia, provides another significant lesson for planners. It was not completed until the later stages of World War II and, of course, the architecture of the great victory was not constructed here, but in the crowded and untidy Munitions Building on Constitution Avenue.

Even today, as the least observant visitor to Washington can see, the most monumental edifices are found to house such derelict organizations as the Departments of Commerce and Labor, while the more active agencies occupy half-completed quarters. Indeed, much of the more urgent business of government goes forward in "temporary" structures erected during World War I, and shrewdly preserved for their stimulating effect on administration. Hard by the Capitol, the visitor will also observe the imposing marble-and-glass headquarters of the Teamsters' Union, completed not a moment too soon before the heavy hand of Congressional investigation descended on its occupants.

It is by no means certain that an influential reader of this article could prolong the life of a dying institution merely by depriving it of its streamlined headquarters. What he can do, however, with more confidence, is to prevent any organization strangling itself at birth. Examples abound of new institutions coming into existence with a full establishment of deputy directors, consultants, and executives, all these coming together in a building specially designed for their purpose.

And experience proves that such an institution will die. It is choked by its own perfection. It cannot take root for lack of soil. It cannot grow naturally for it is already grown. Fruitless by its very nature, it cannot even flower. When we see an example of such planning— when we are confronted for example by the building design for the United Nations—the experts among us shake their heads sadly and tiptoe quietly away.

INDEX